I0810647

Carving Bottlestoppers

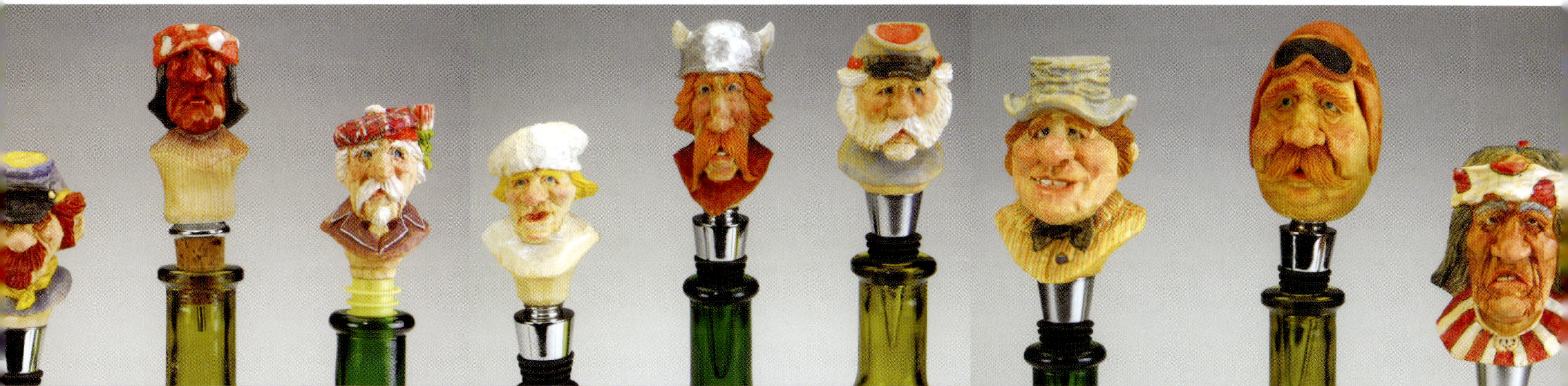

with Tom Wolfe

Schiffer Publishing Ltd

4880 Lower Valley Road, Atglen, Pa 19310

Schiffer Books are available at special discounts for bulk purchases for sales promotions or premiums. Special editions, including personalized covers, corporate imprints, and excerpts can be created in large quantities for special needs. For more information contact the publisher:

For the largest selection of fine reference books on this and related subjects, please visit our web site at **www.schifferbooks.com**
We are always looking for people to write books on new and related subjects. If you have an idea for a book please contact us at the above address.

Published by Schiffer Publishing Ltd.
4880 Lower Valley Road
Atglen, PA 19310
Phone: (610) 593-1777;
Fax: (610) 593-2002
E-mail: Info@schifferbooks.com

This book may be purchased from the publisher.
Include $5.00 for shipping.
Please try your bookstore first.
You may write for a free catalog.

In Europe, Schiffer books are distributed by
Bushwood Books
6 Marksbury Ave.
Kew Gardens
Surrey TW9 4JF England
Phone: 44 (0) 20 8392-8585; Fax: 44 (0) 20 8392-9876
E-mail: info@bushwoodbooks.co.uk
Website: www.bushwoodbooks.co.uk
Free postage in the U.K., Europe; air mail at cost.

Library of Congress Control Number: 2008936025

Designed by RoS
Type set in Brittanic Bold/Zurich BT

ISBN: 978-0-7643-3222-7
Printed in China

Introduction

For the carver looking for fresh ideas, bottlestoppers fit the bill, especially if you do caricature carving like I do. Actually you can find a lot of old carved pieces, many from Anri and other European carvers, with corks on the bottom to serve the same purpose. But today's new hardware that is available to carvers brings everything up to date...and just in time for the new interest in wines and other spirits!

Being a bust, these are a little simpler to carve than a full figure, so they are good projects for inexperienced carvers to cut their teeth on. At the same time the possibilities for creativity are endless, which will appeal to old hands like myself. For the professional carver, the market for these fun, useful pieces seems unlimited.

So I hope you enjoy this carving and will experiment figures of your own.

Cheers!

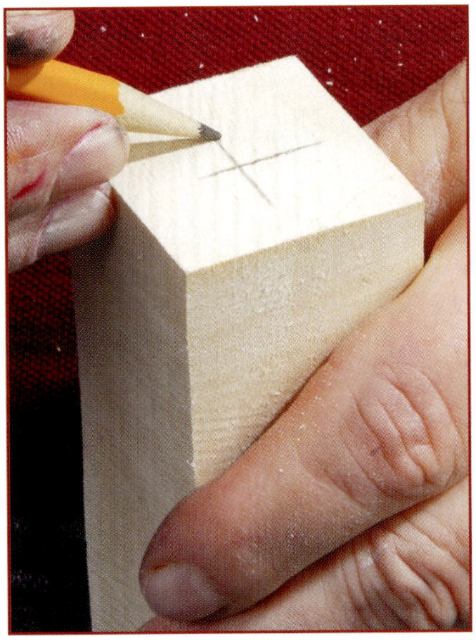

Find the center of the end of a square block. The length or width depends on your particular idea. With your finger acting as a depth gauge draw lines parallel to each side.

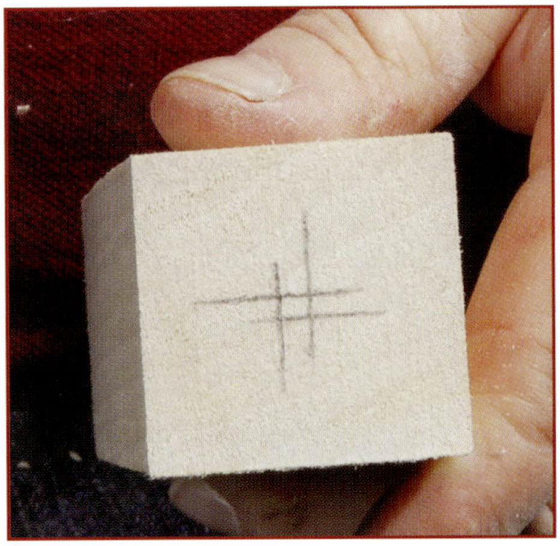

This will give you the center.

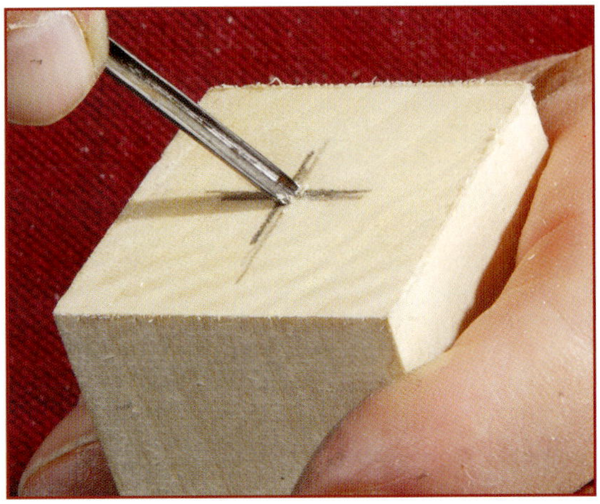

Repeat on both ends. Working on the base, pop out a little hole in the center to help align the drill bit.

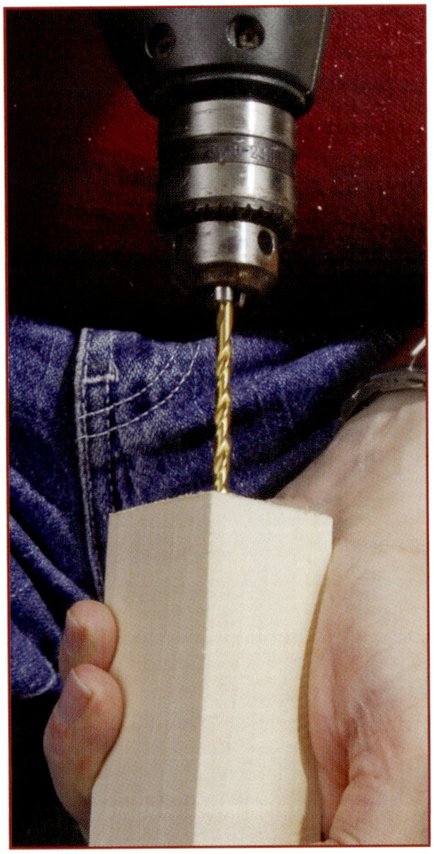

It is best to drill using a drill press. If you can't do that, use a smaller bit for a pilot hole, align the bit with one edge of the block, drill a little bit, give the block a quarter turn, realign, and drill a little more. Repeat this turn, align, drill routine until pilot hole in the base is the depth…

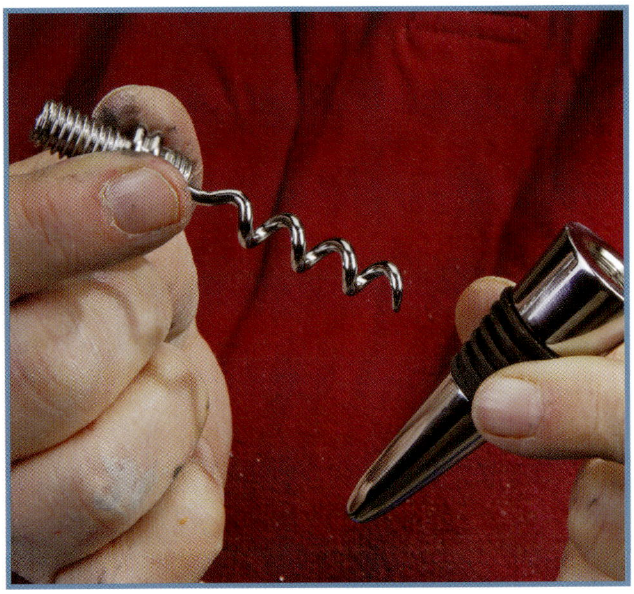

…of the screw on the bottle stopper hardware. This hardware is a combination stopper and corkscrew and can be purchased from Penn State Industries at www.pennstateind.com. Other stoppers are available from most woodworking suppliers.

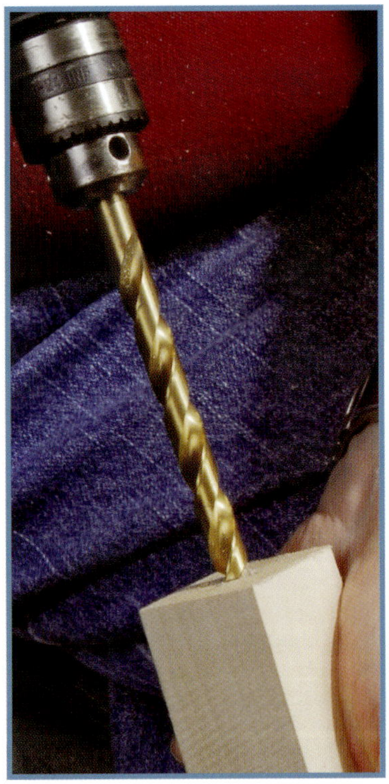

Switch to the a bit that is the size of the hardware screw and widen the hole. I start by running the drill backwards, creating a small countersink that prevents tearing. I then follow the same sequence, turn, align, drill procedure as with the pilot hole.

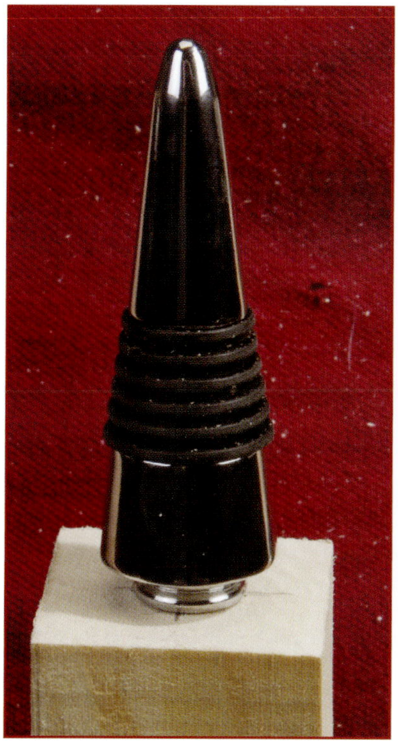

Test fit the stopper hardware in the base.

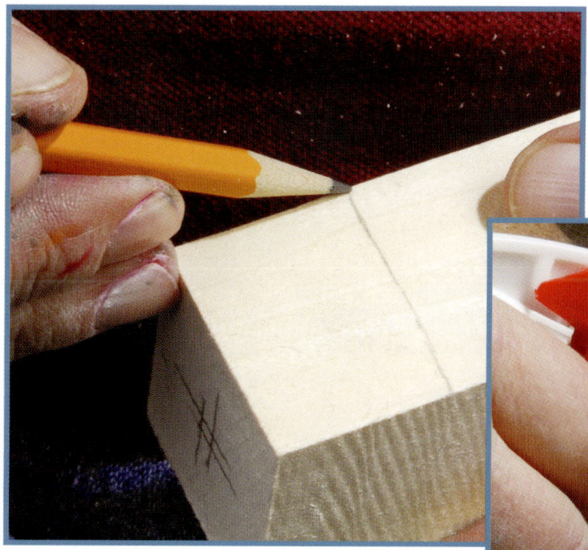

At the other end, mark the brim of the hat all around. I use a finger as a depth gauge, running along the end of the block.

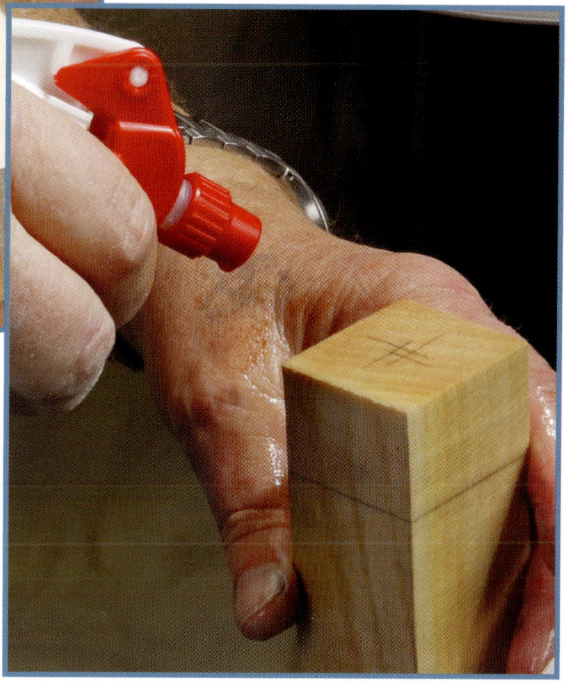

Spraying the block with a 50-50 mixture of rubbing alcohol and water makes it easier to carve.

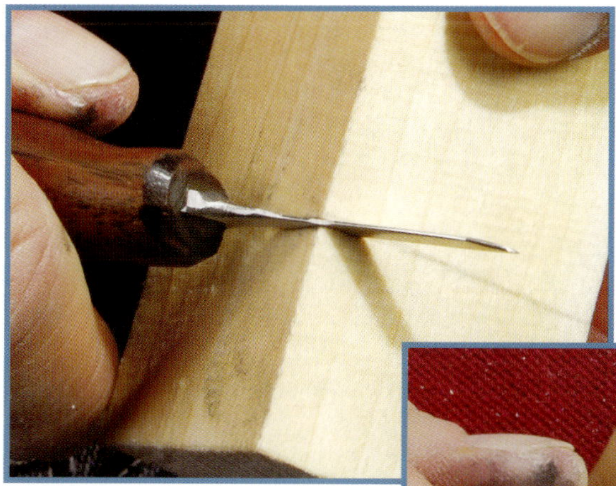

Make a stop in the corner...

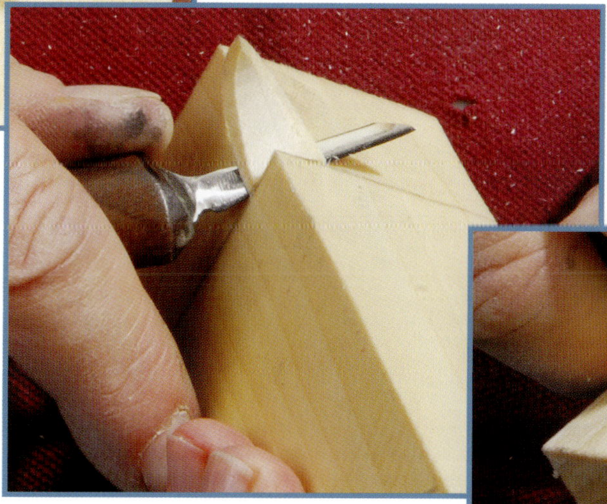

...and cut back to it from the hat.

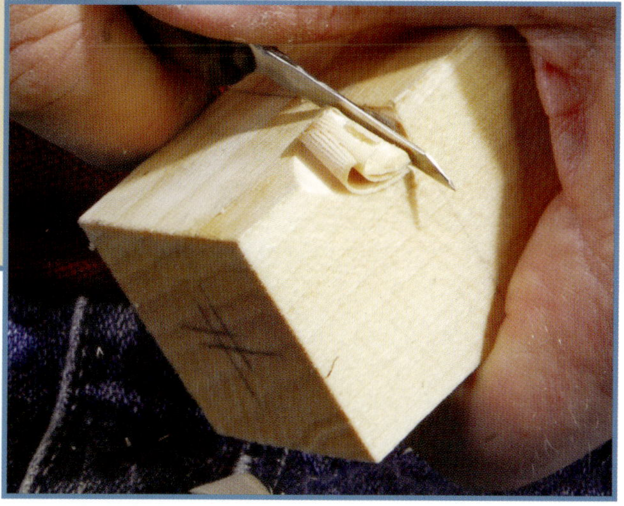

Repeat on all four corners, trying to get them kind of equal.

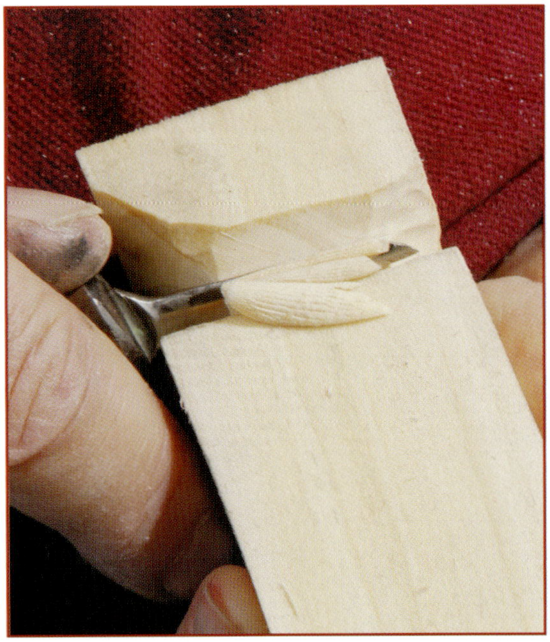

As you get deeper, join the corners across the surface.

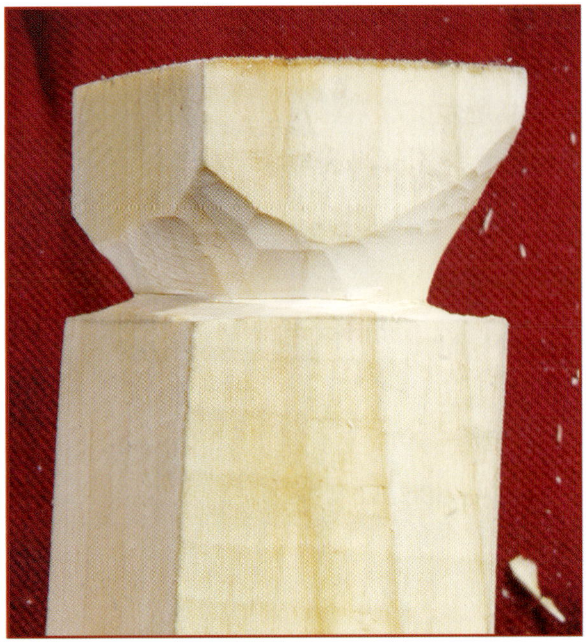

Progess

I want to knock the corners off to shape the hat into an octagon shape. This intermediate step helps keep things round.

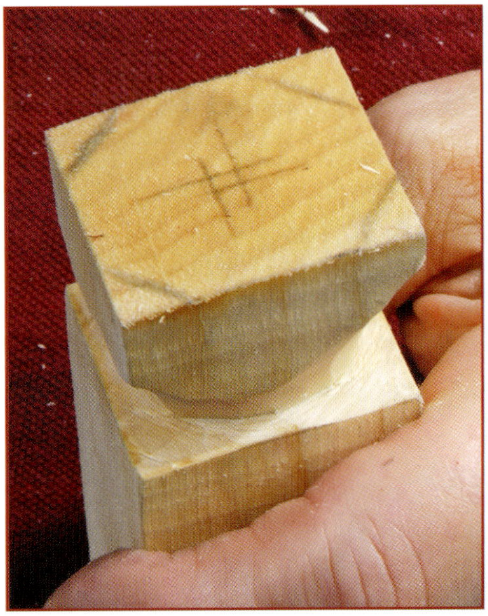

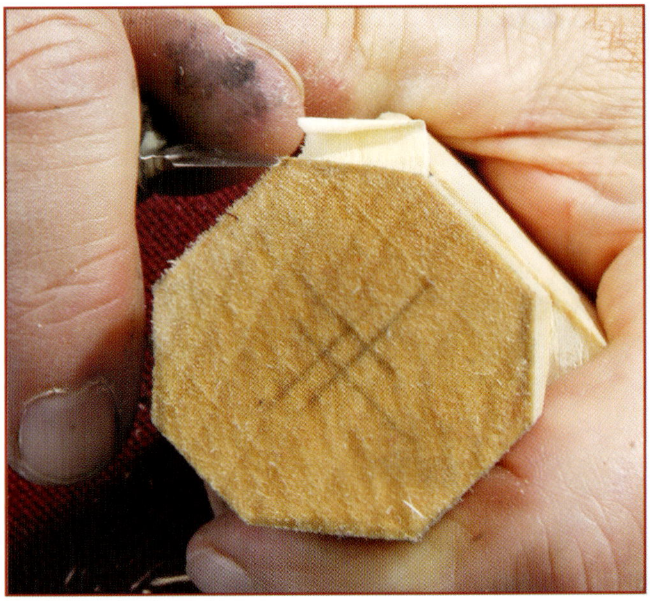

Carve the corners.

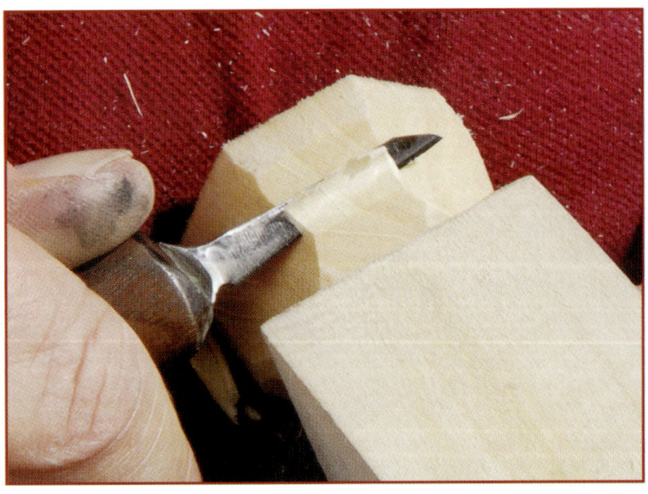

Continue working around the hat.

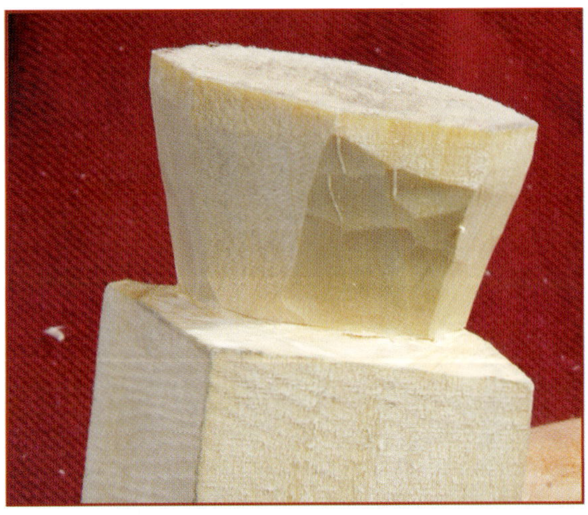

Progress. Now I'll shift for a while to the area under the brim.

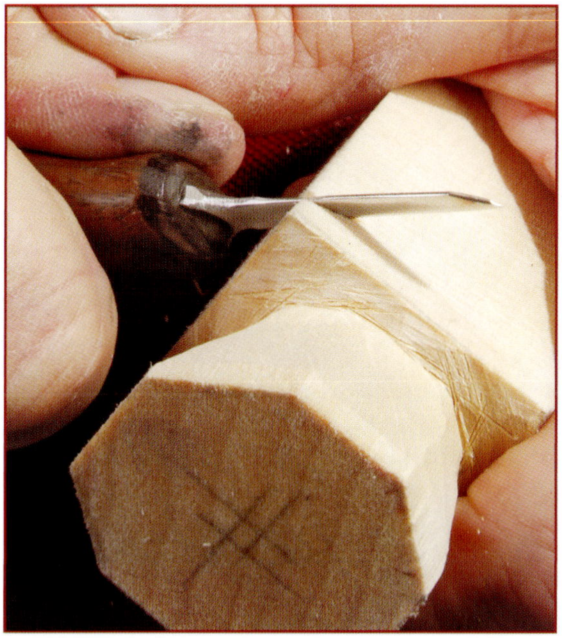

On the nose corner, cut a stop under the brim. I leave the brim pretty thick for now so I have wood to work with it later.

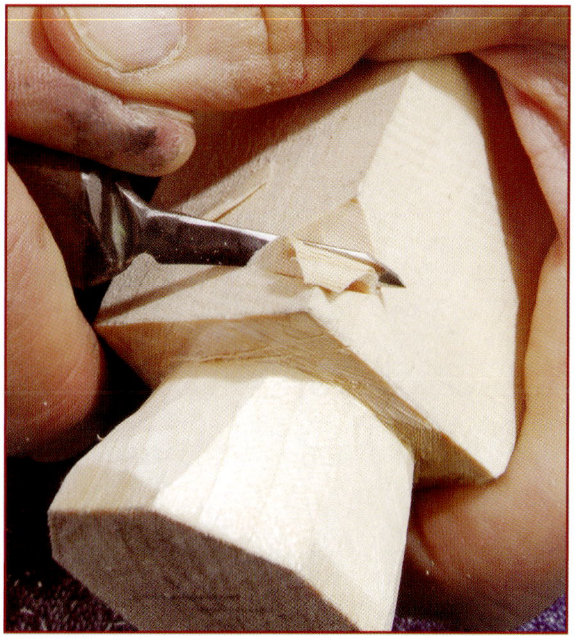

Trim back to the stop from below.

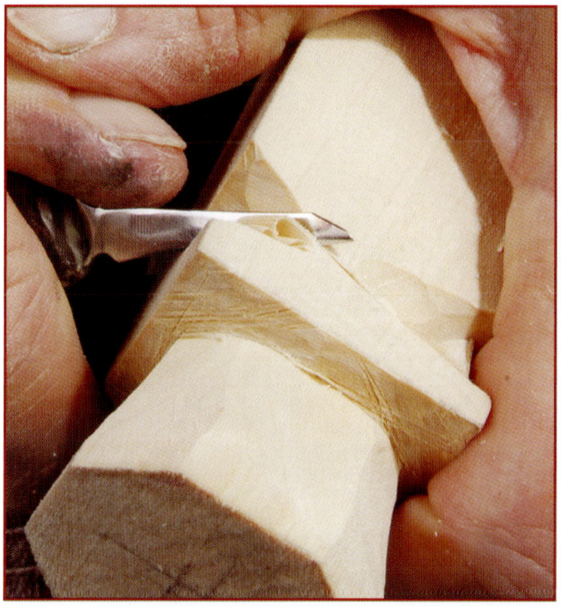

Repeat on the other three corners.

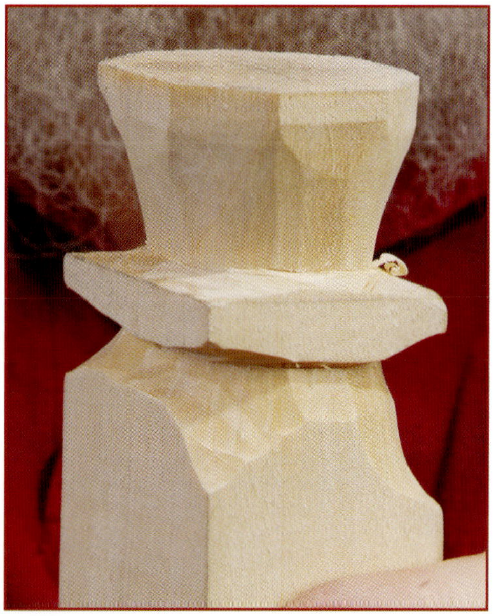

Progress

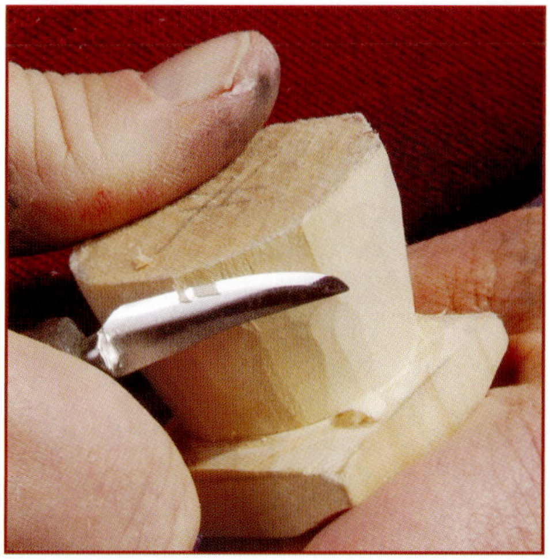

Having now made the hat octagonal I can round it off easily.

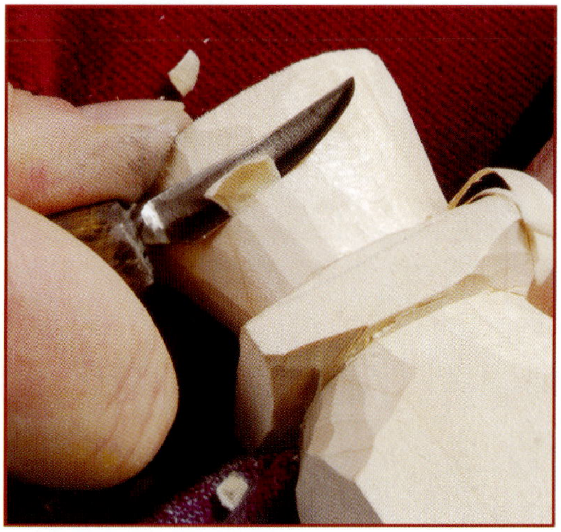

Smooth the hat, working down to the brim.

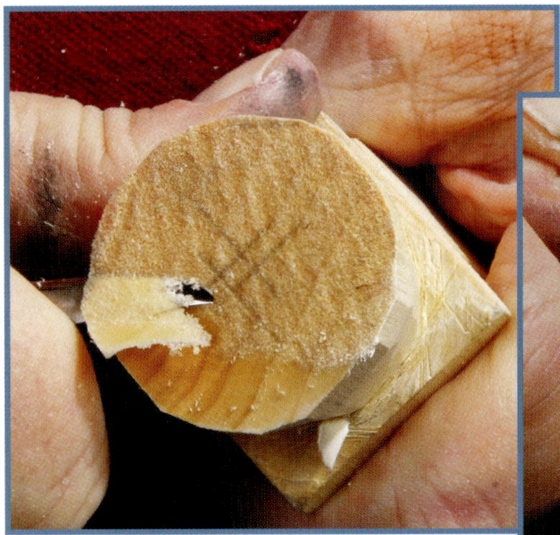

I'm going to give the top of the hat a slight dome. It will still look flat, but will be cleaned up.

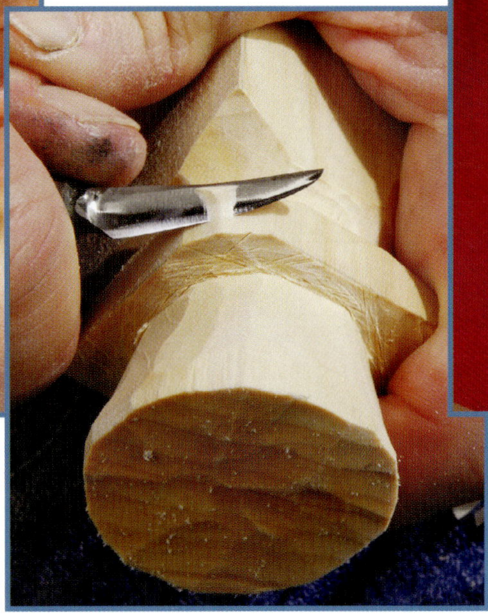

Knock the corners off the brim.

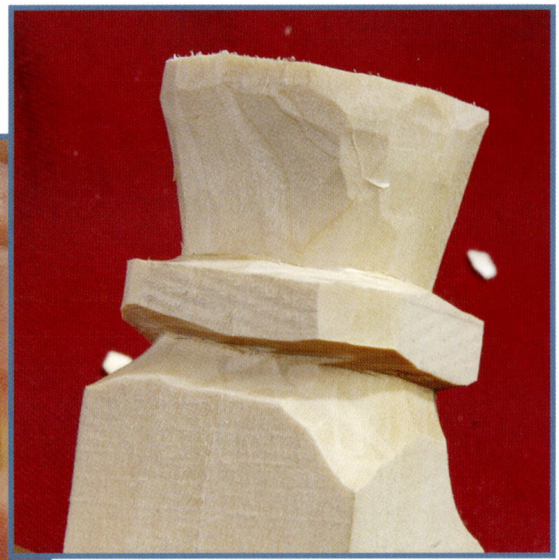

Progress.

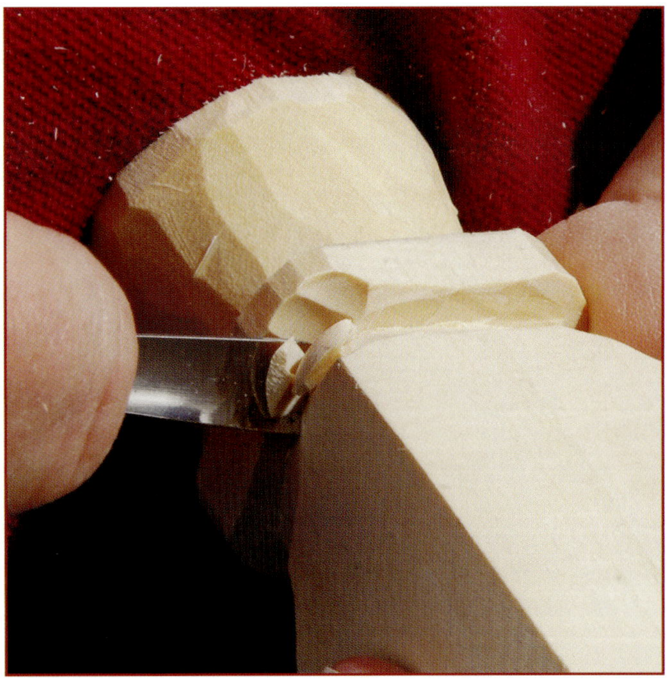

The hat brim will undulate. I undercut it with a gouge, here on the corner above the nose.

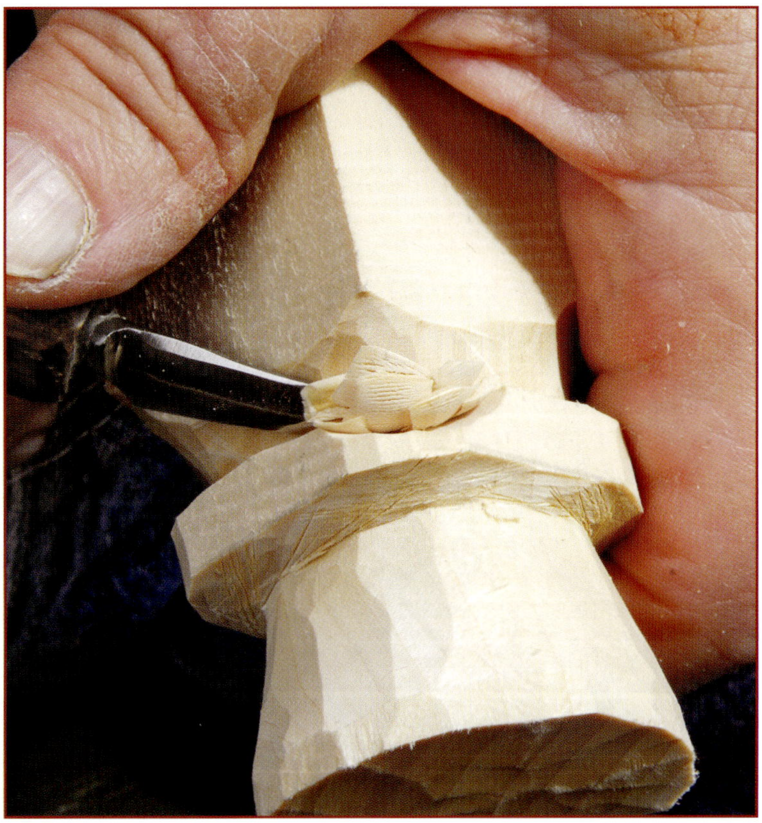

Trim off the chips with a knife.

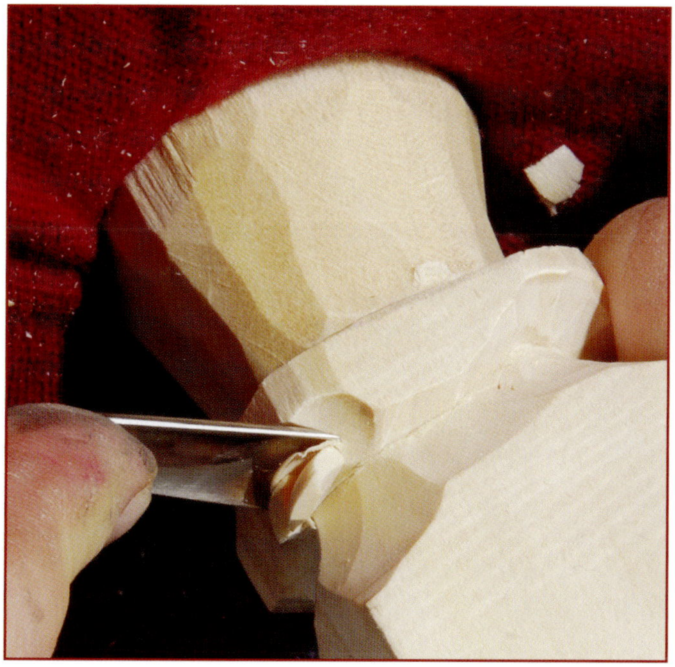

Repeat on all four corners…

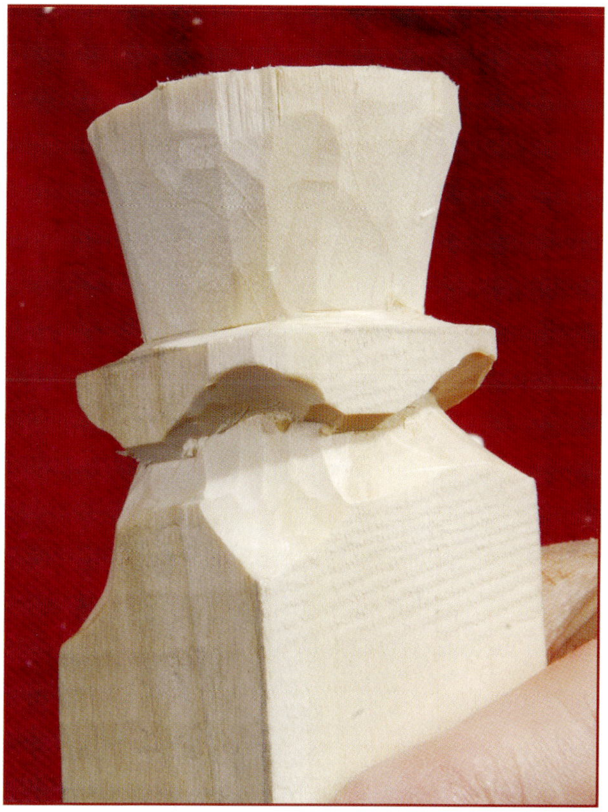

…for this result.

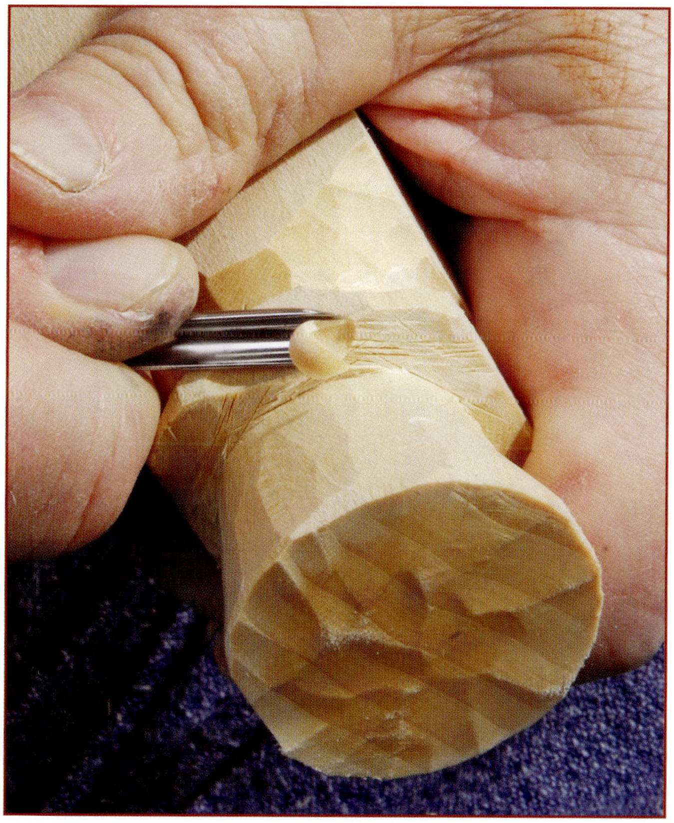

On the top of the brim, gouge out between the high spots…

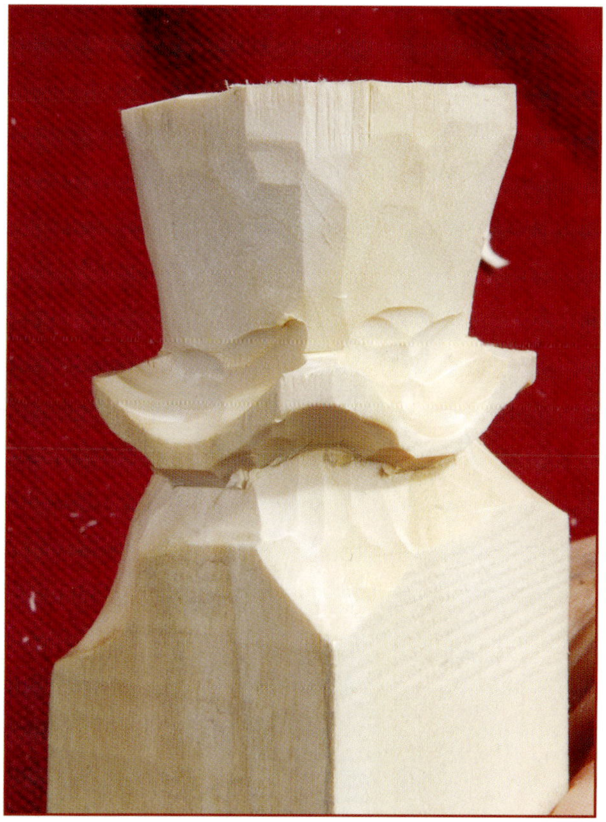

…for this result.

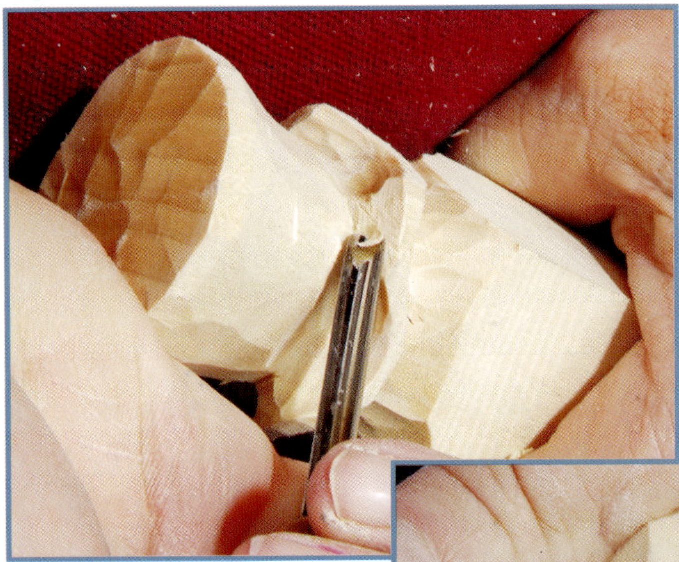

Run a gouge on the top of the brim to cup behind the high spots, shaping it. Work from one side…

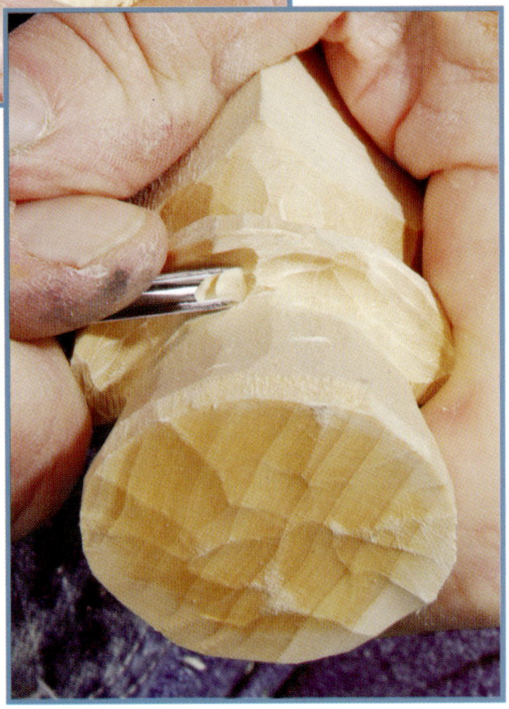

…then the other so you are always cutting uphill, to avoid putting too much stress on the brim.

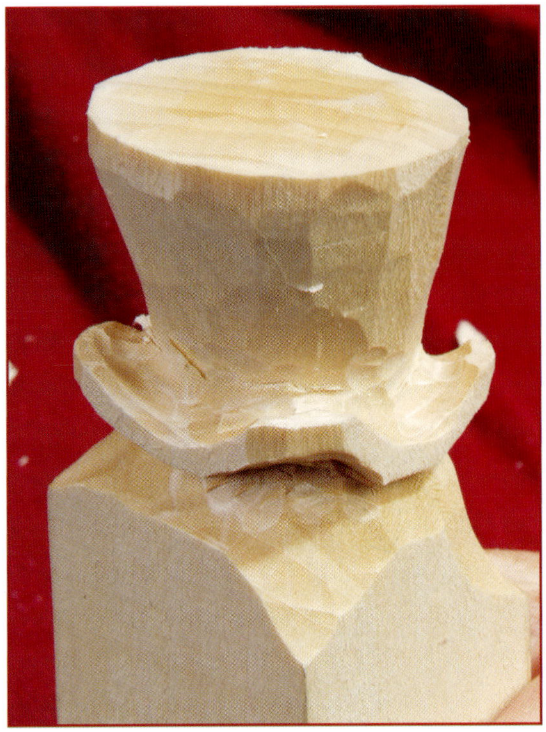

The result.

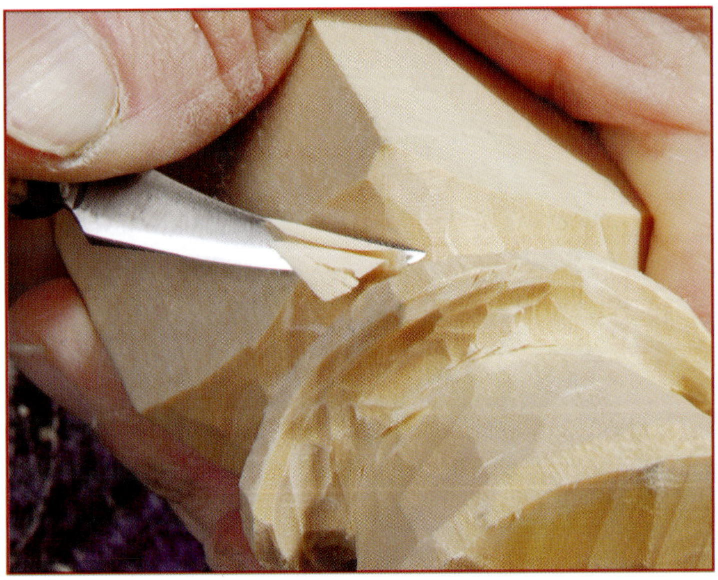

Make a scoop cut…

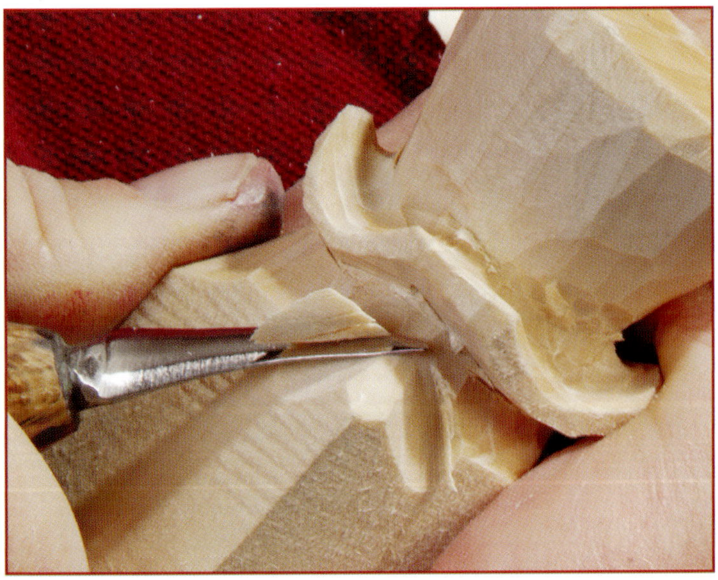

…on each side of the nose.

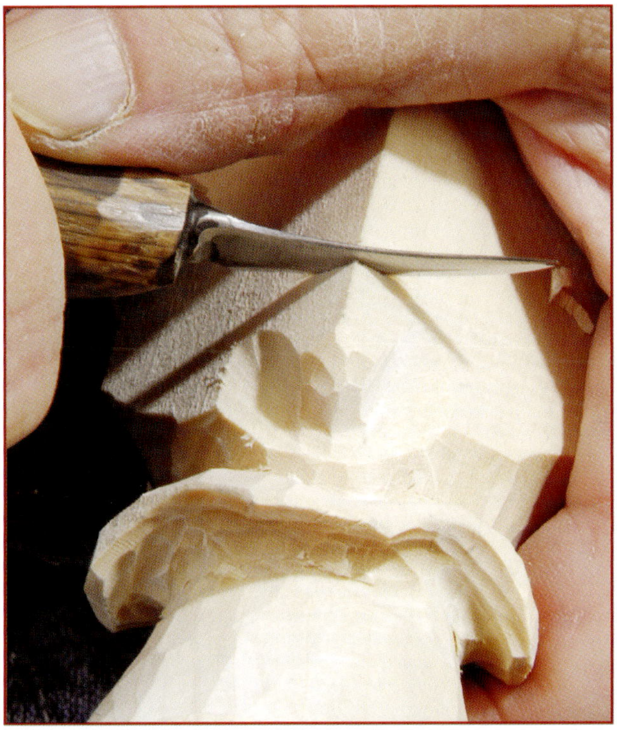

Cut a stop straight in at the bottom of the nose.

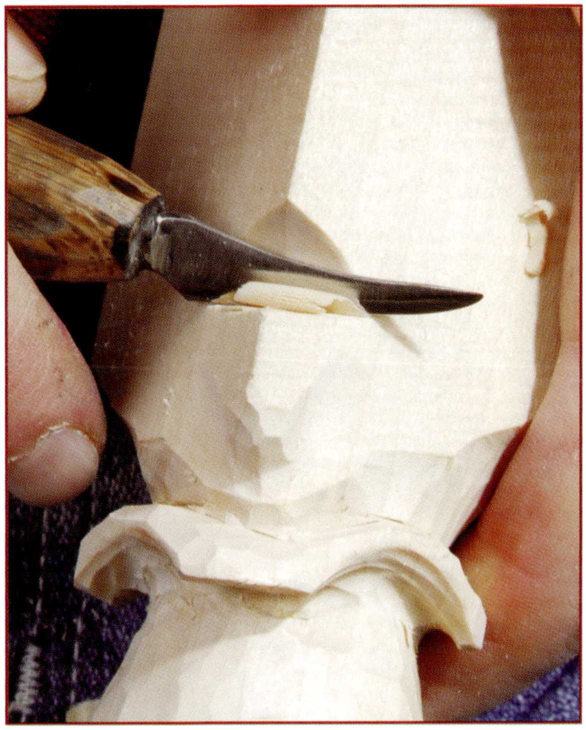

Trim back to it from the lip.

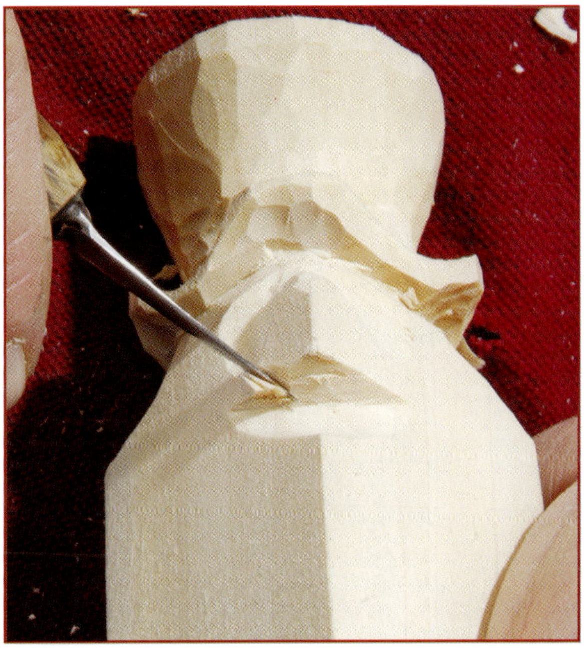

Nip the corner of the nostril at an angle…

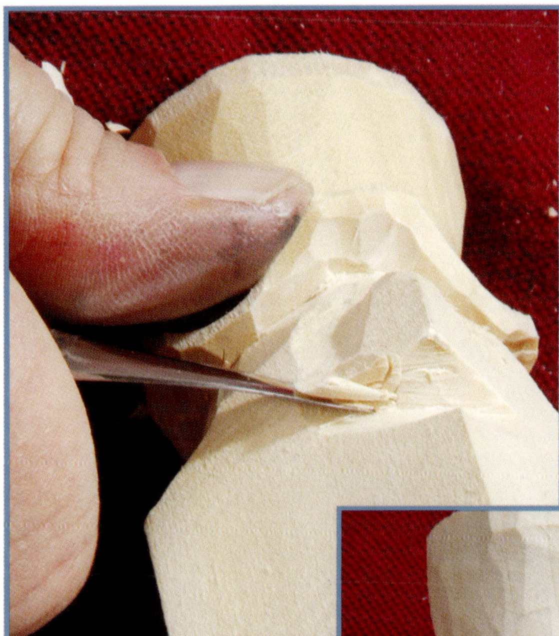

…and clip back to it from the lip. Repeat on the other side.

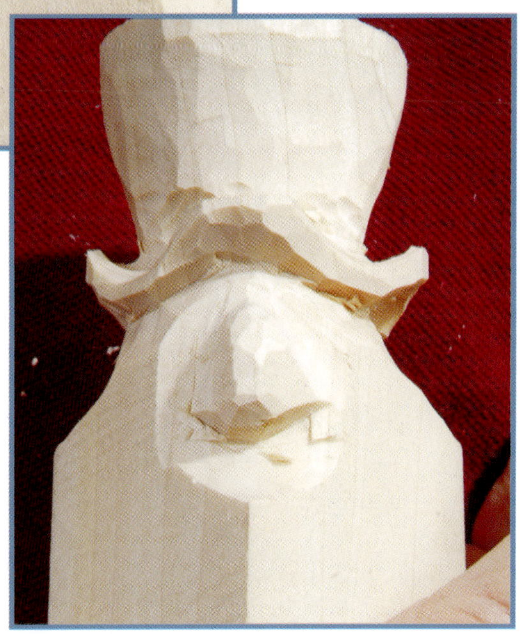

Progress.

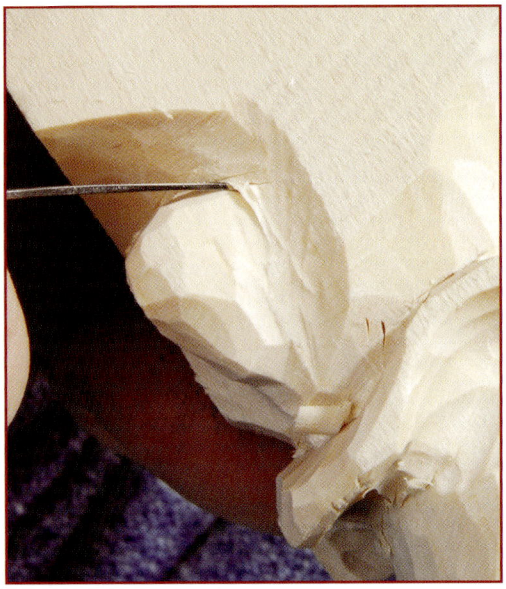

Cut a stop along the back of the nostril.

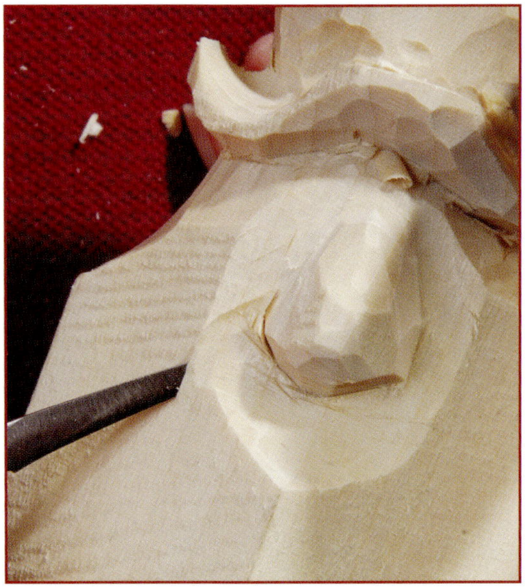

Trim back to it along the cheek…

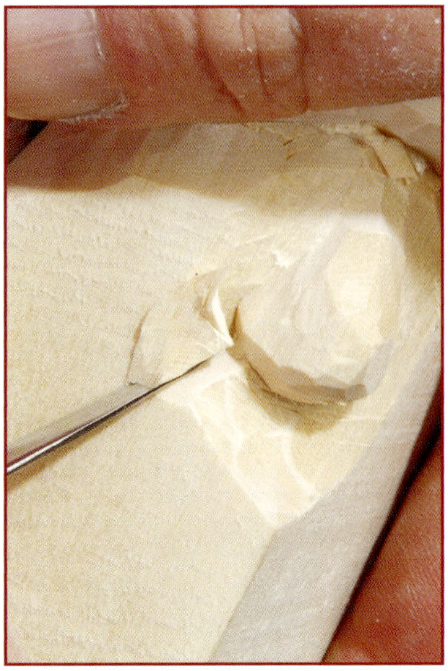

…and up from the lip. The piece should pop out.

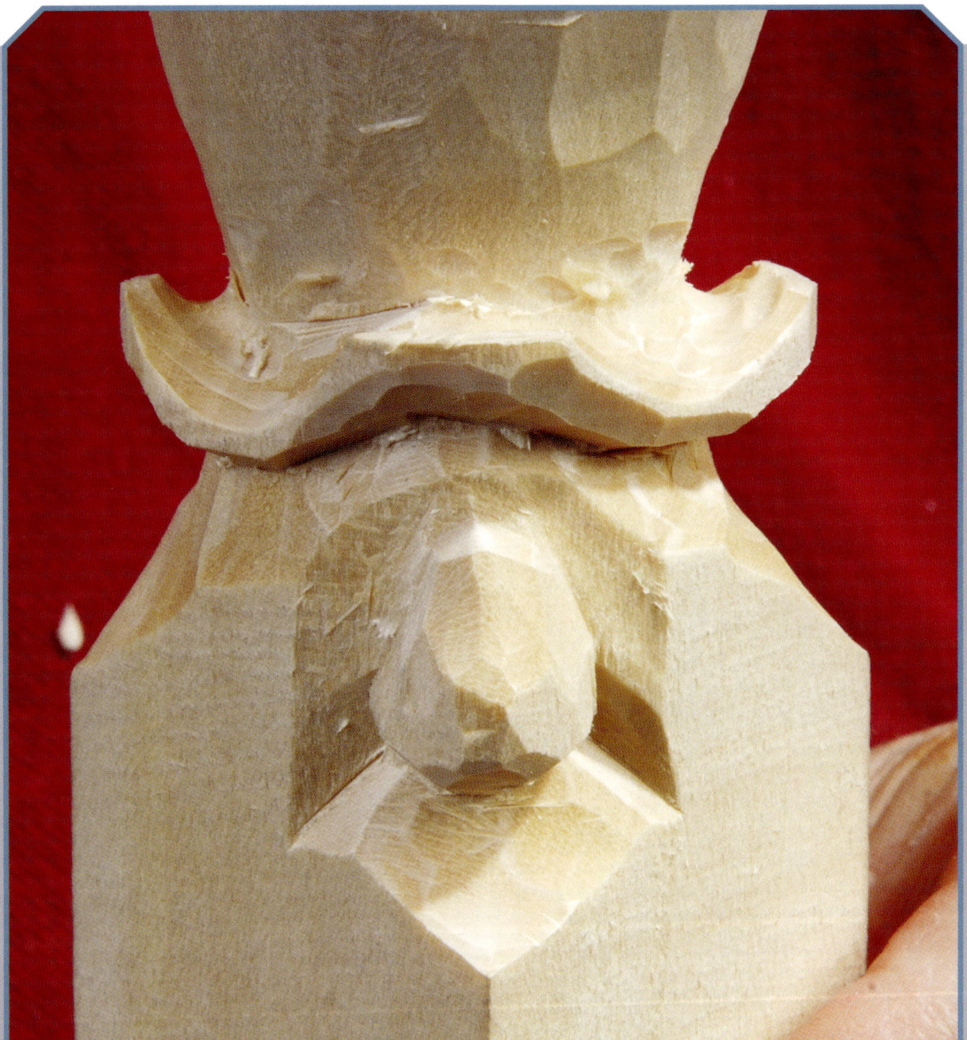

The result.

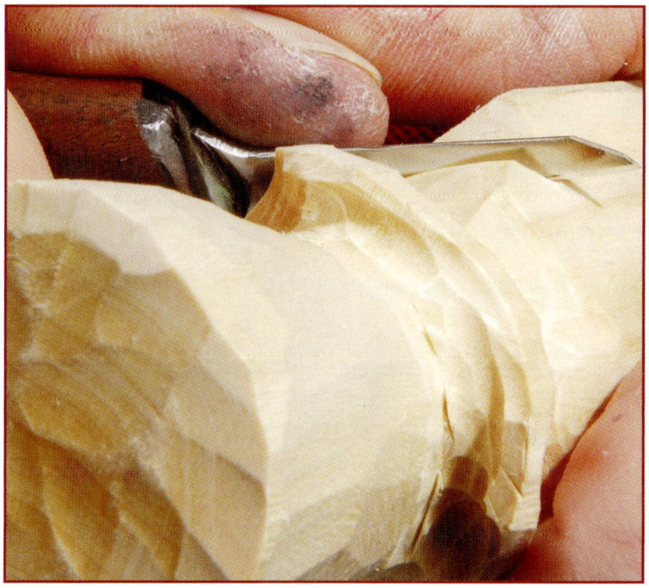

Cut a stop at the bottom of the hairline on the side of the face. Make it about halfway down the ear so the ear will show.

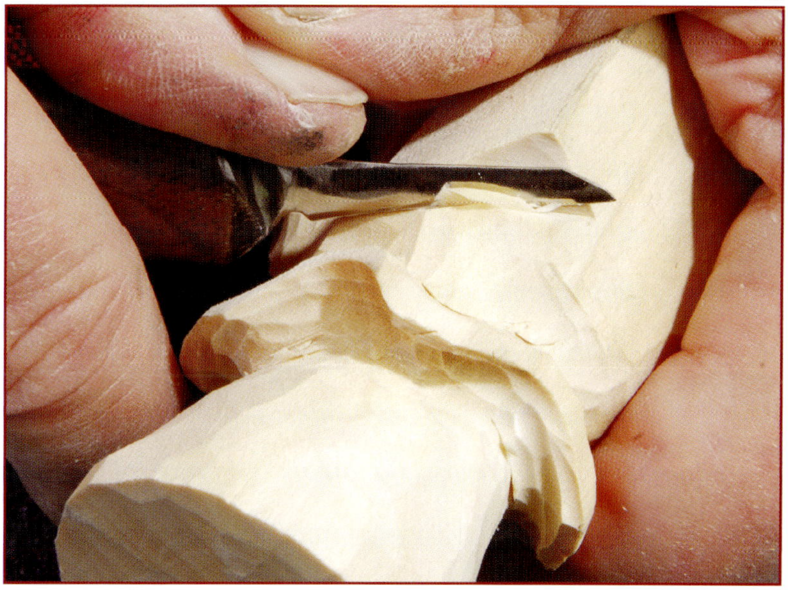

Trim back to it from below.

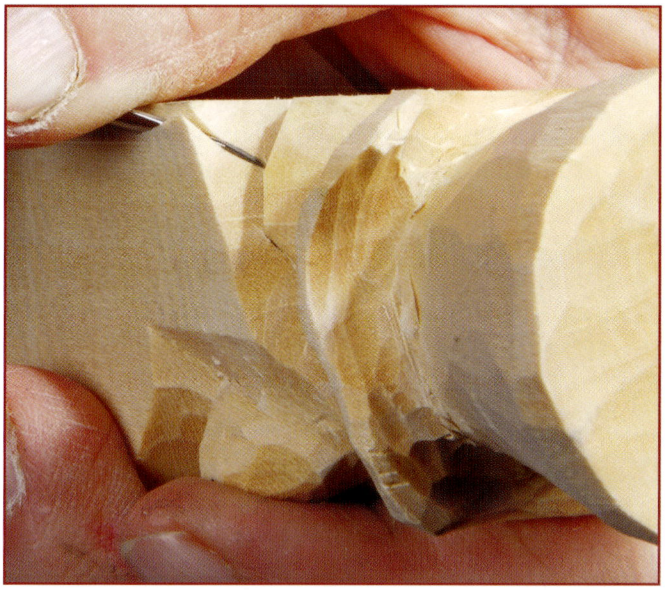

Cut a stop in the corner, which is the line of the front of the ear and the back of the sideburn

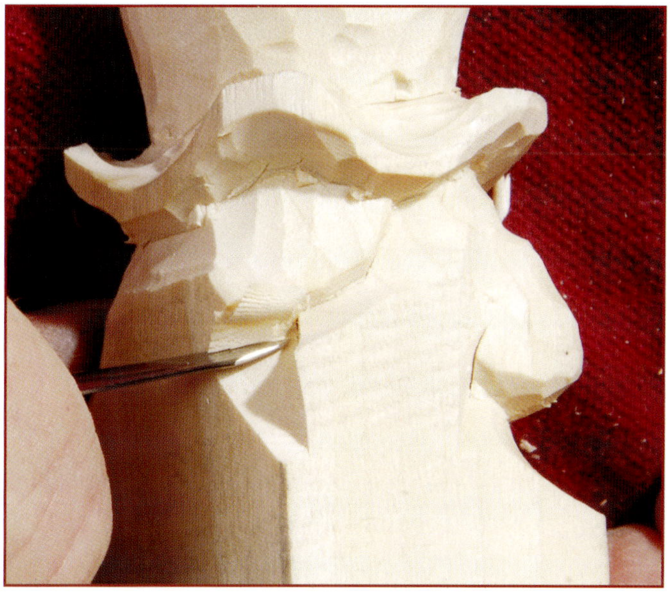

Behind the stop trim away for the ear.

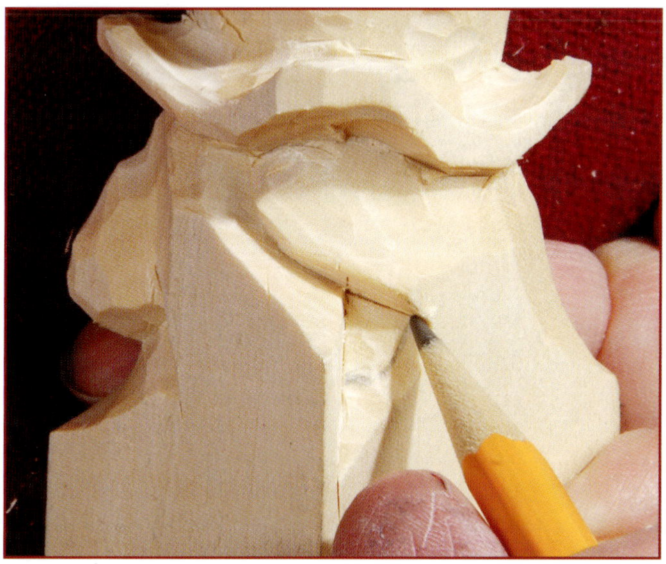

The bottom of the ear should be about even with the bottom of the nose. Draw it in.

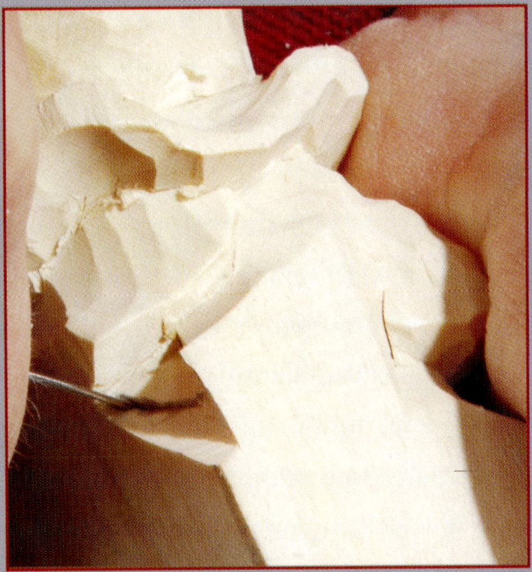

Make a stop on the line...

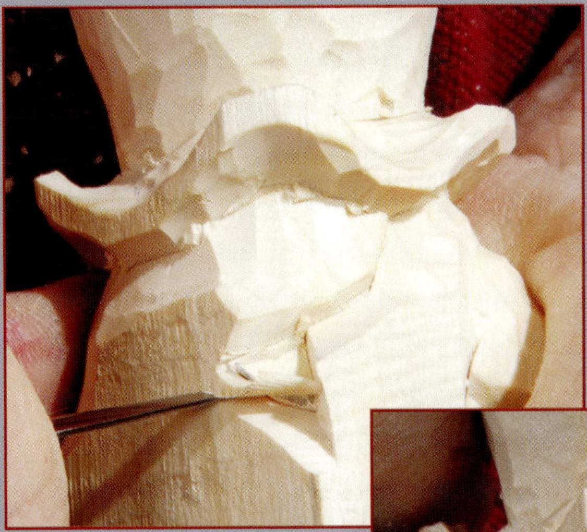

...and trim back to it from the neck.

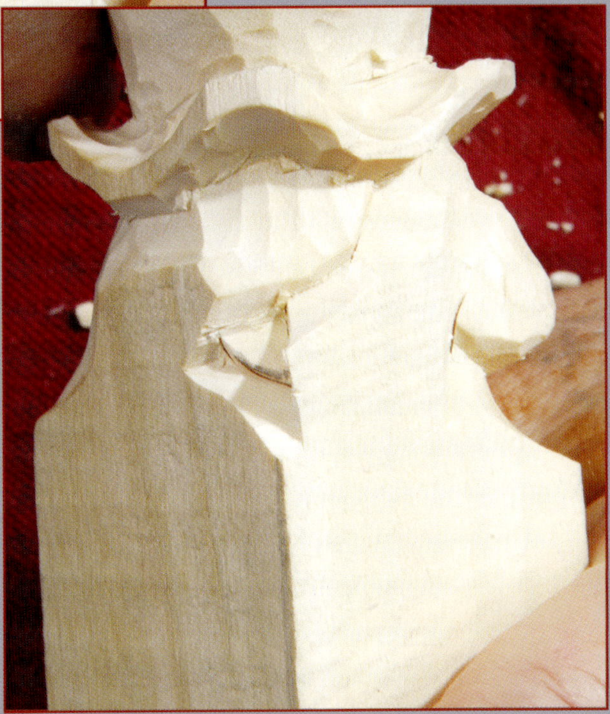

The result. This about all of the ear that will show.

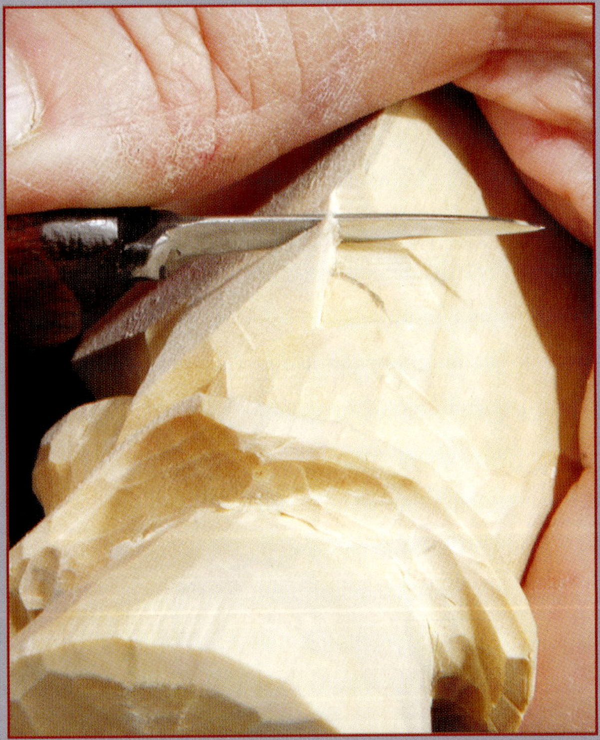

The sideburn ends just a little below the ear. Cut a stop there...

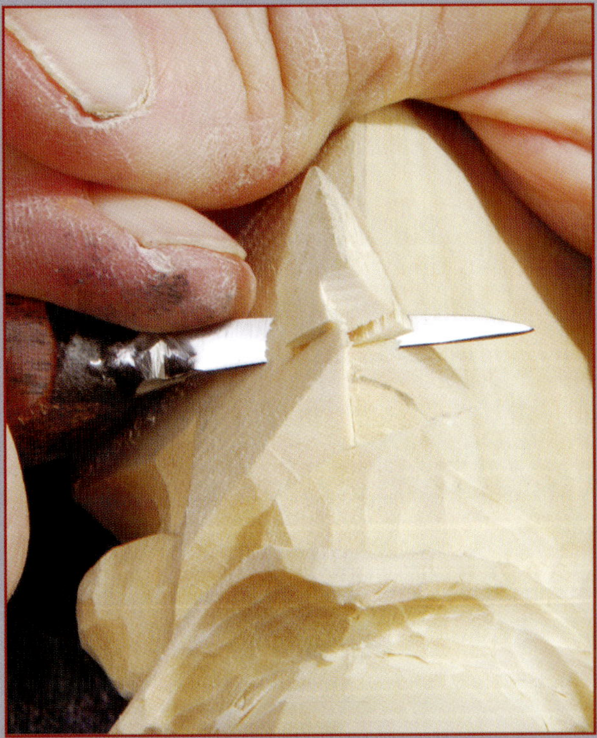

...and trim back from the shoulder.

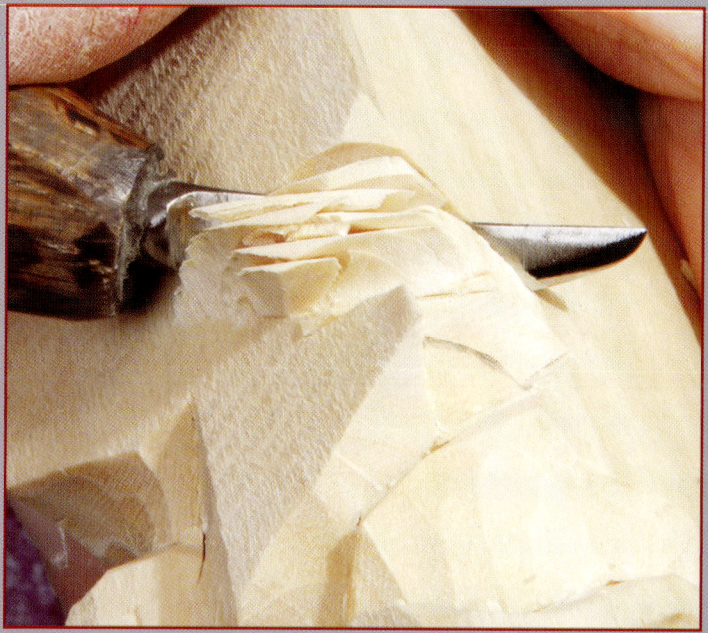

Make several cuts on the shoulder...

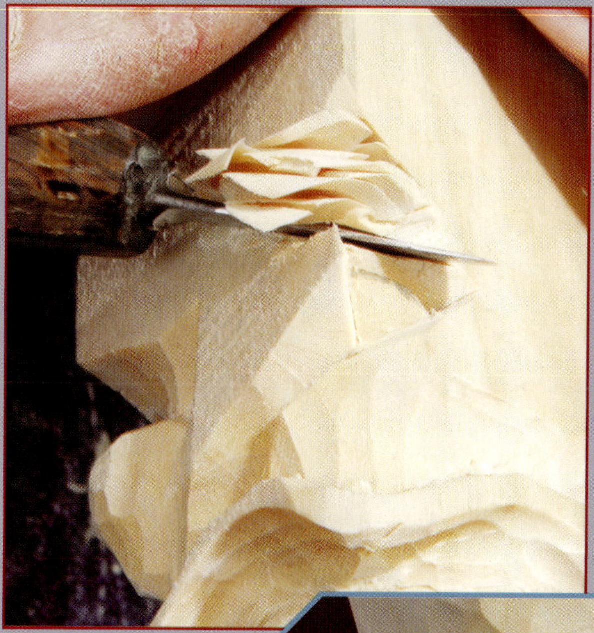

...and wack them off.

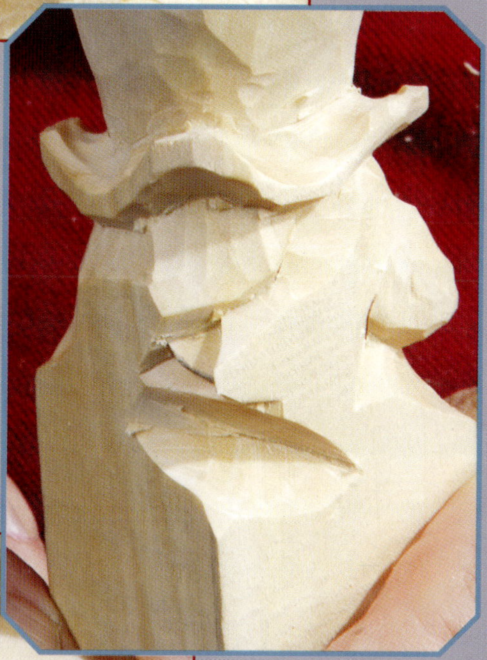

Progress.

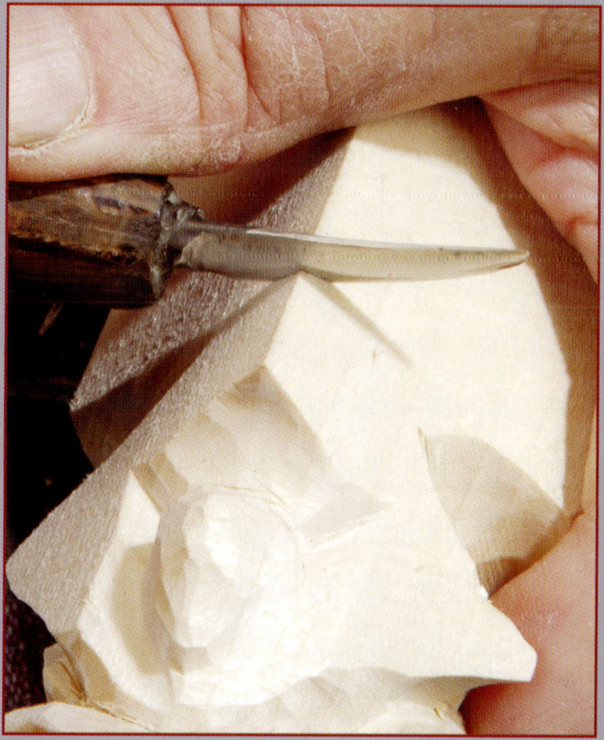

Make a stop at the bottom of the whiskers.

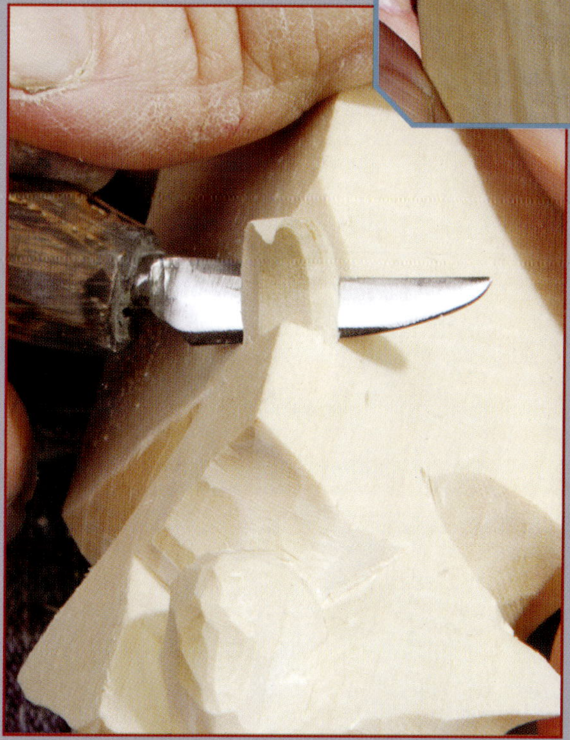

Trim back to it from the chest.

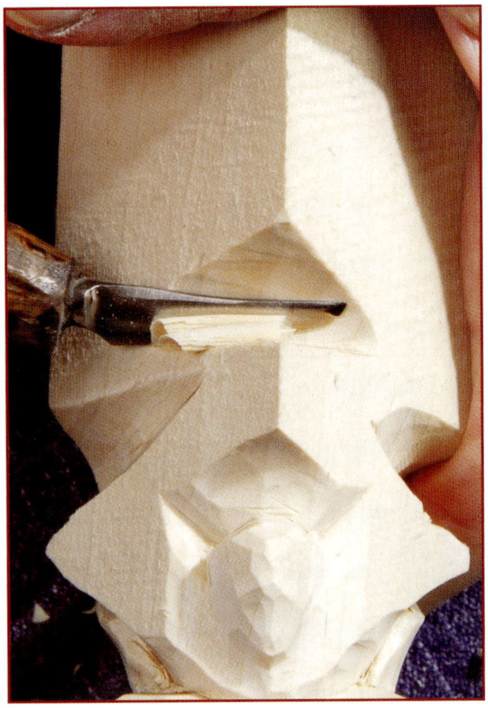

This cut is going all the way back to the chest, so it will be pretty deep.

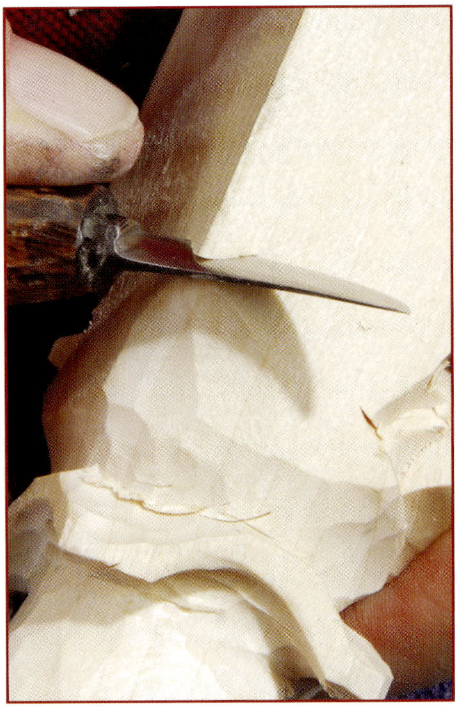

At the back, make an angled stop at the hairline. This allows for a little flip in the hair at the back.

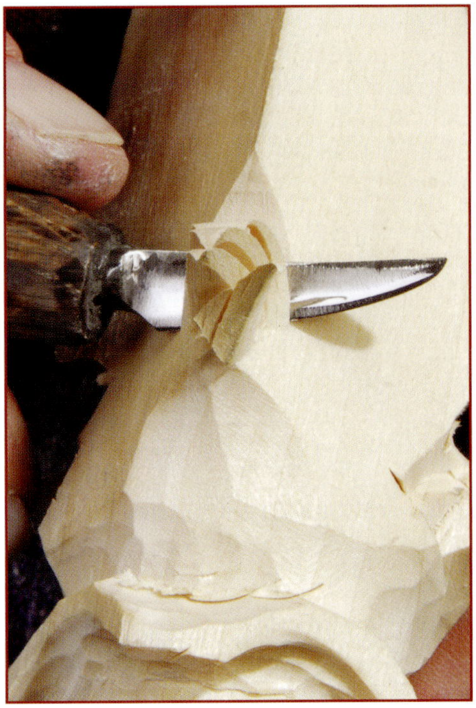

Trim back to it from the back, going in to where the collar will be.

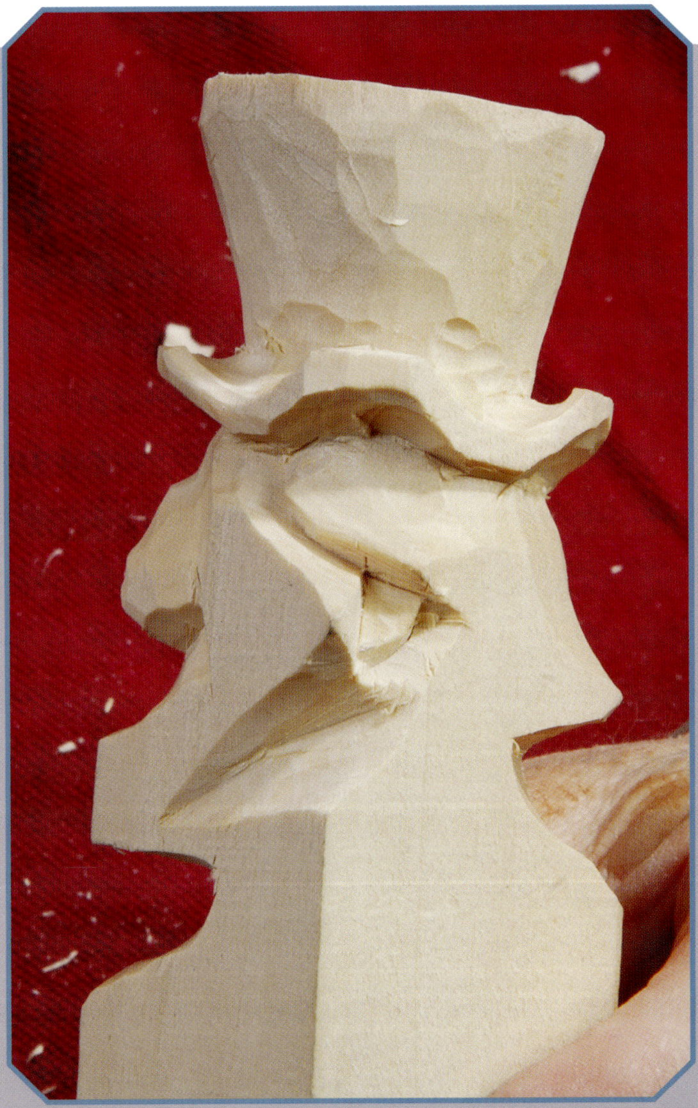

Progress.

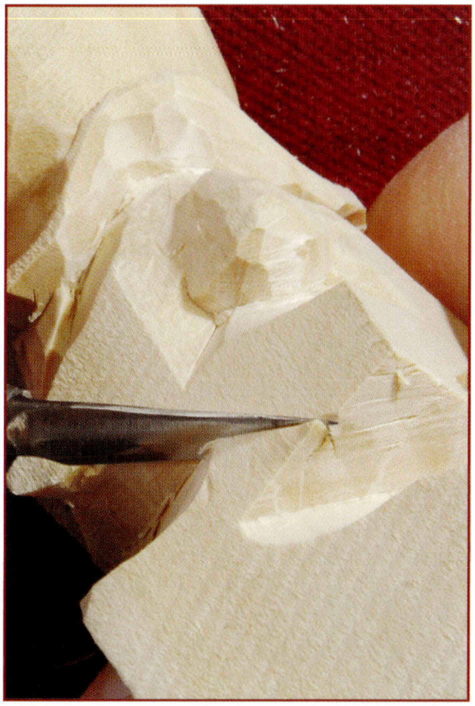

Make a stop in the jaw line.

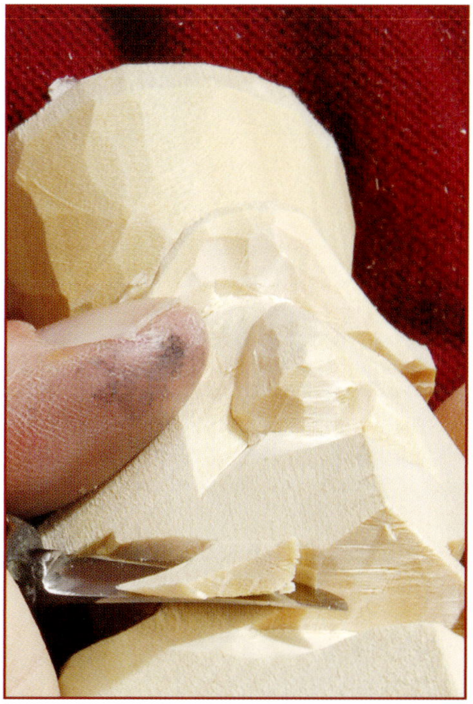

Trim back to it from the chest.

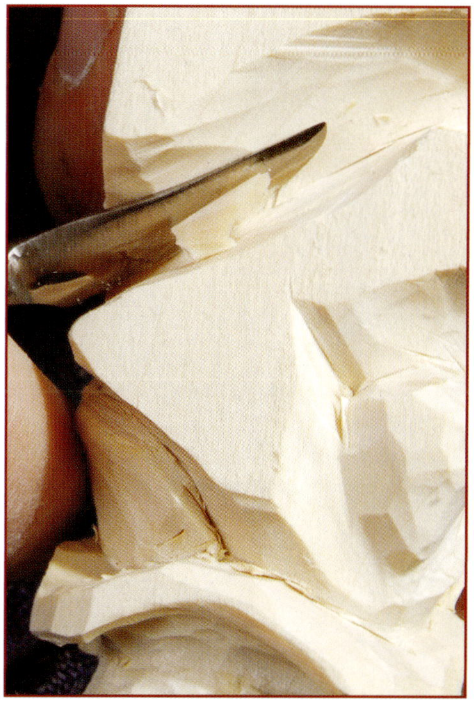

Deepen to the neck.

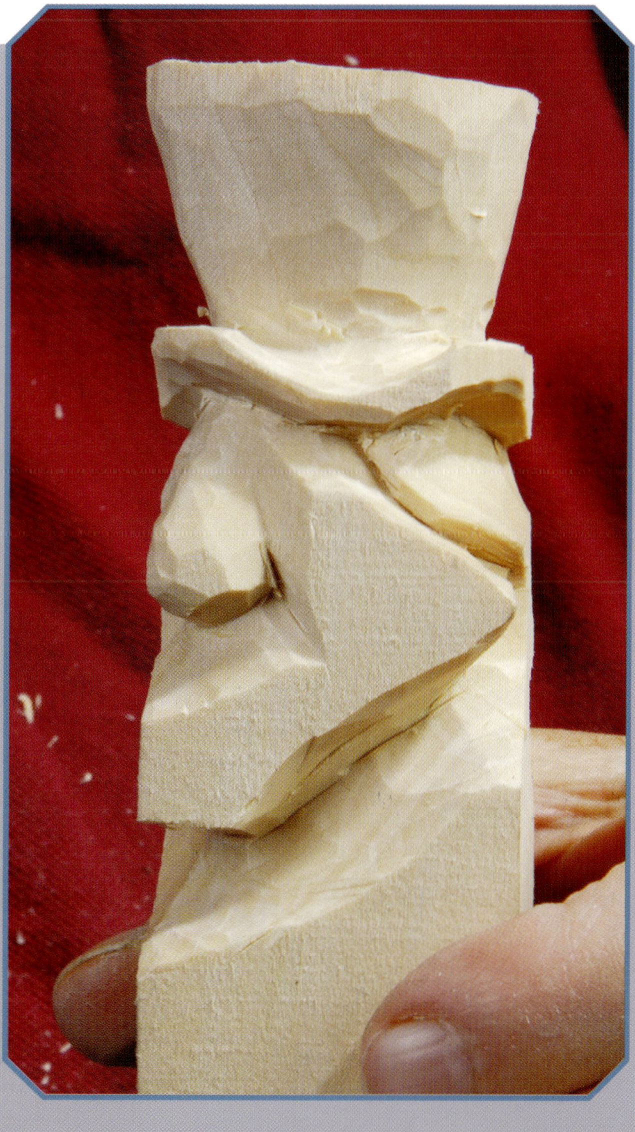

Progress.

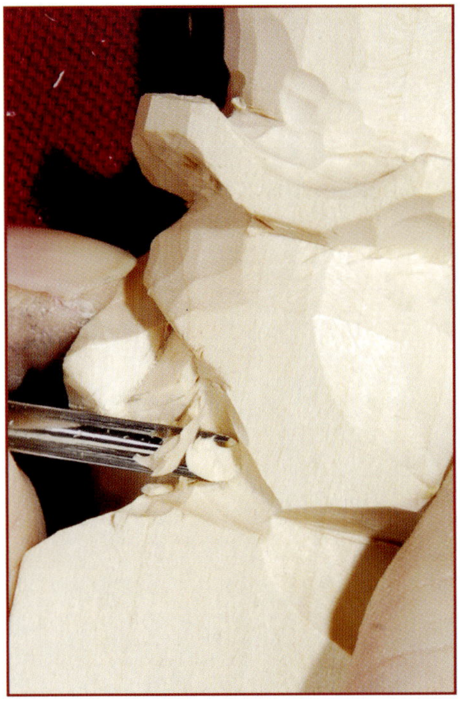

Clean up behind the ear to take it back to the neckline.

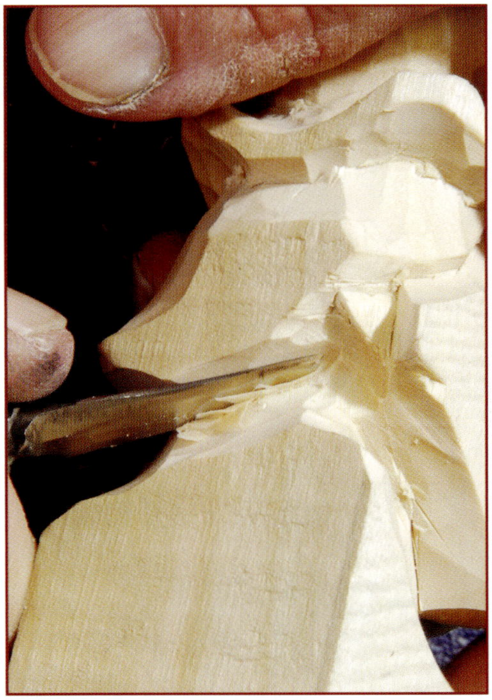

Continue the neckline from behind the ear to the back.

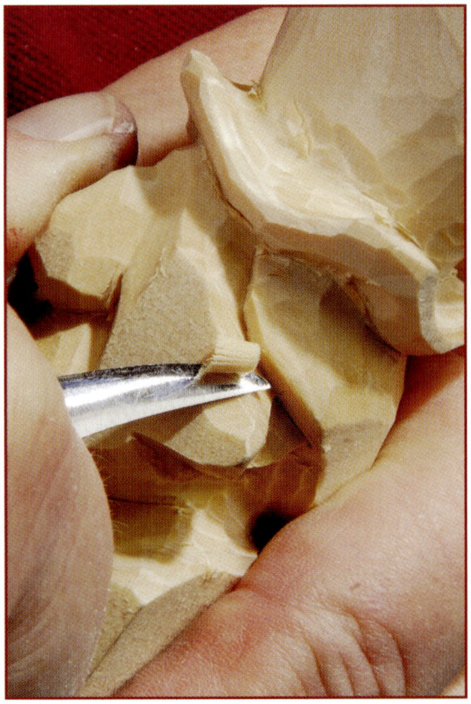

Cup the sideburns so they flare out a bit.

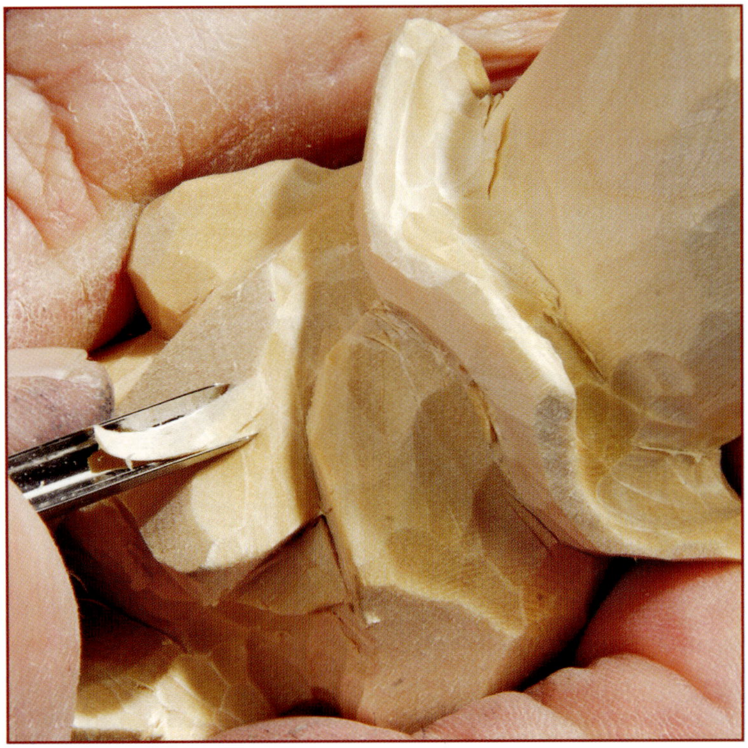

Cut in front of the sideburn with a gouge…

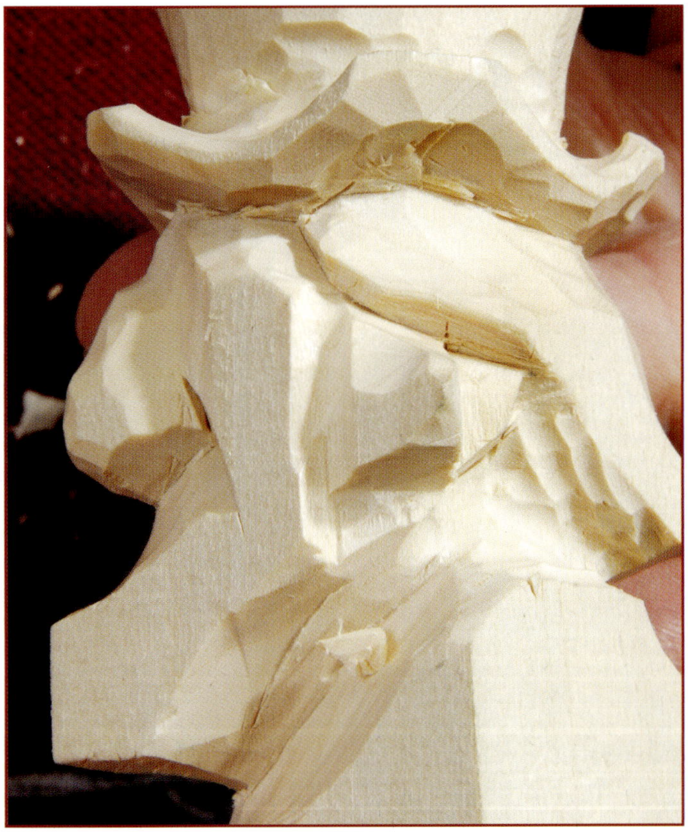

…to separate it from the face.

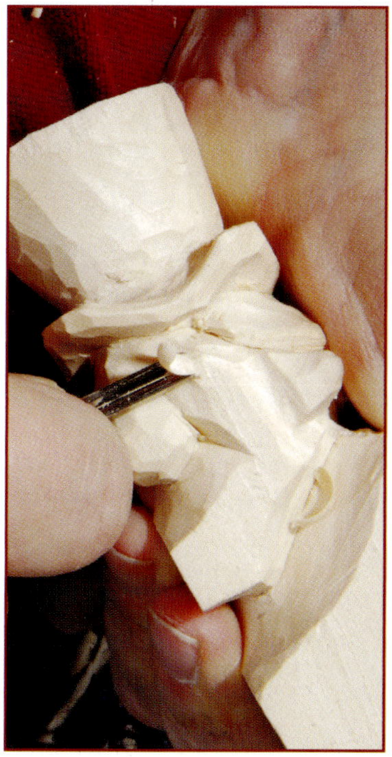

Gouge out the eye area, cutting from the bridge of the nose to the outside of the cheek.

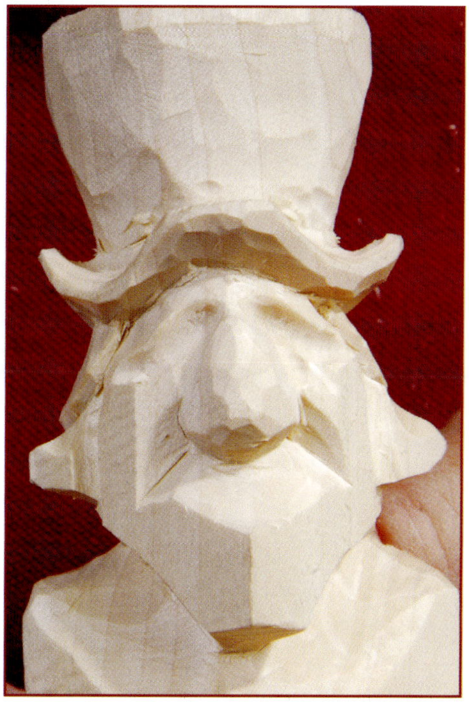

The result

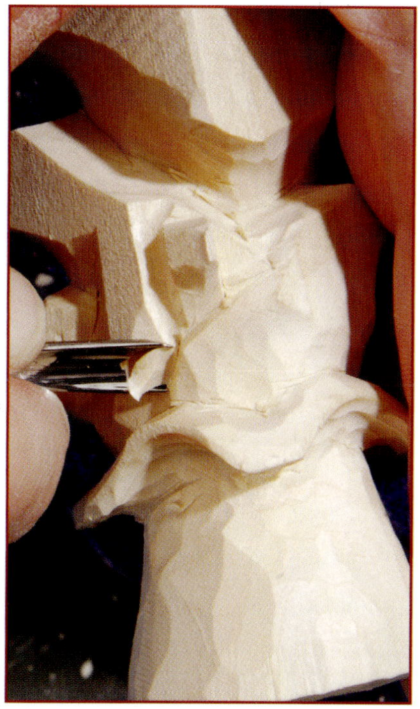

Switch to a wider gouge and continue the line straight in at the temple to the sideburn.

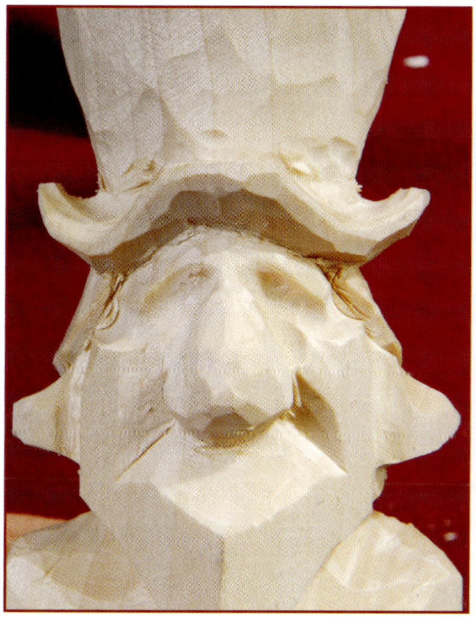

Progress

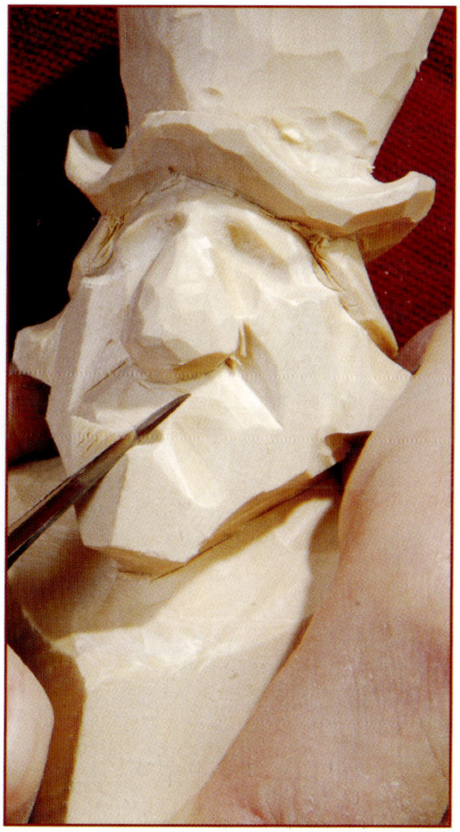

Scoop out on each side of the upper goatee.

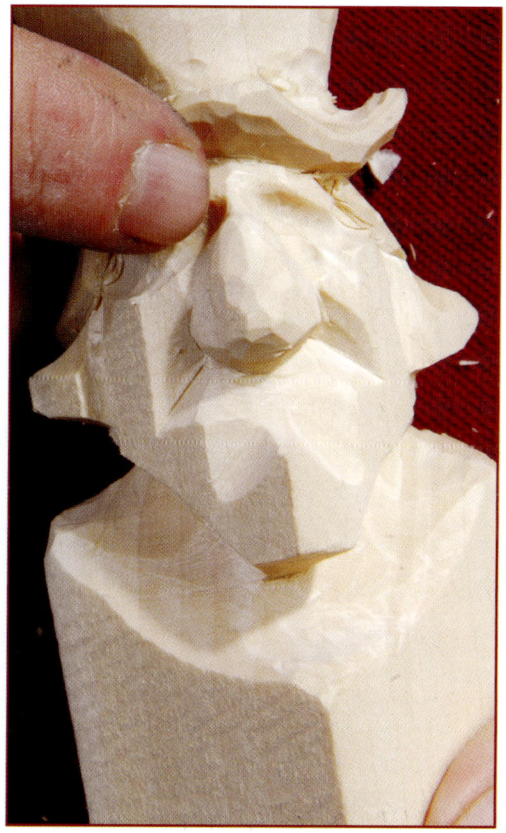

The result.

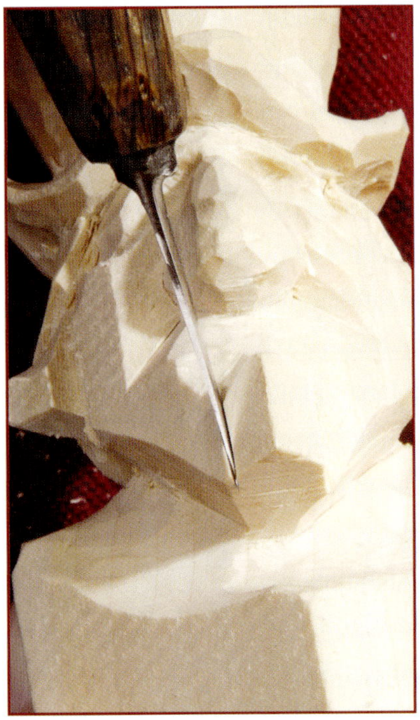

From there make a stop cut along the side of the goatee down to the chin…

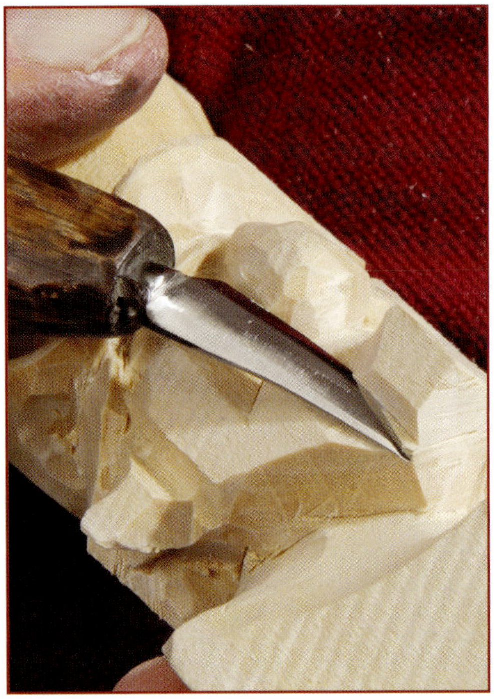

…and trim back to it.

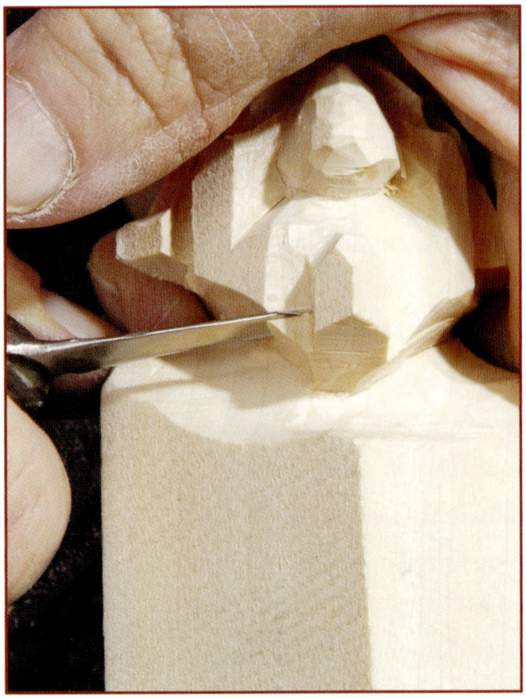

At the side of the goatee cut in at the chin line and pop off the piece below it.

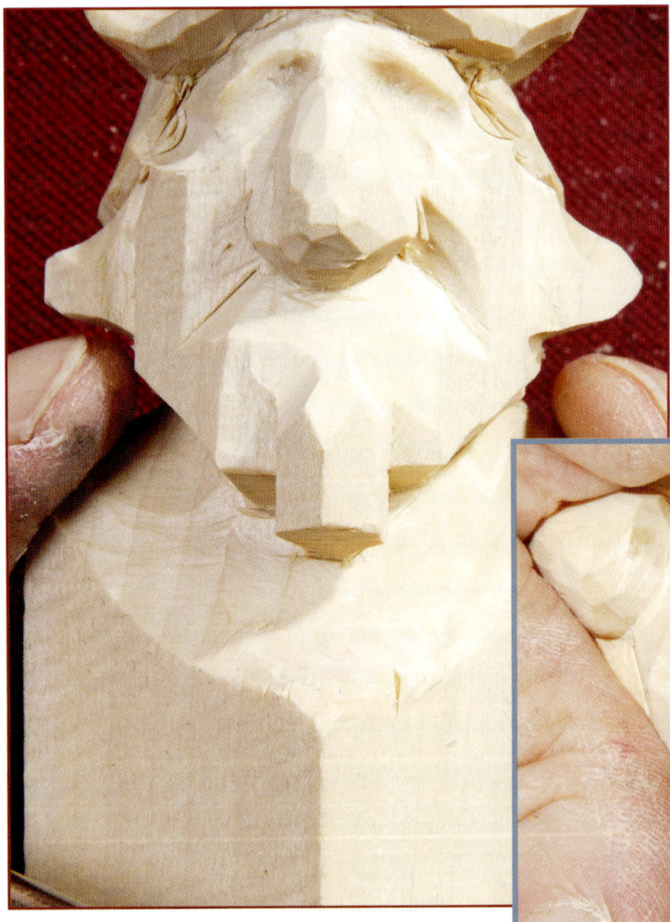

This is the result.

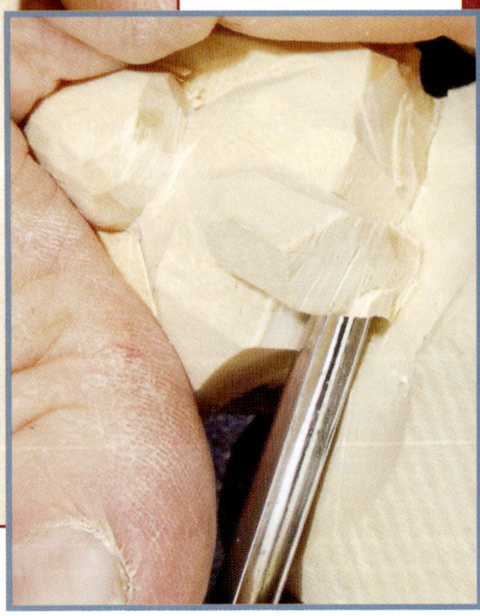

Work behind the goatee to clean out the area behind it to the neck.

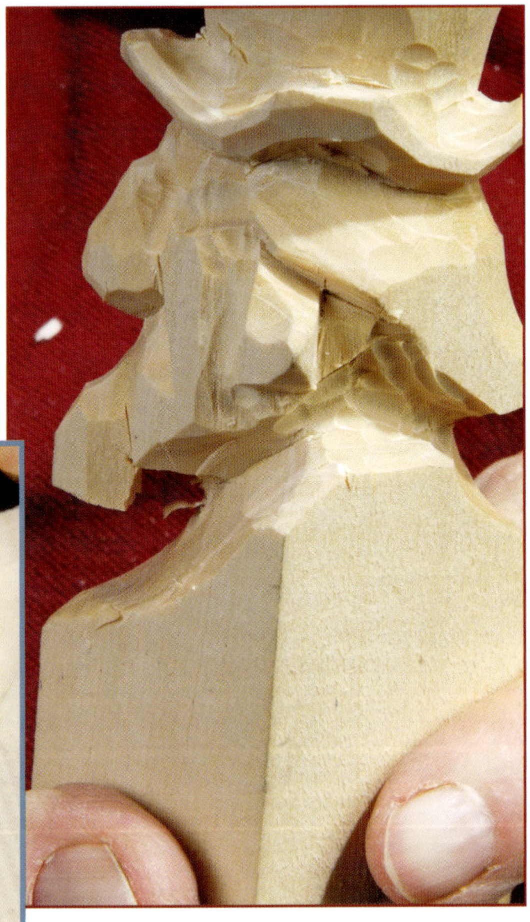

The result.

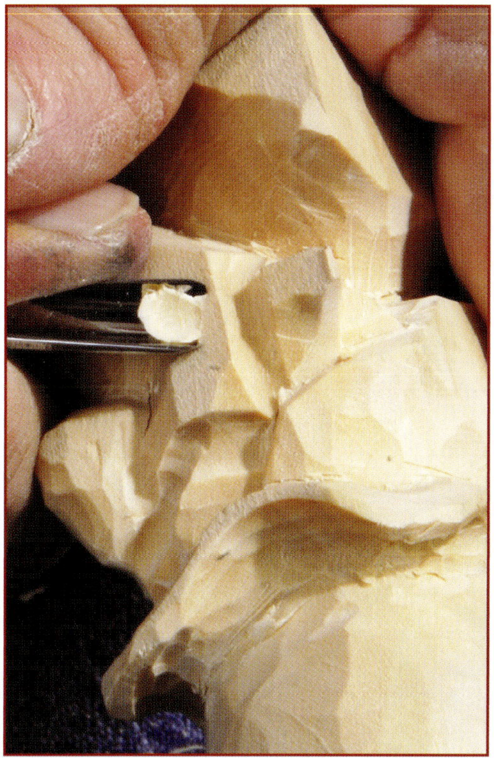

Starting at the edge of the nose making an arcing cut with a gouge to define the bottom of the cheek.

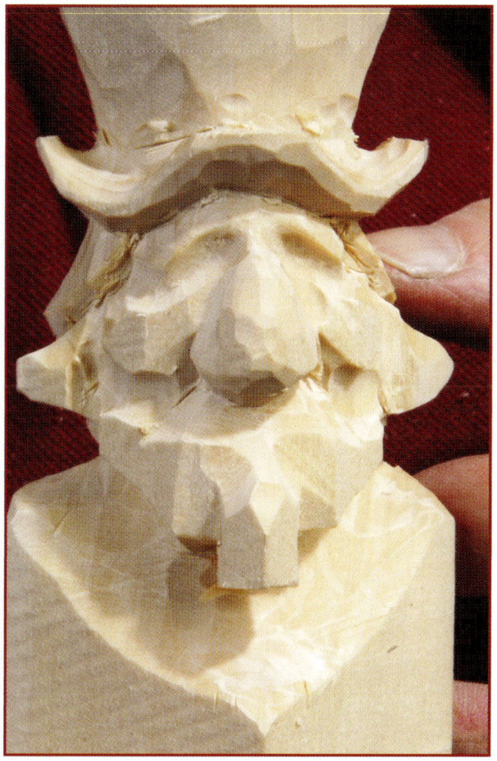

The result .

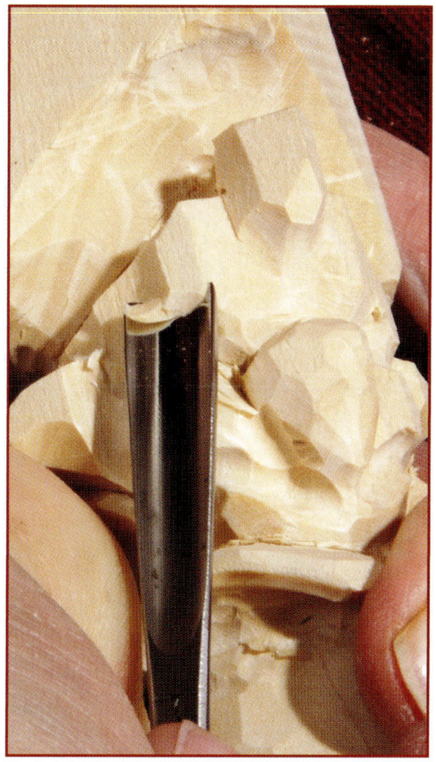

With a wide gouge, cut under the cheek bone to narrow the jaw.

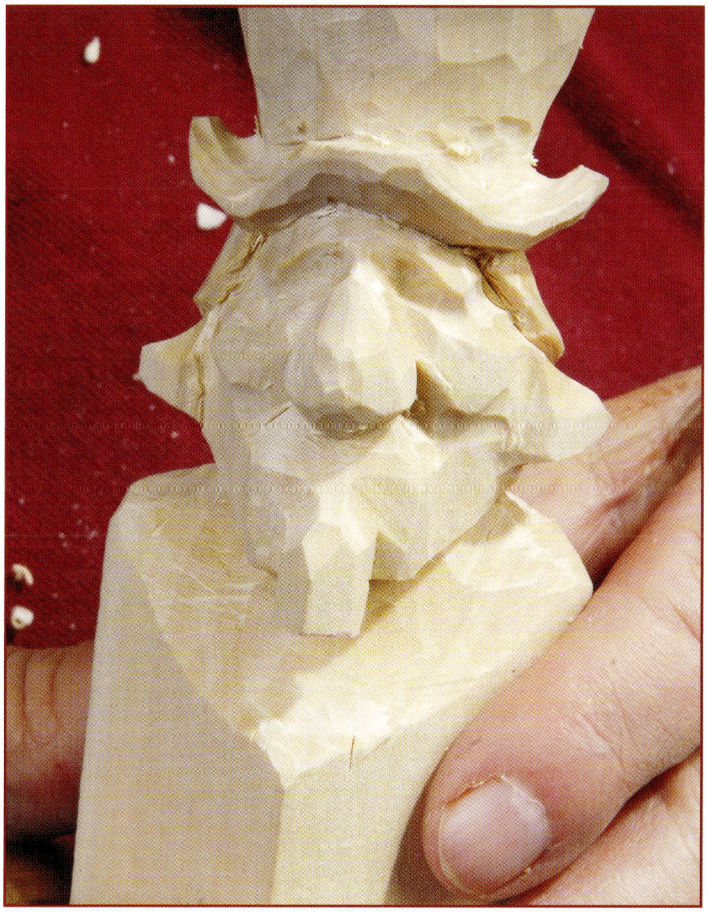

Progress.

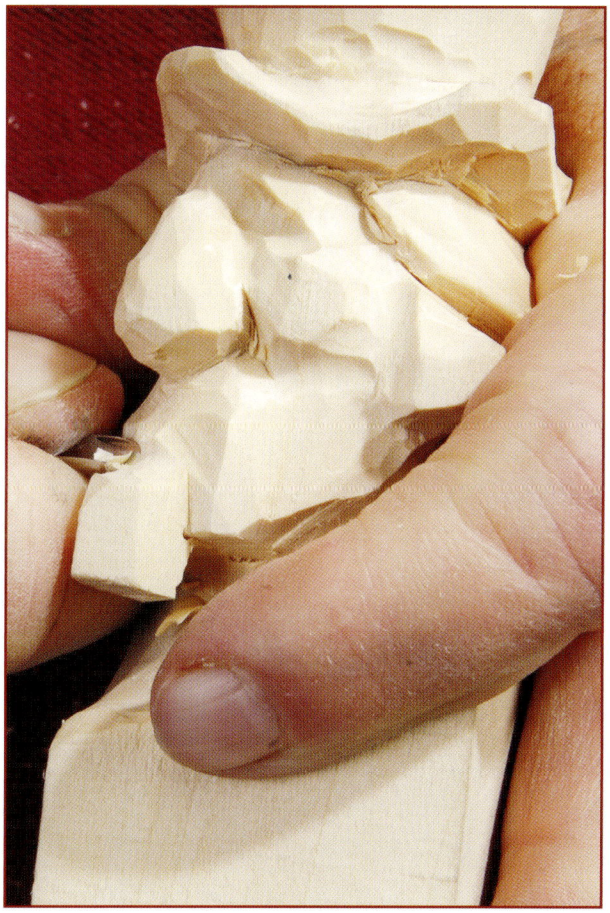

I want to trim a little off the top of the goatee to give me more room for the mouth.

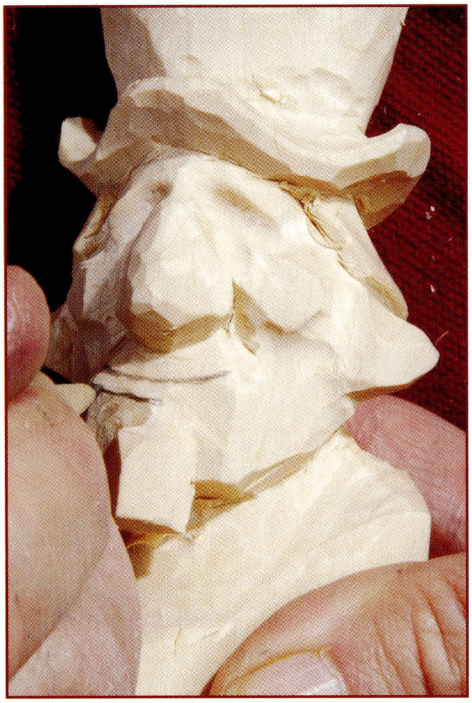

Draw in the mouth. I'm hoping to have room for a toothy grin.

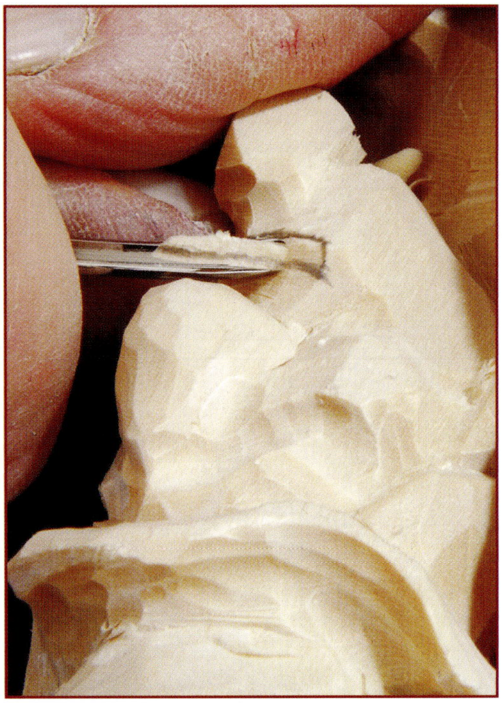

Go across the top line with a v-tool...

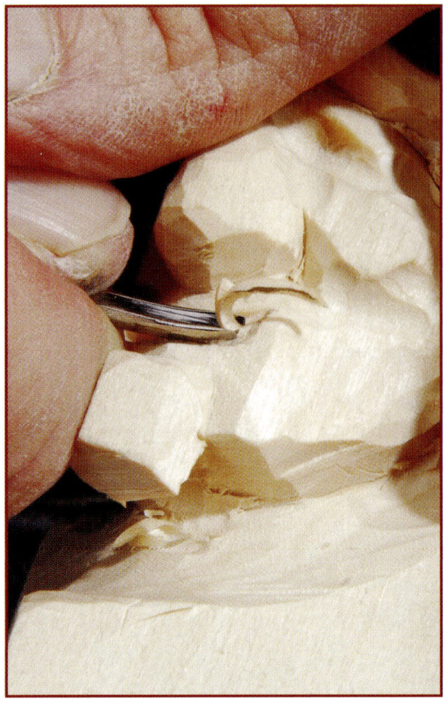

...and do the same thing on the bottom line.

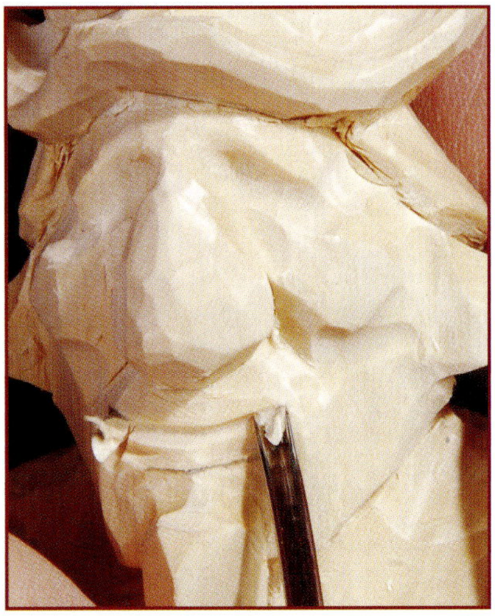

Bring the corner of the lower line up to the upper line. This will create the inside of the mouth.

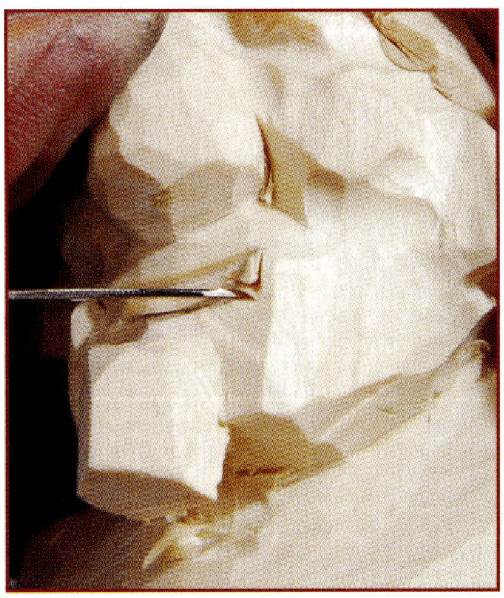

Use a knife to clean up the corner.

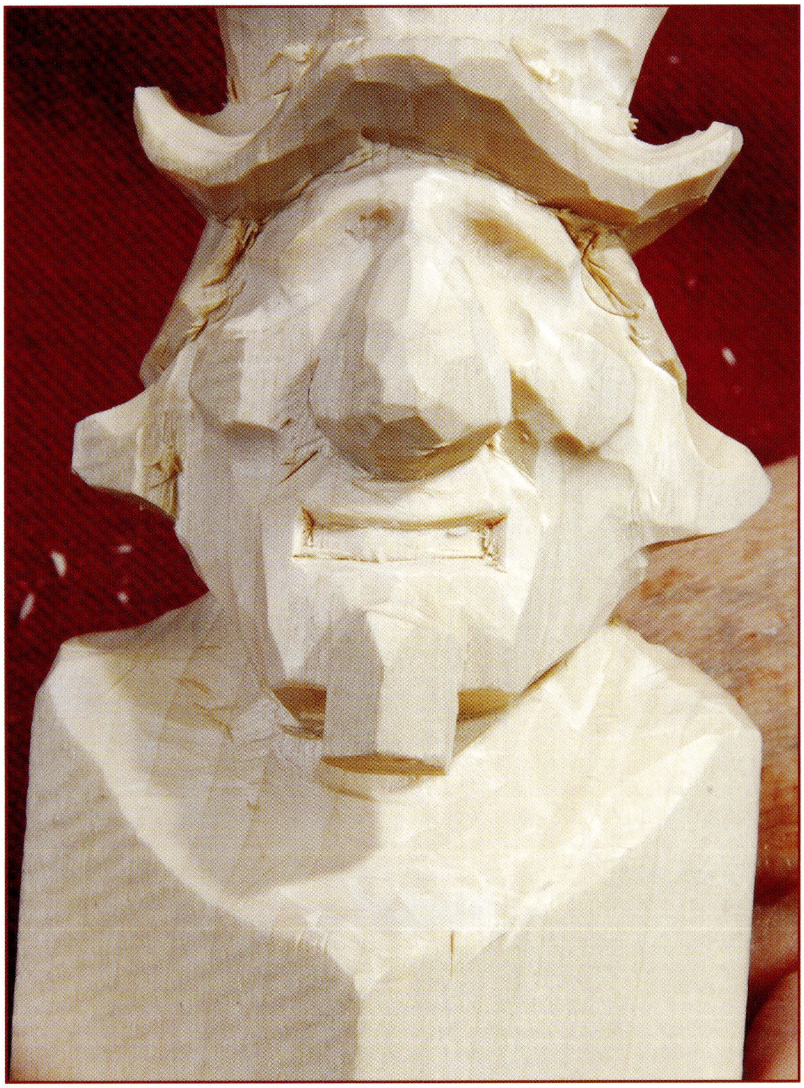

Progress.

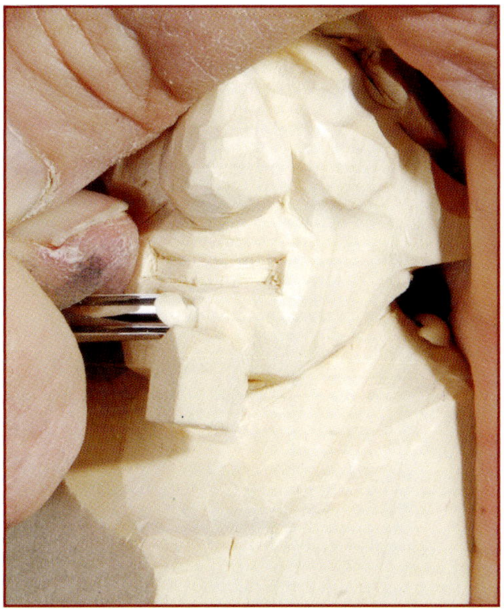

Go under the lower lip with a small gouge to bring it out.

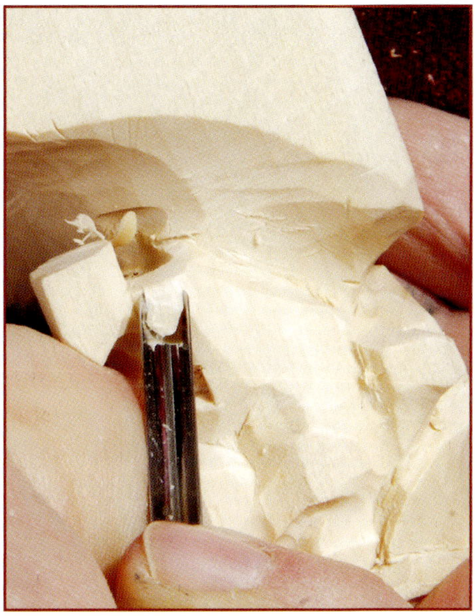

Gouge down from the corners of the mouth to bring out the chin.

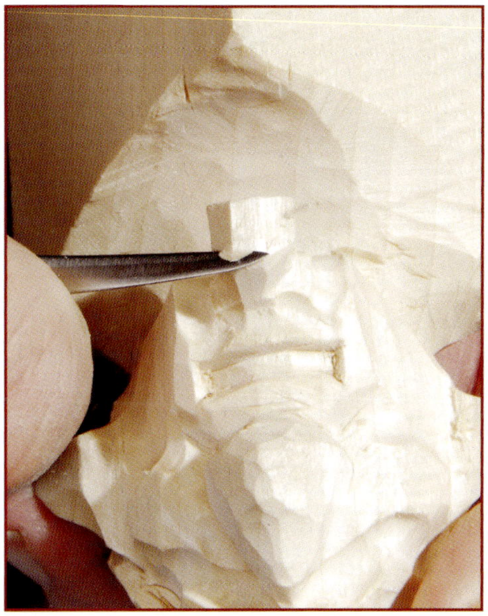

Shape up the goatee.

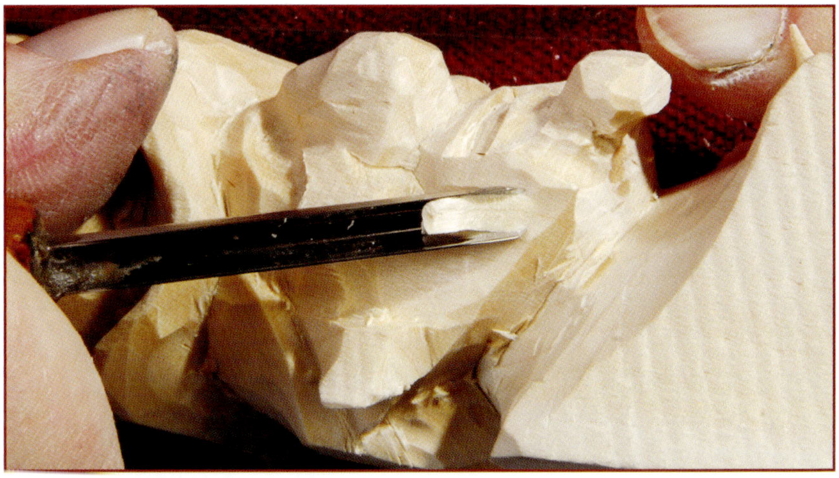

Now bring the smile line down to the jaw…and a little underneath to give him something of a waddle.

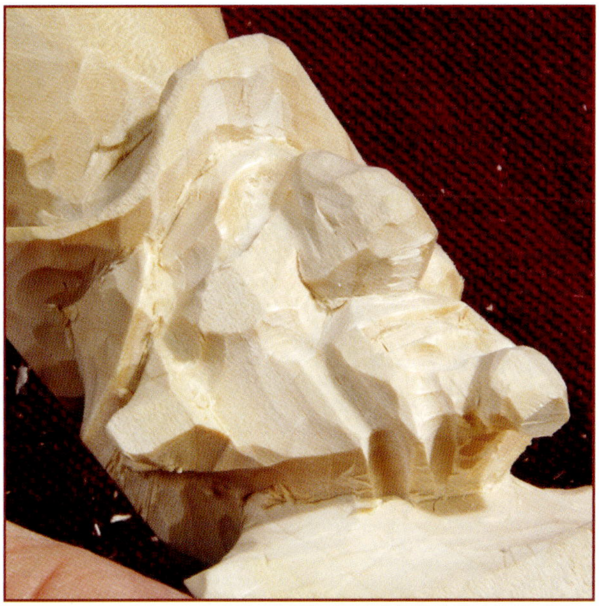

The result.

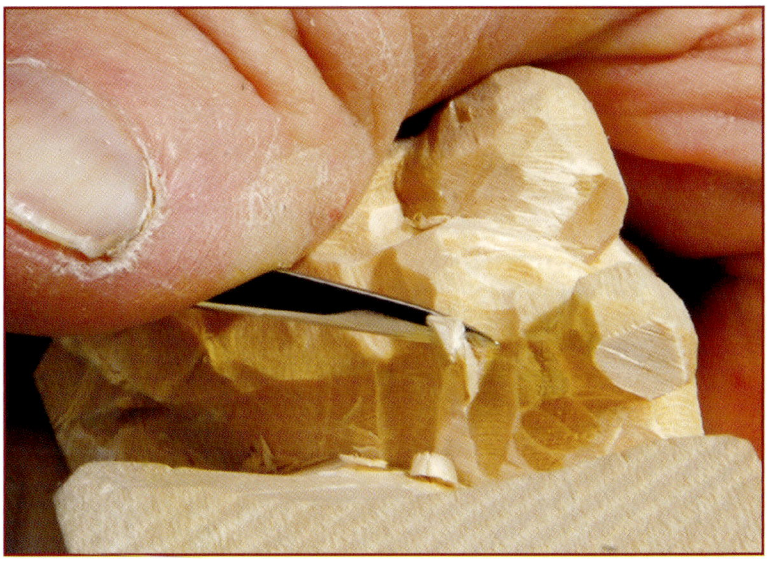

Soften the waddle up with a knife.

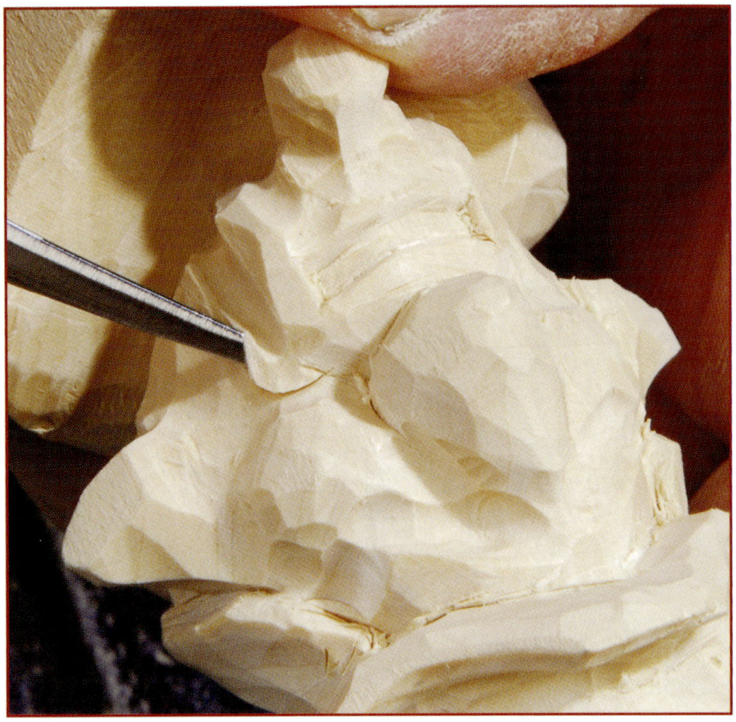

Exaggerate the smile line with a curved cut...

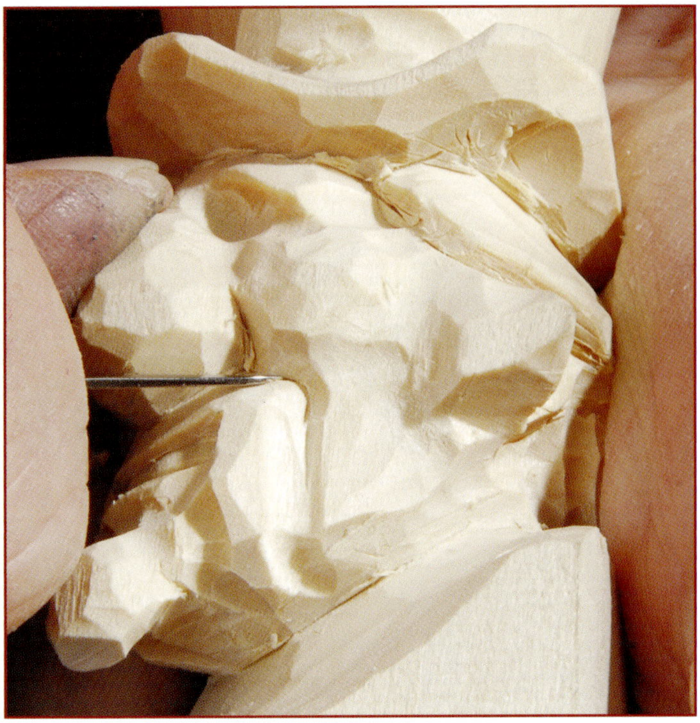

...trimmed off from the upper lip.

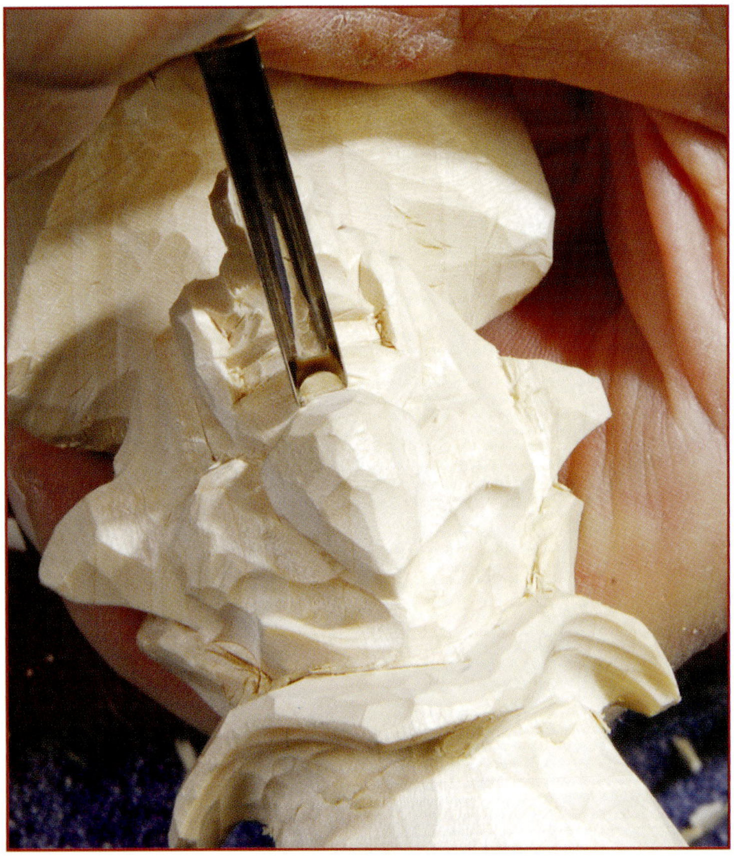

Use a gouge to create a philtrum in the upper lip.

Progress.

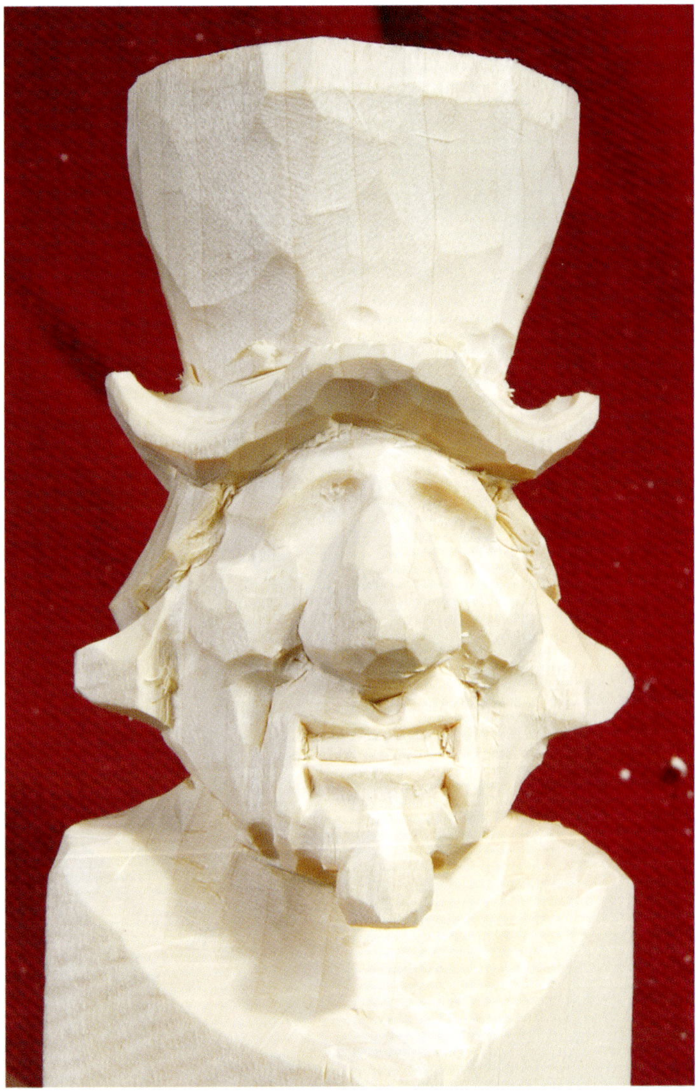

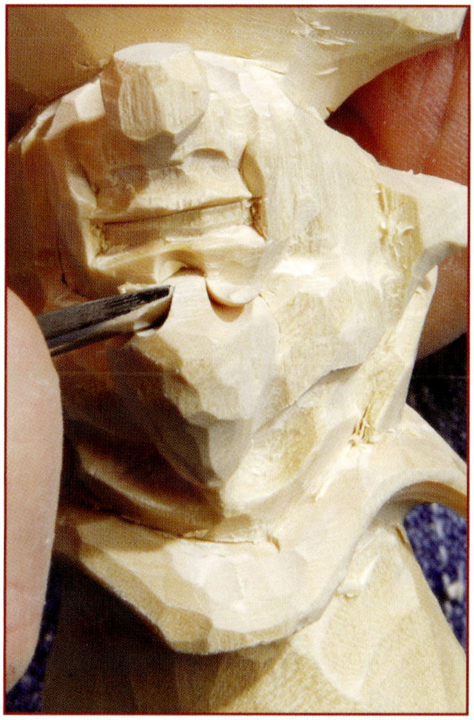

A gouge pushed straight in creates the nostrils.

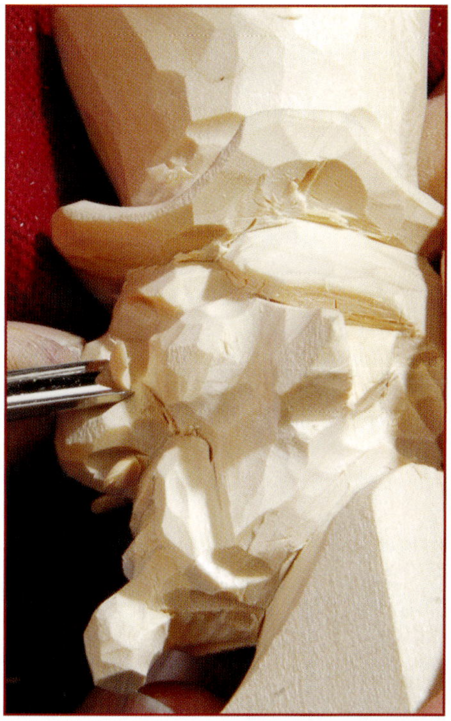

Go over the outside of the nostril with the same gouge.

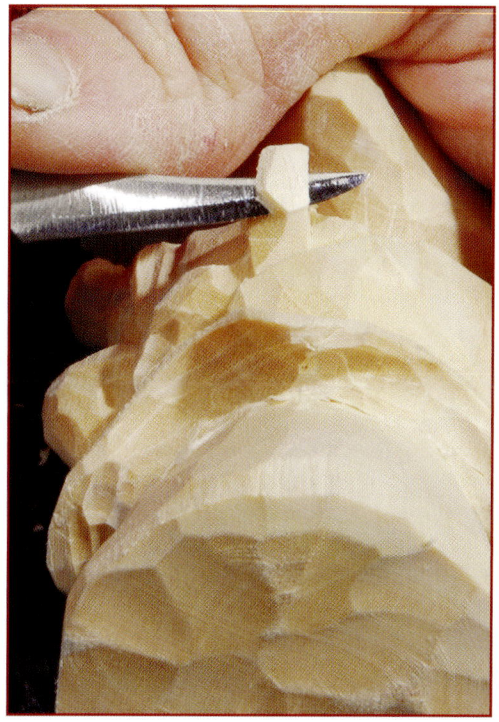

Shape the sideburns.

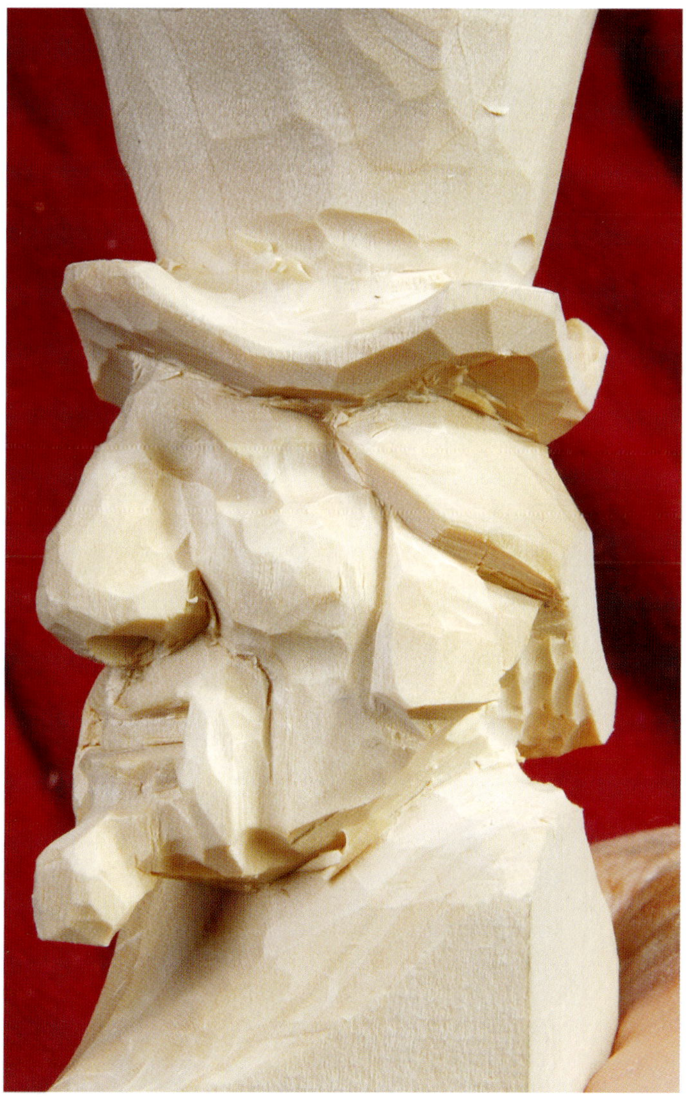

The result.

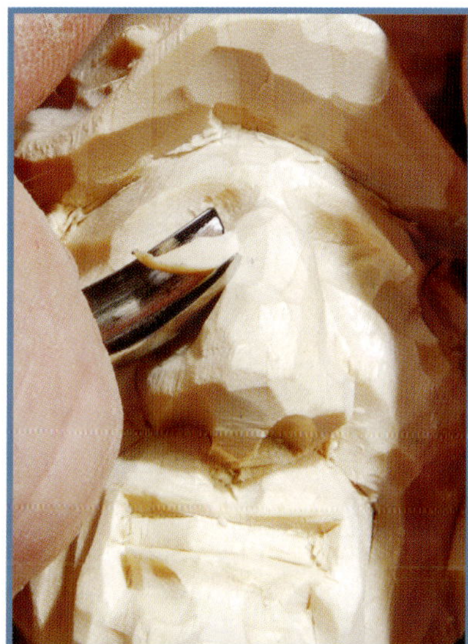

I don't like the thickness of the nose, so I'll use a gouge to narrow it some.

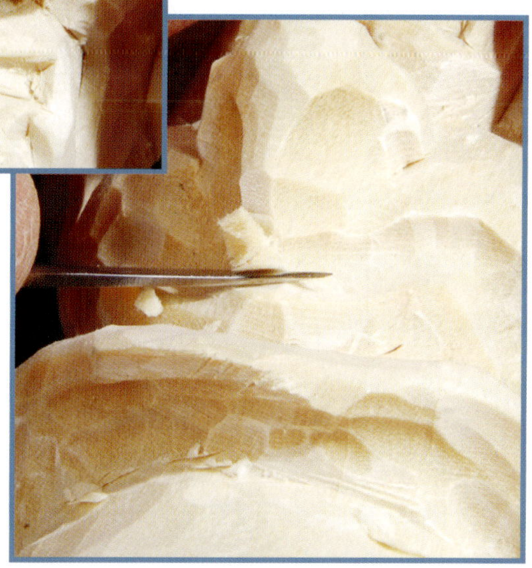

I'll define the bridge with the knife.

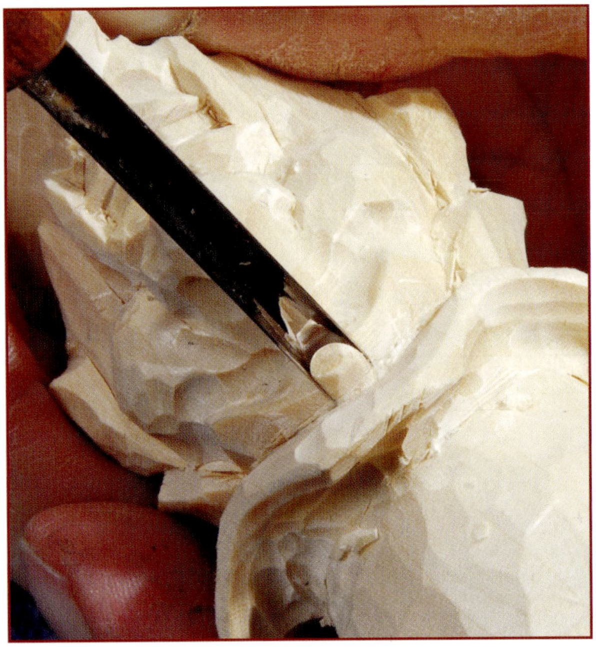

From the bridge use a gouge to separate the eyebrows.

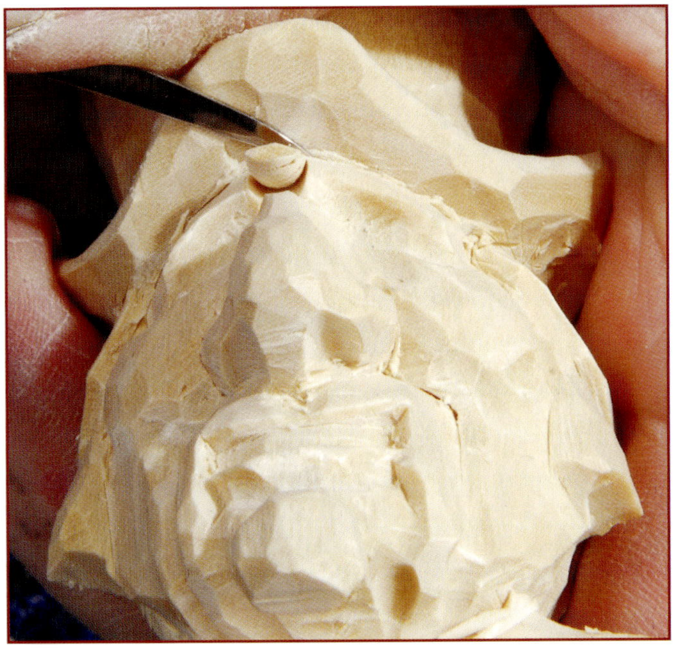

Snap the chip out with a knife.

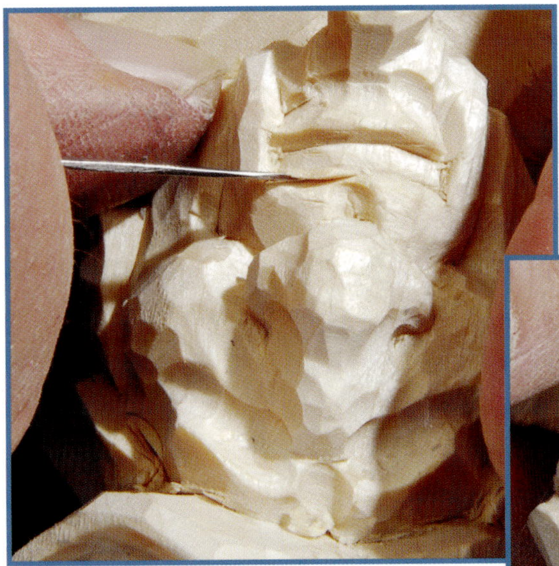

The upper lip needs a bow. Cut a curved stop from the middle...

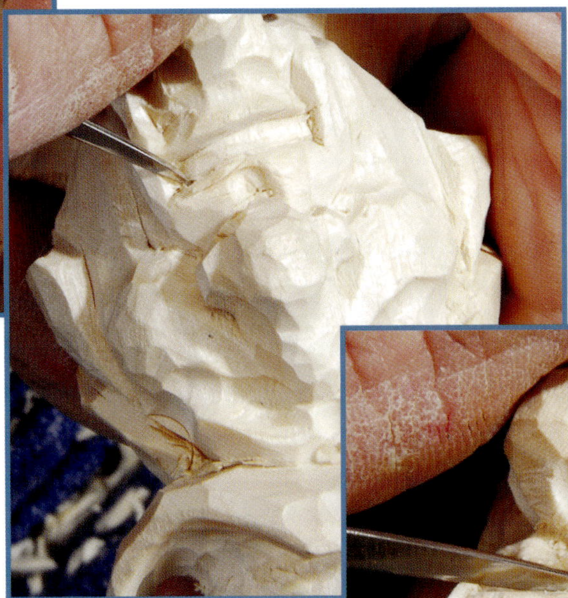

...and clip it out from the teeth. Repeat on the other side.

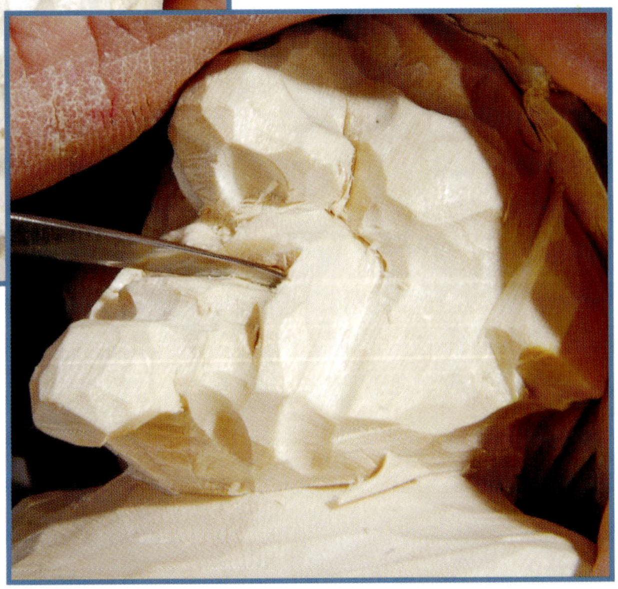

Two slices make a shadow line under the teeth.

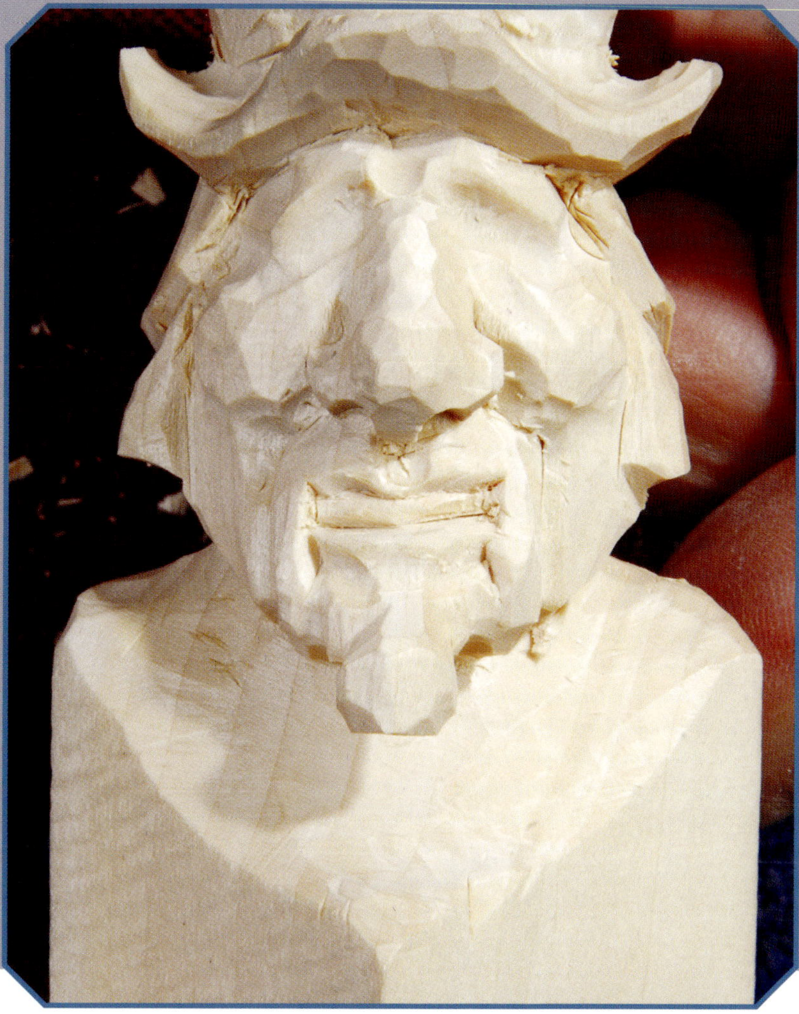

Progress.

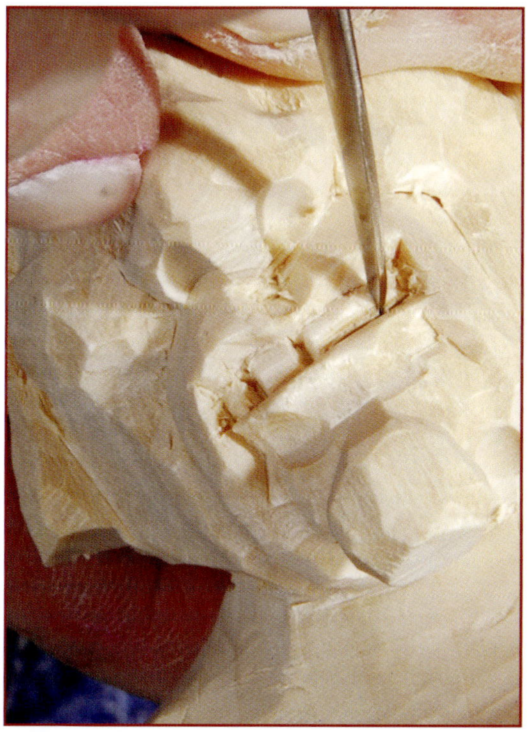

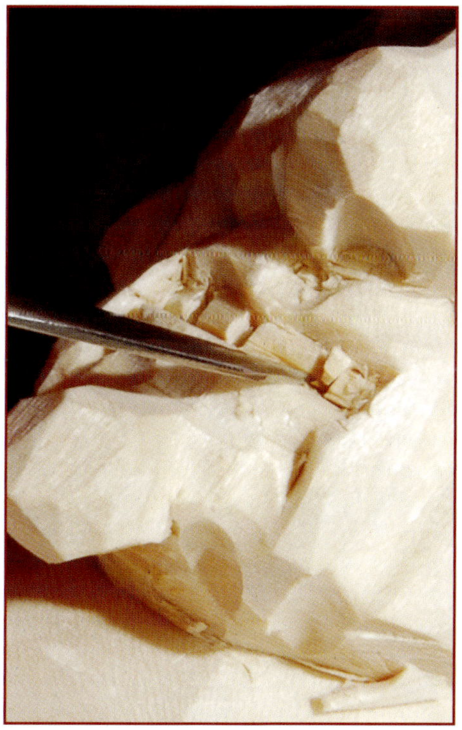

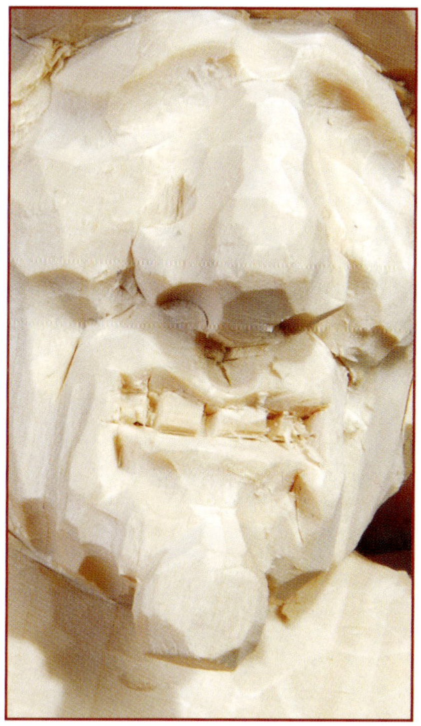

The teeth are separated from the middle out. Make a double slice between the teeth…

…and pop out the chip.

The teeth formed.

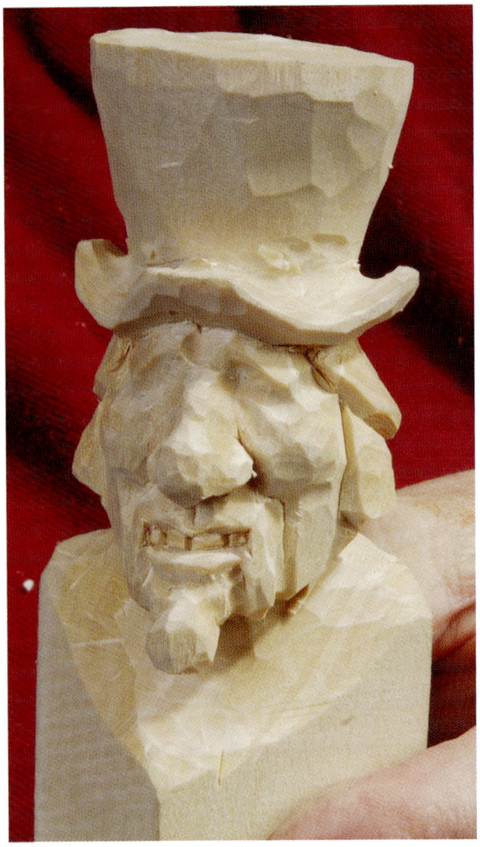

Progress.

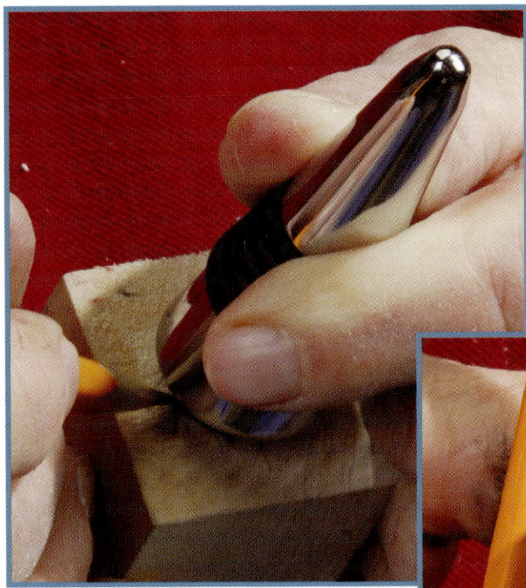

Mark around the bottom of the stopper hardware.

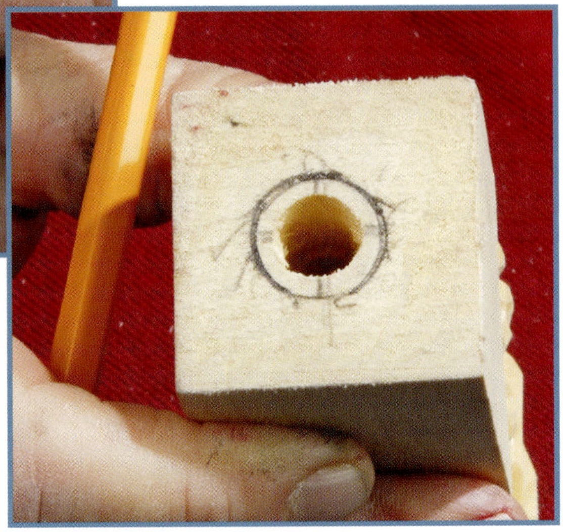

This gives me the limit of my carving.

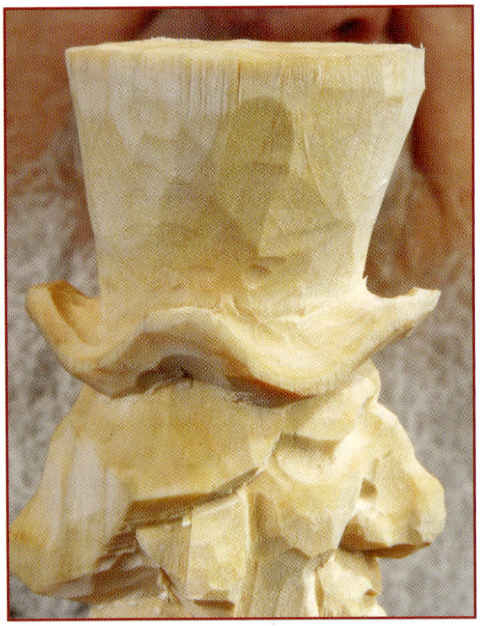

I don't like the line of the front of the hat. It should match the back.

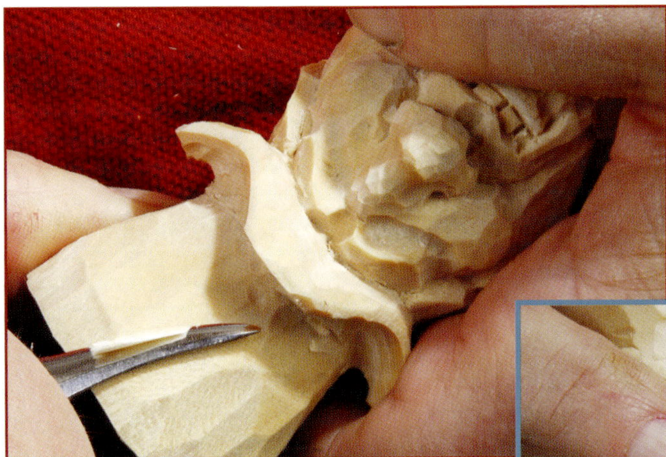

So I just trim it back.

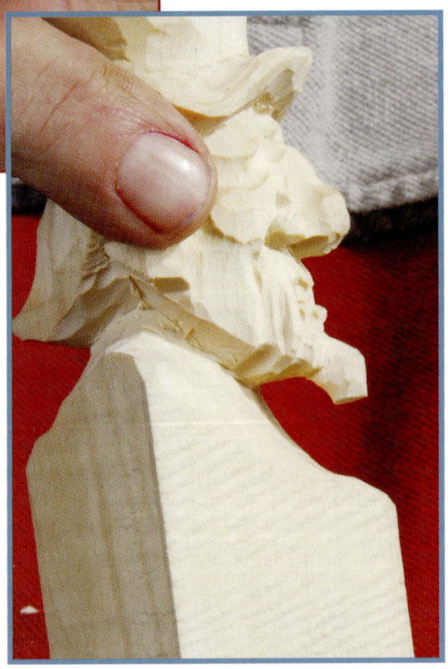

I'm going to flatten the upper chest...

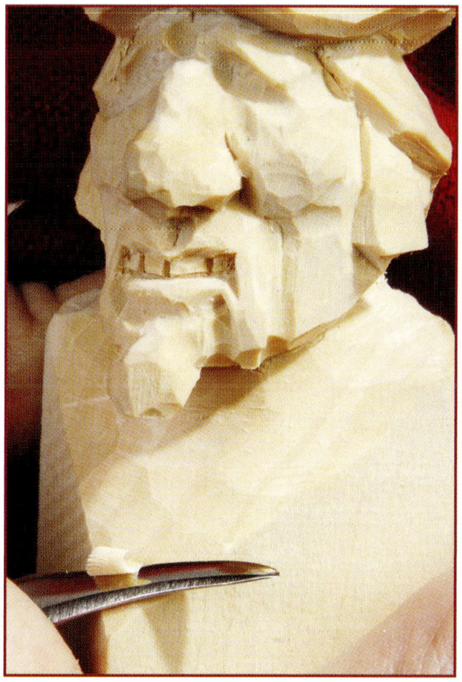

...to get rid of the ski slope look.

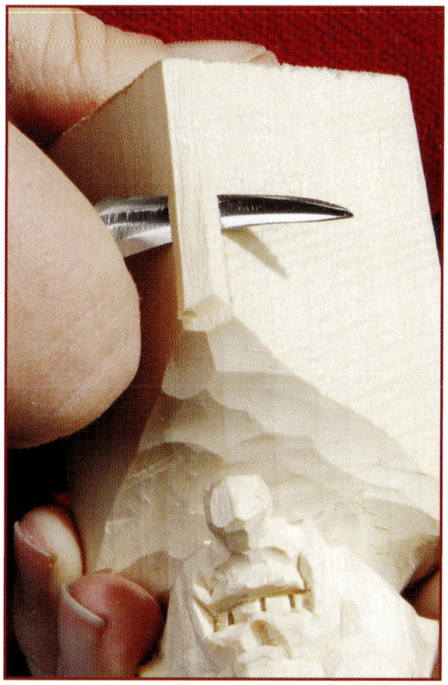

Knock off the front corner of the base.

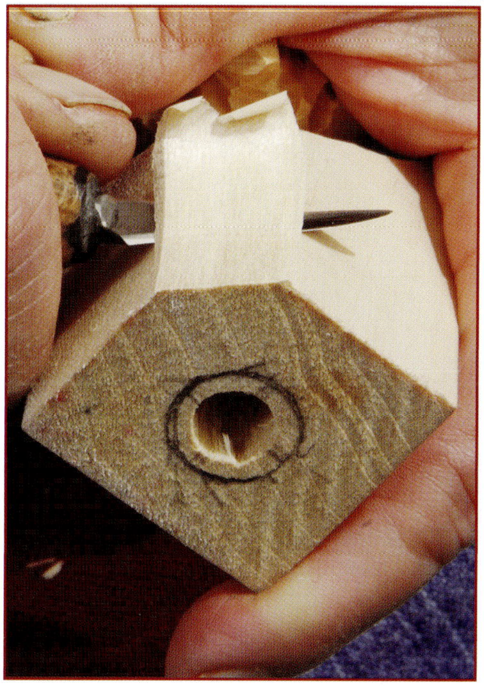

Gradually I taper it down to the black ring.

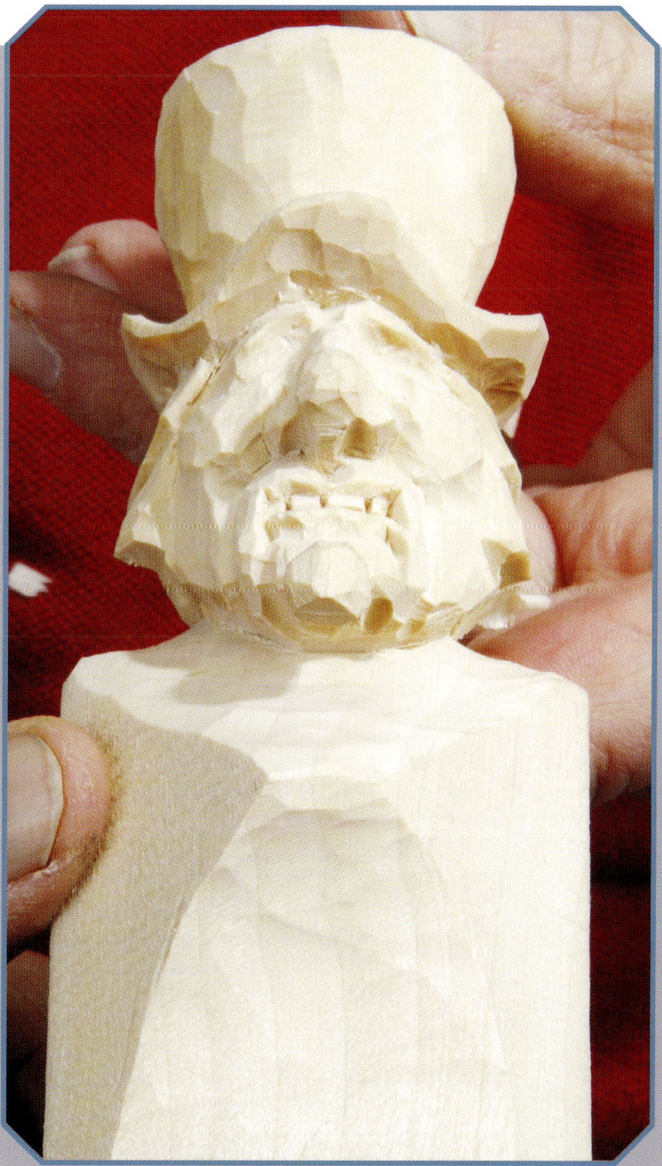

The result.

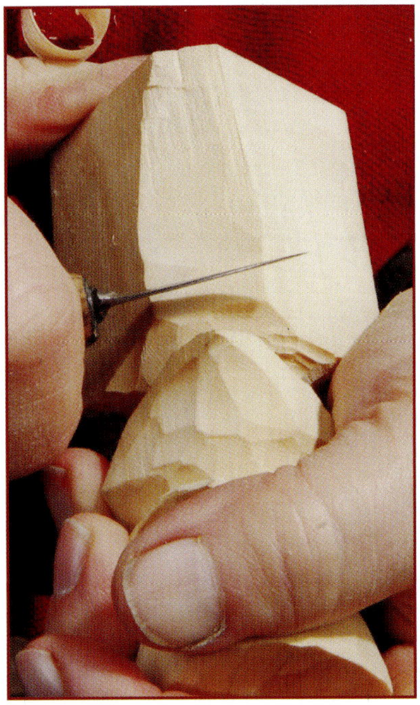

Repeat the process on the back.

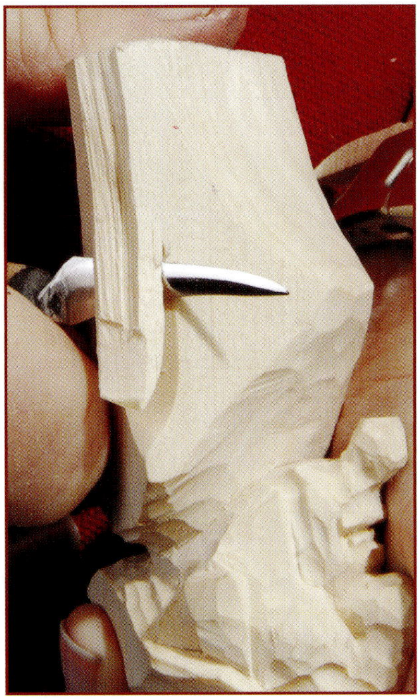

Next, taper the sides in the same way. Start a little bit under the shoulder.

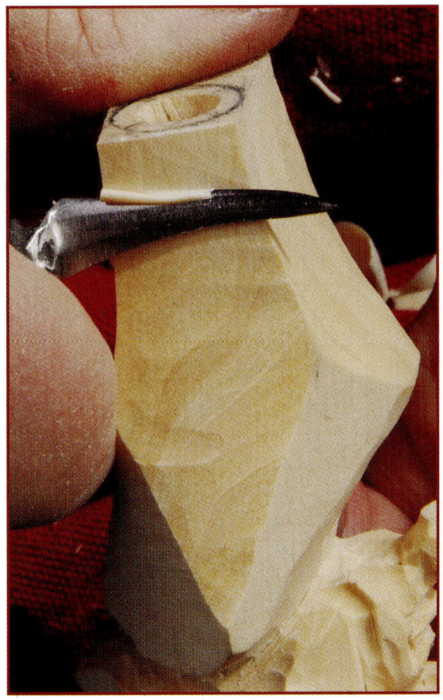

Bring it down to the same ring.

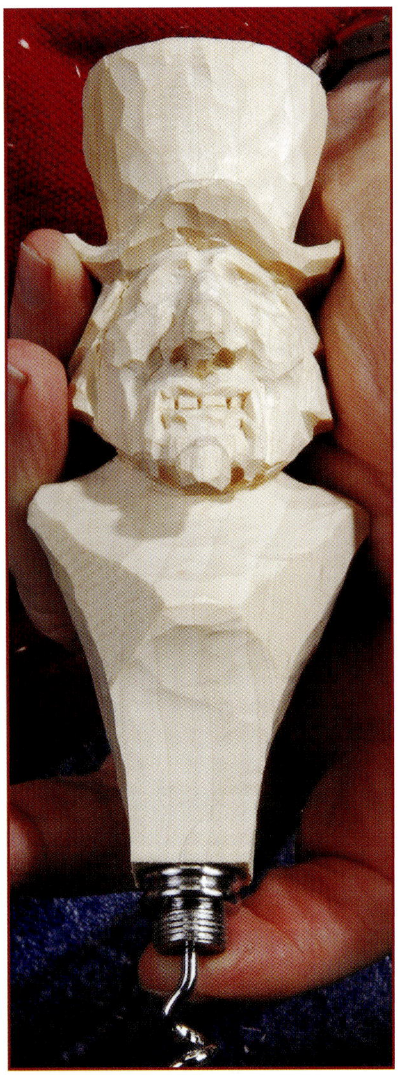

With the corkscrew/stopper in place check the flow of the line.

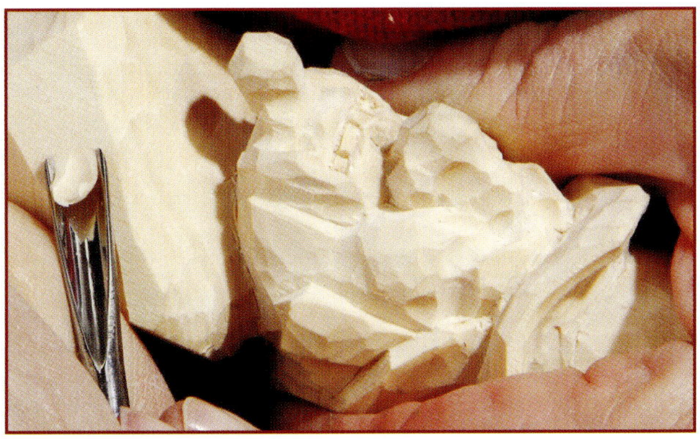

Undercut around the perimeter of the shoulders.

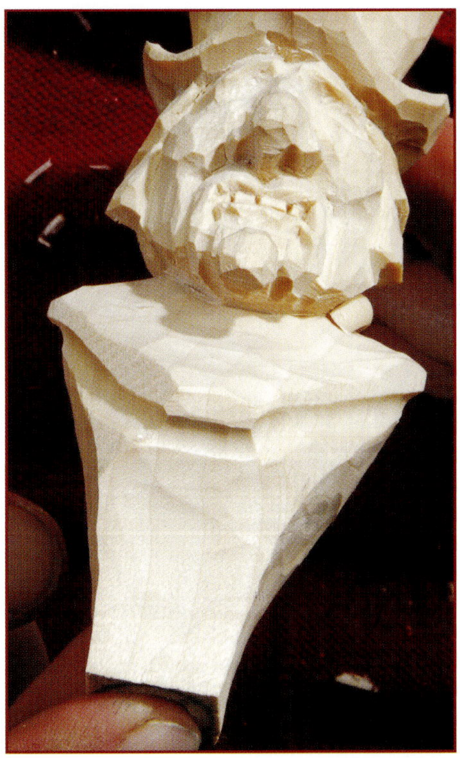

The result.

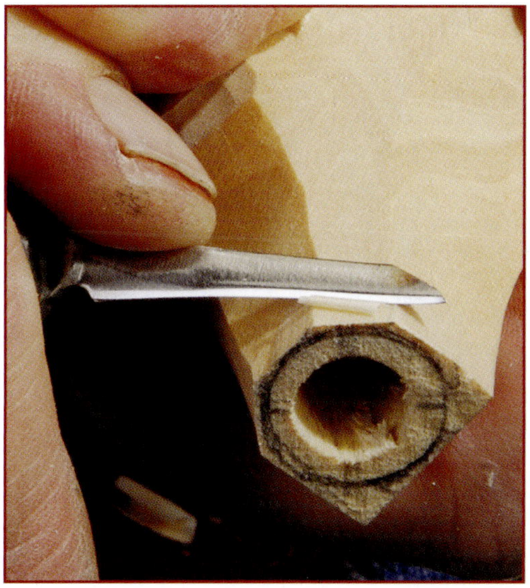

From there the base blends down toward the base. I first go to an octagonal shape. I may decide to keep it that way or continue to round it off.

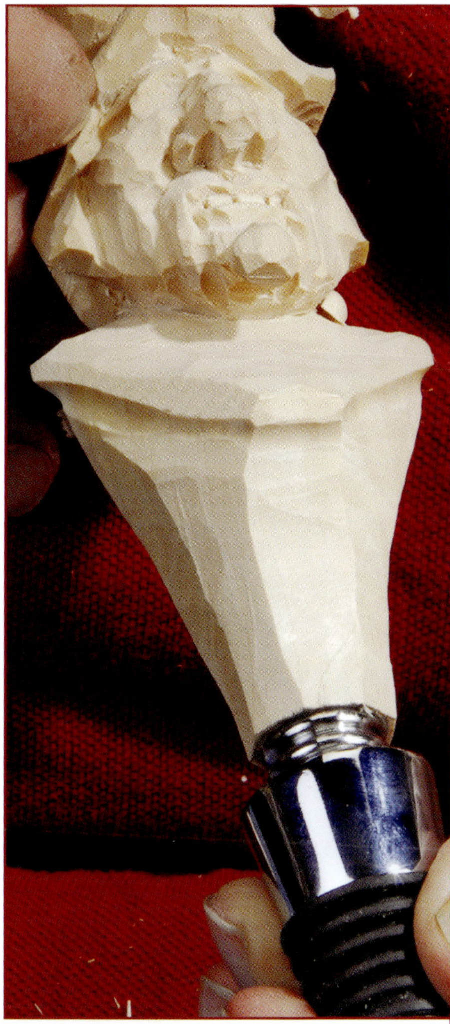

I don't like how the octagonal shape ends at the round stopper, so I'll round it off.

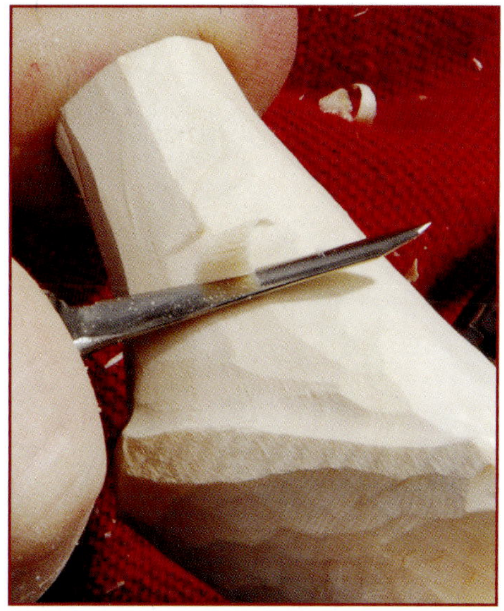

Work around the base until it is round.

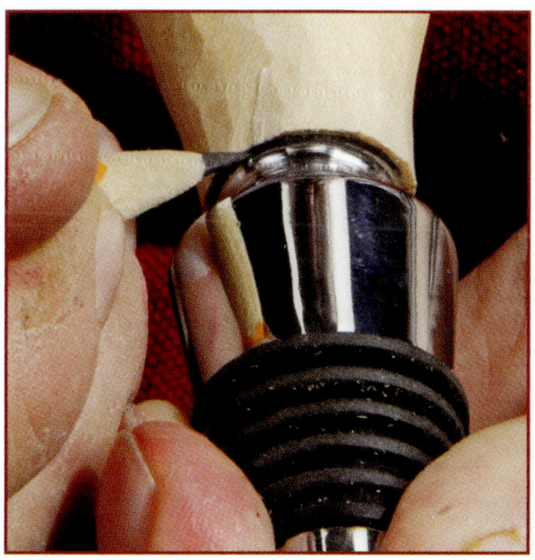

Remark around the stopper to get a good black line.\

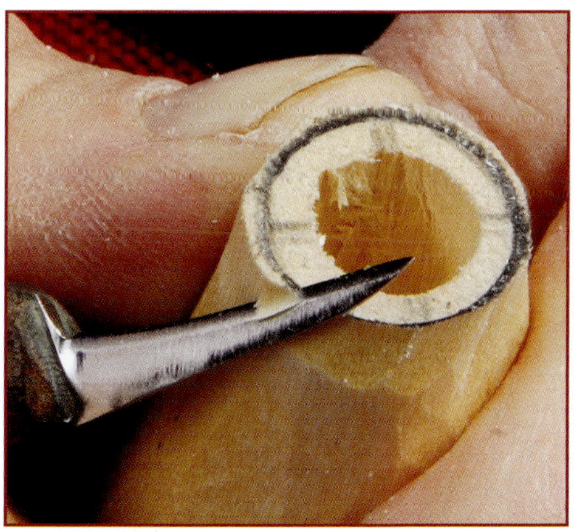

Carve back to take the line out and get a snug fit.

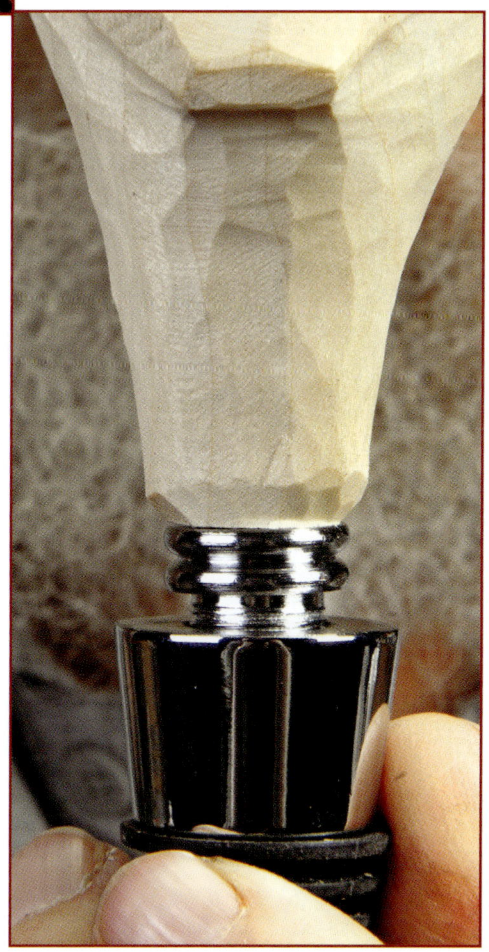

The result.

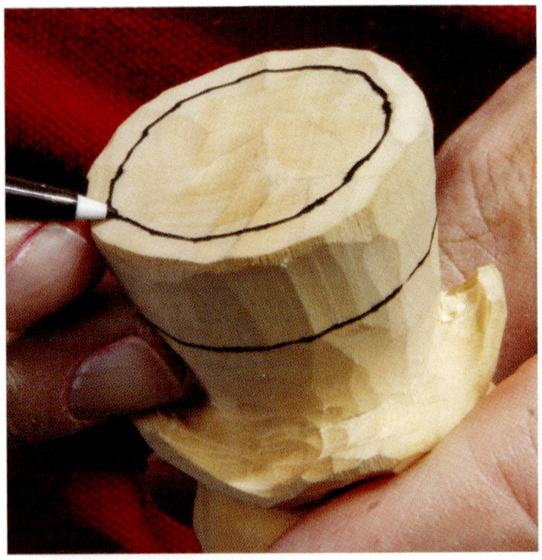

Draw a paint line in the crown of the hat…

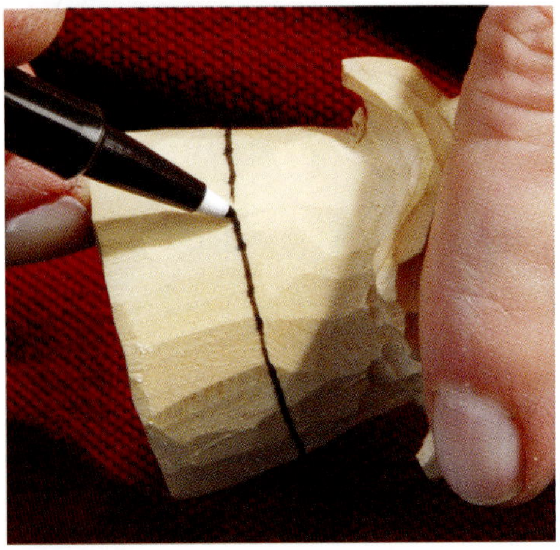

…and a hat band around the side. Note I use a Flair® brand pen for this, which is compatible with oil paints, but not with acrylics or water-based paints.

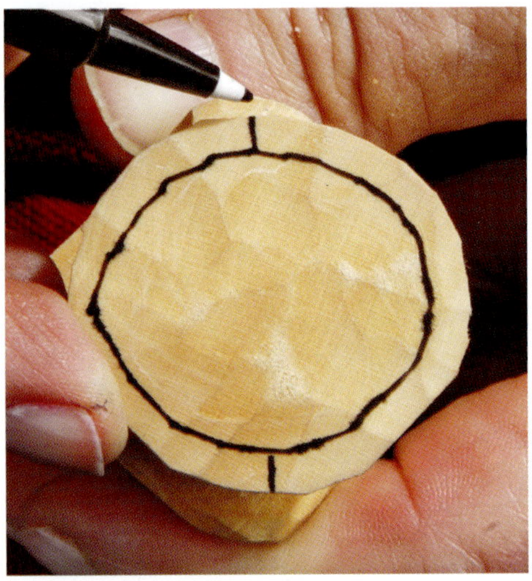

The stripes are drawn by the "halving method." This way you will always end up right with alternating white and red stripes. On the crown, halve the circle.

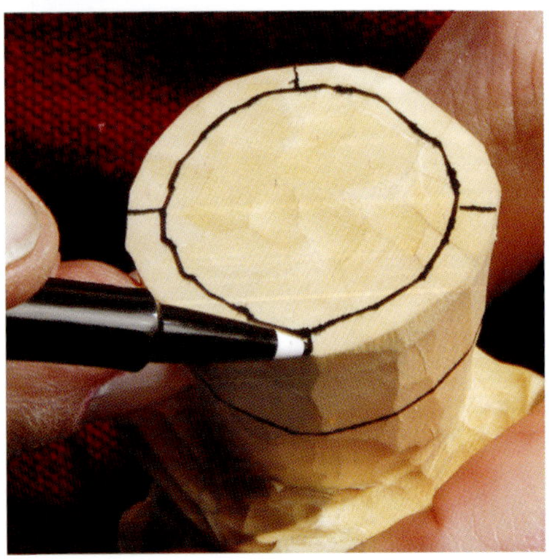

Halve the two arcs.

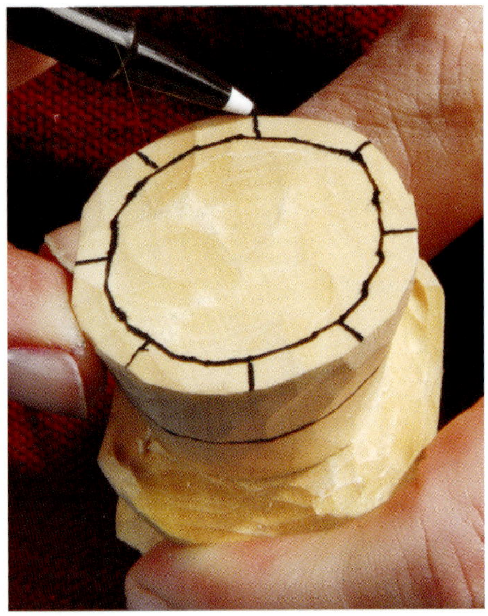

Halve the quarter circles.

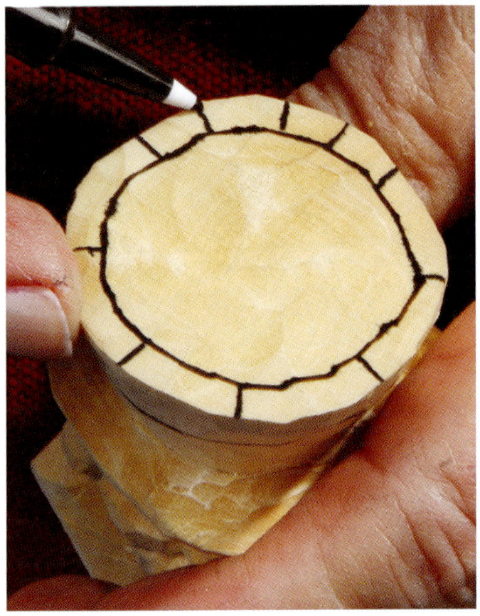

and, finally, halve the eight arcs, giving you 16 segments.

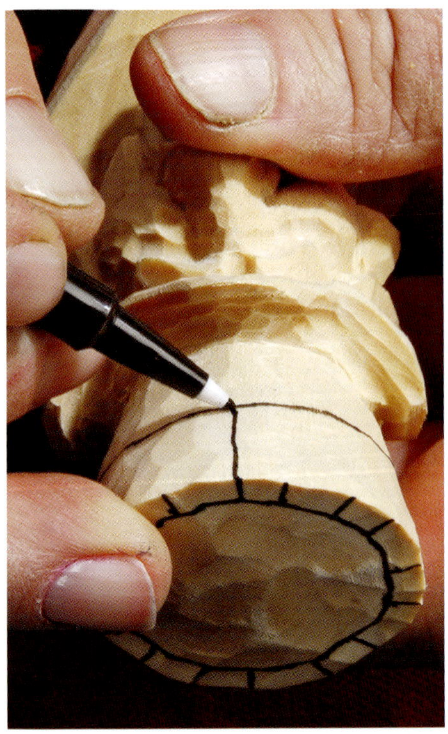

Carry the lines down the side to the hatband.

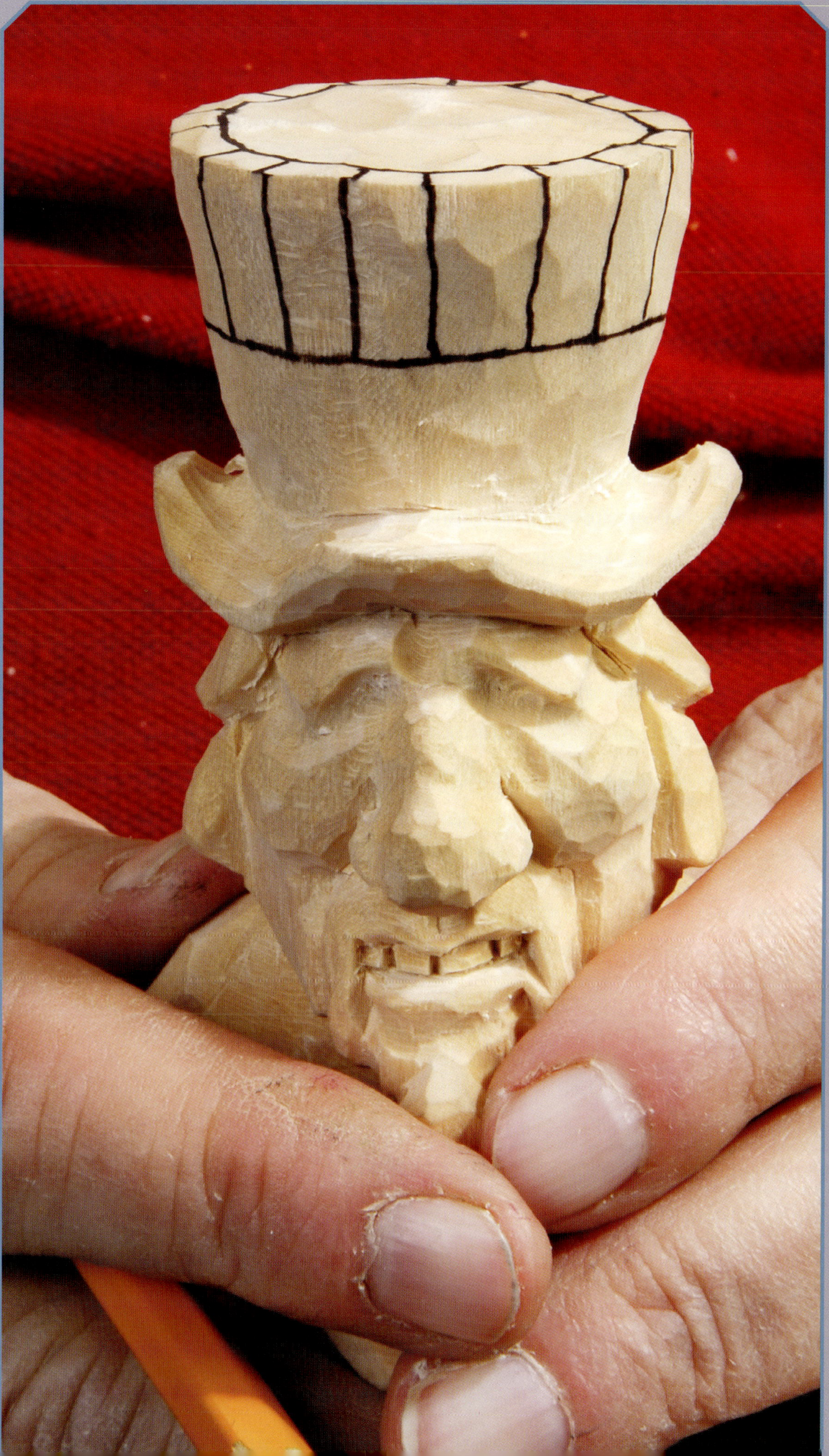

The result.

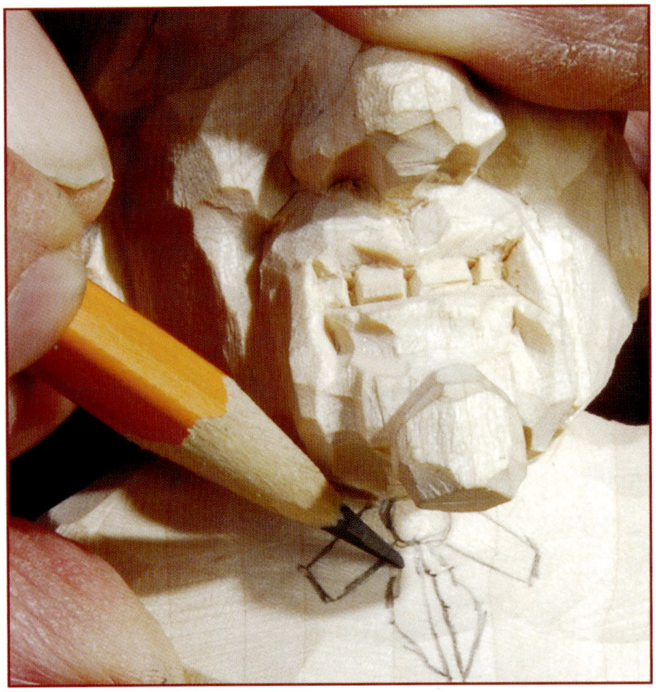

Draw in the string tie...

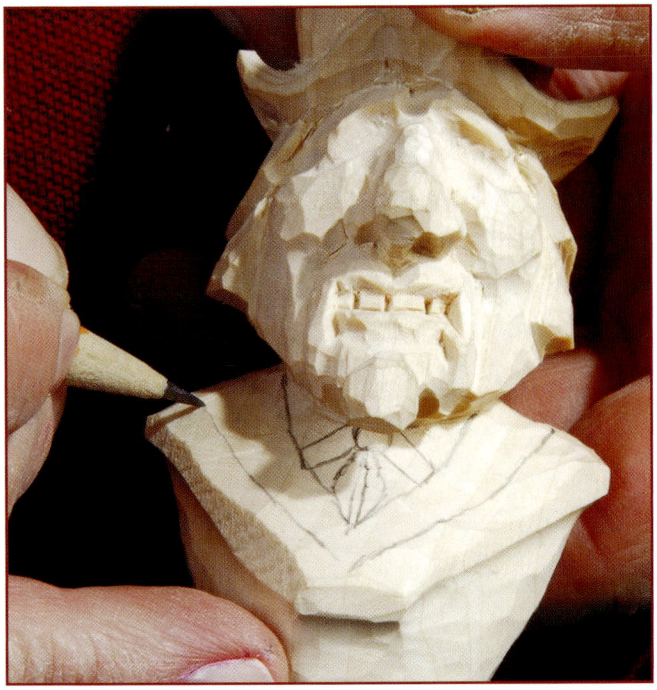

...and the collar line.

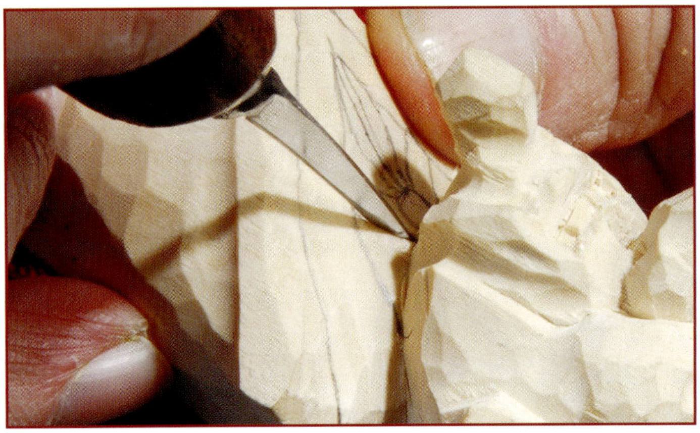

Make stops on the line of the tie and the neck line...

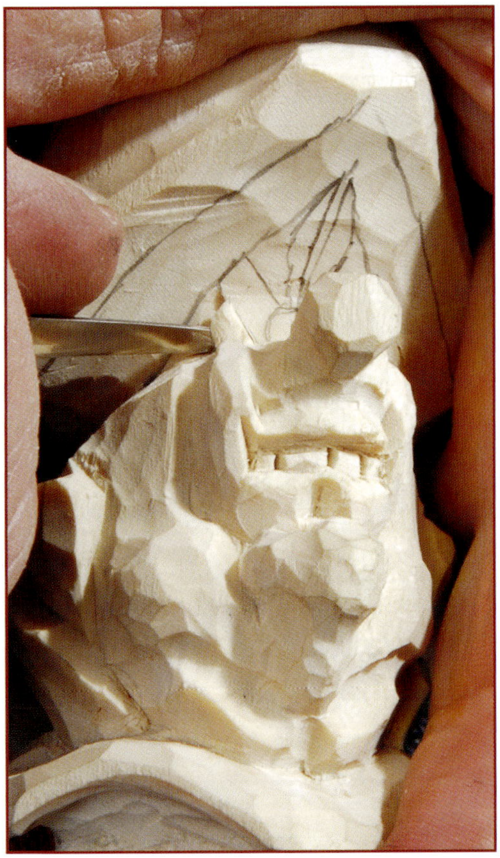

...and slice back to it from the collar line. Continue in the same way around the tie.

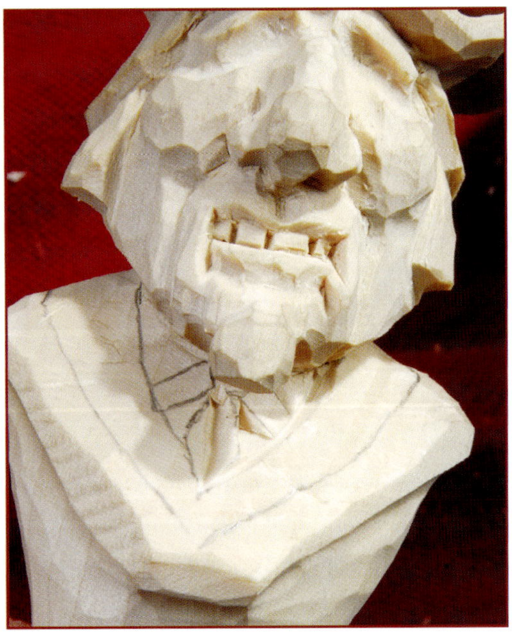

The result. Repeat on the other side of the tie.

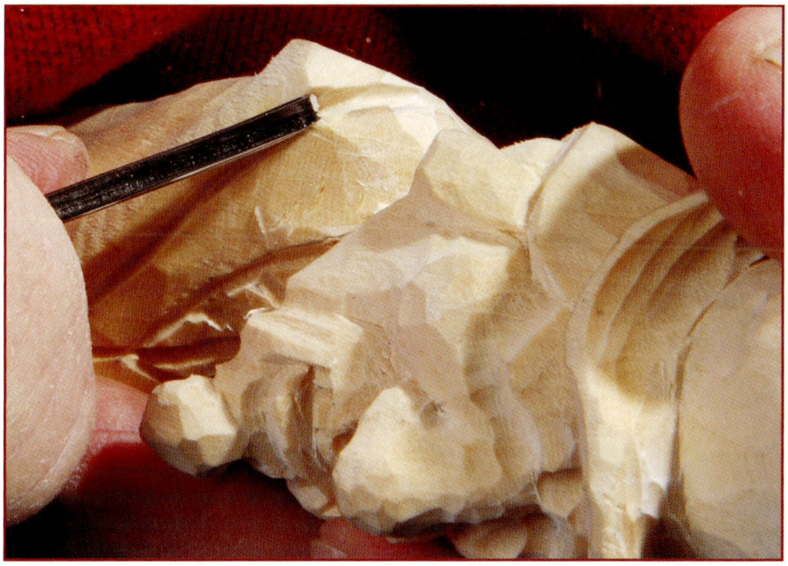

Go around the collar with a V-tool.

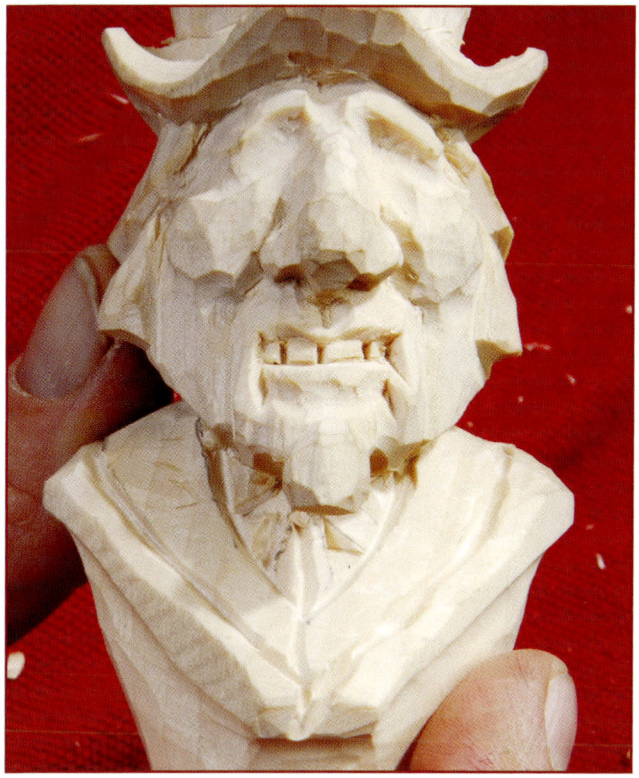

Progress.

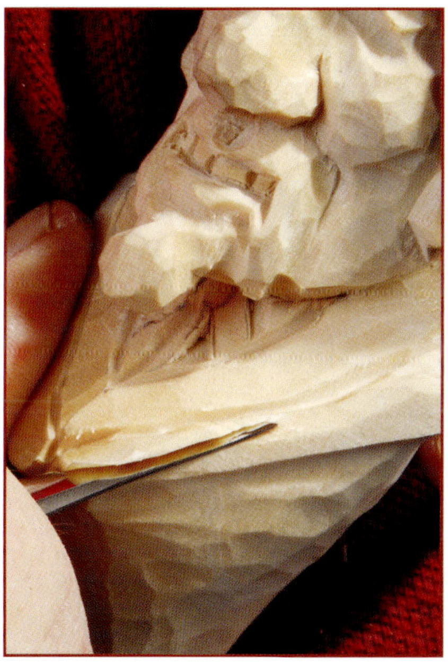

Trim back to the collar from the chest.

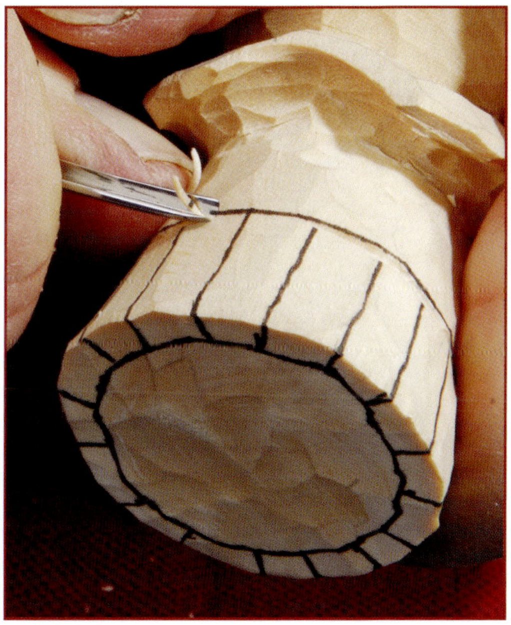

Follow the top of the hat band with the V-tool.

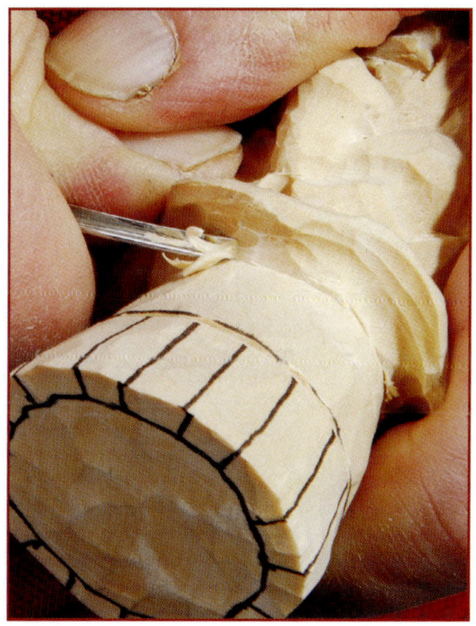

Go around the bottom of the hat band with the same tool, following the natural line of the brim.

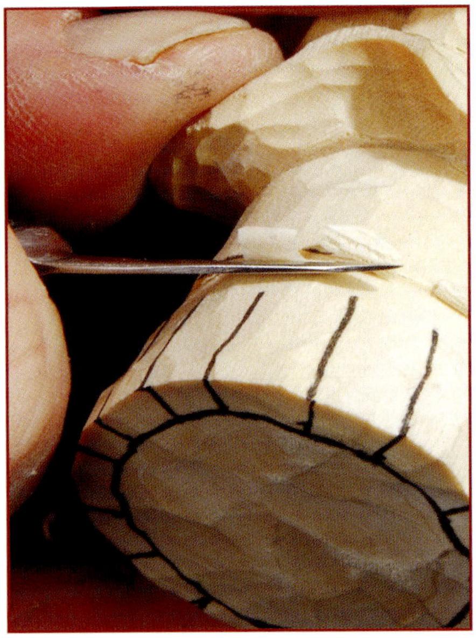

Cut back to the upper line from the crown to make the hat band stand out.

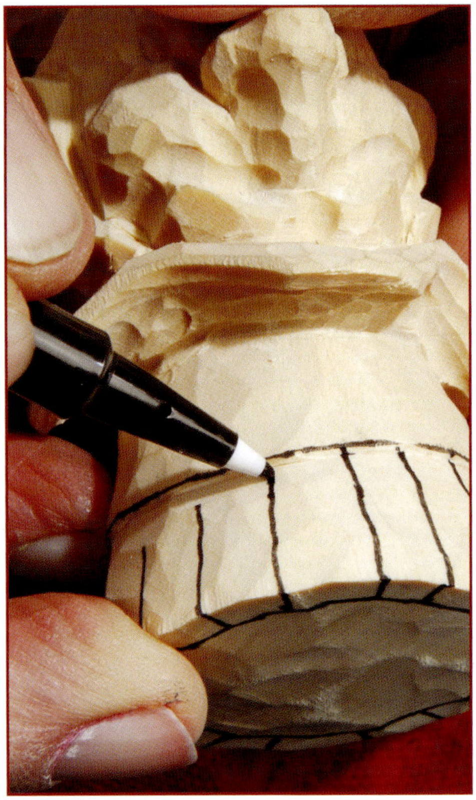

Dress up the lines.

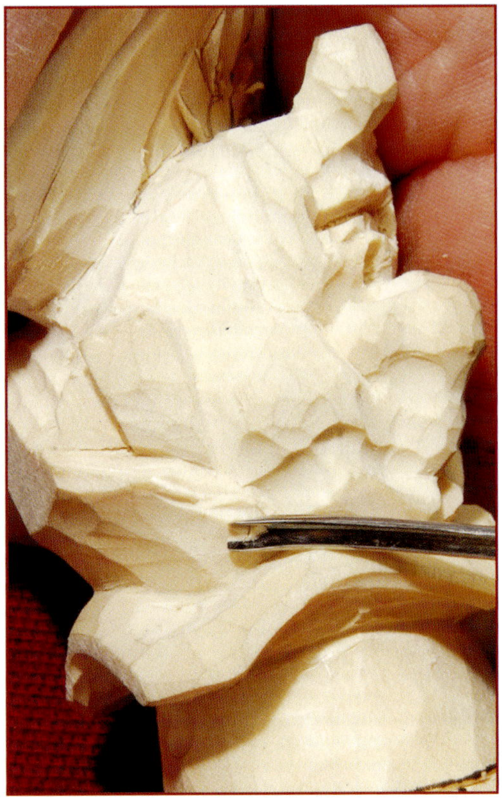

Use a V-tool to create hair lines. It always seems better to start at the face and go back. It's the way the Lord made water to run off your face.

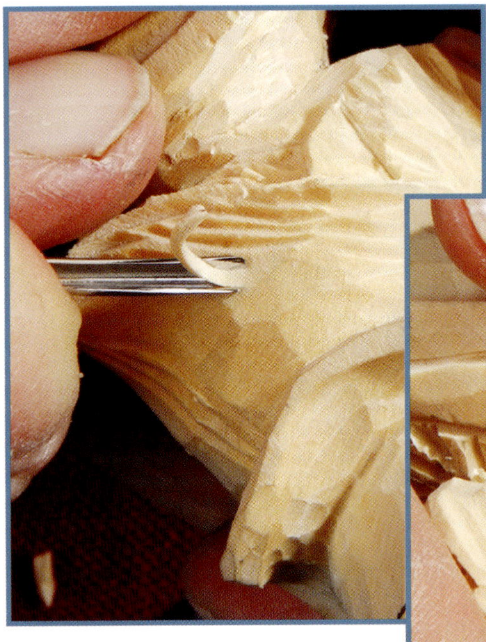

Progress

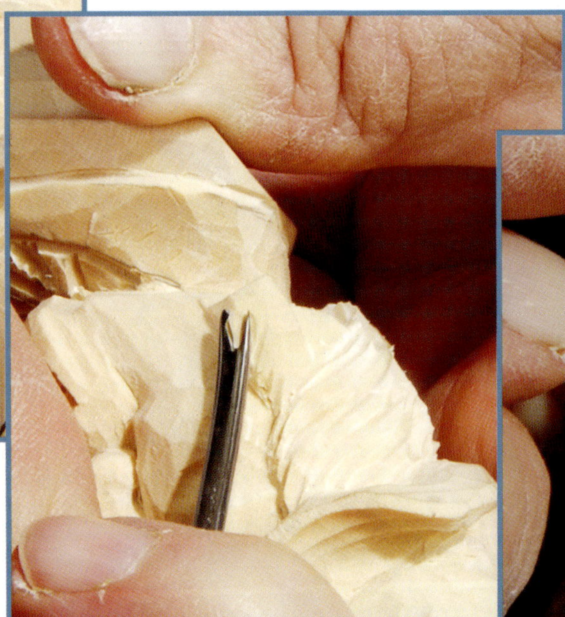

Continue with the sideburns.

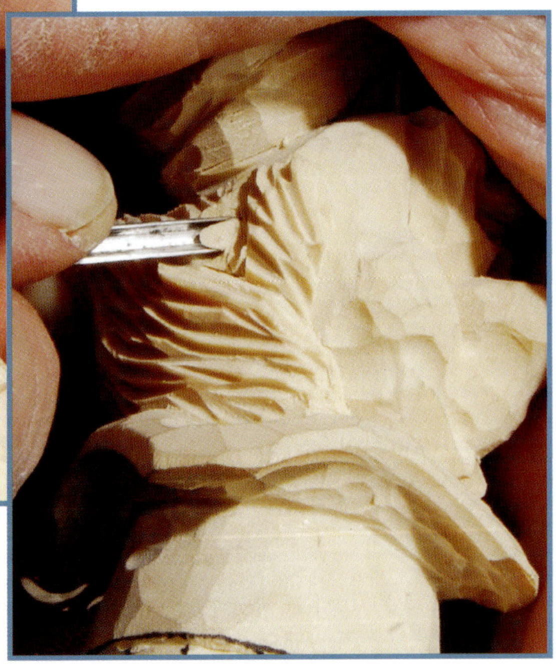

With a gouge, form the ear with one cut back to the sideburns

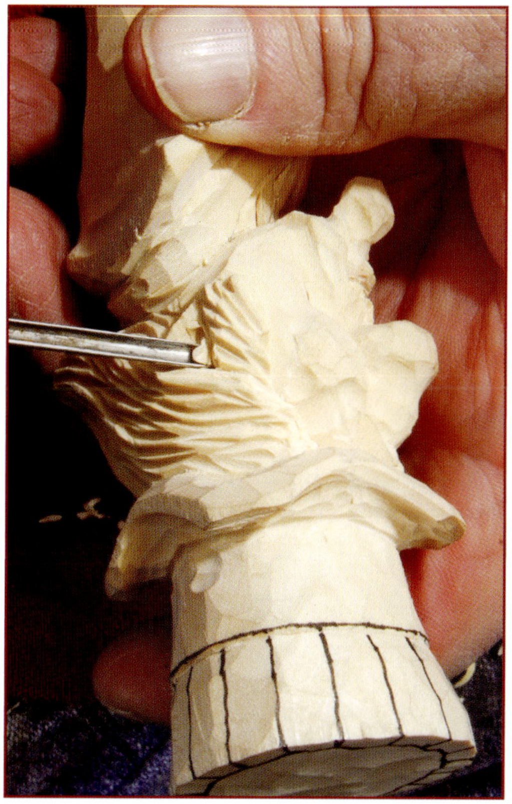

...and another above the first.

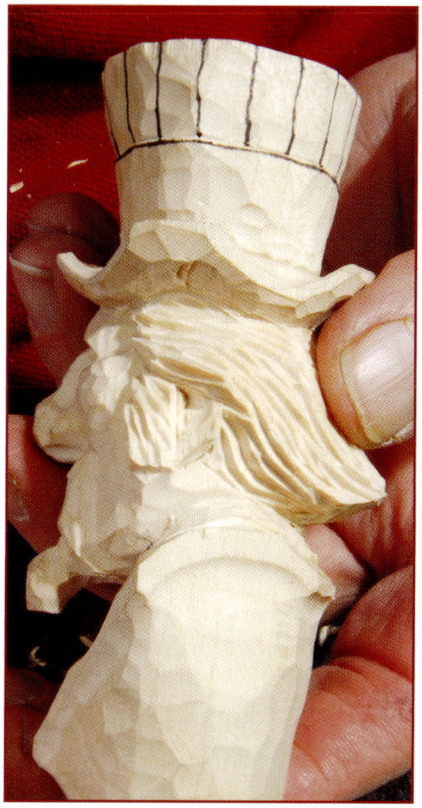

The result.

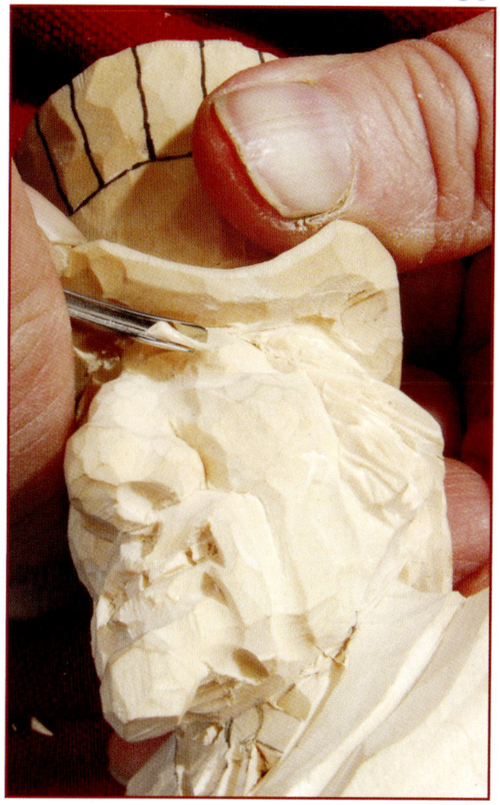

Undercut the eyebrow with a small gouge.

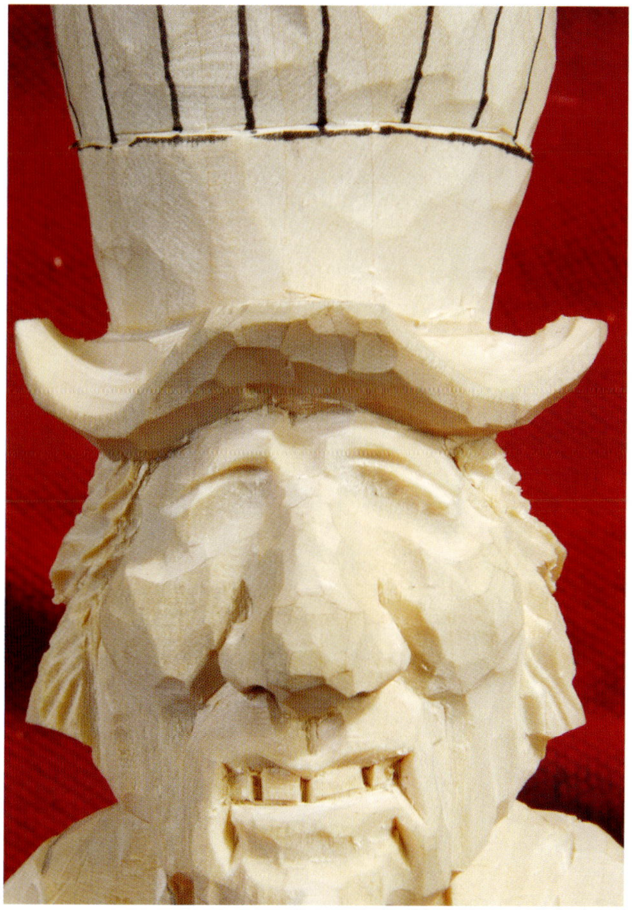

The result.

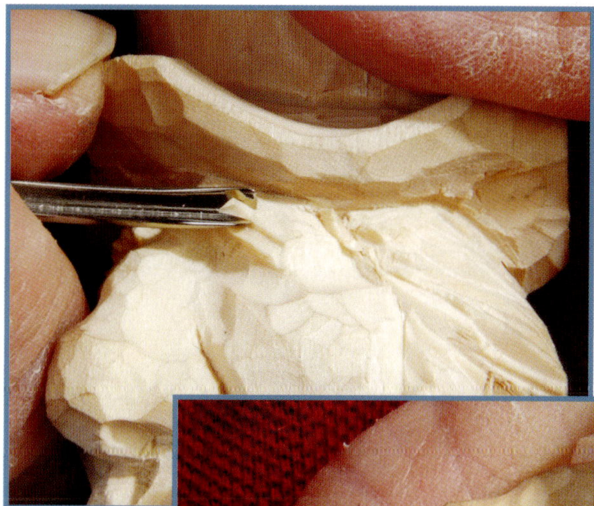

Add hair to the eyebrow...

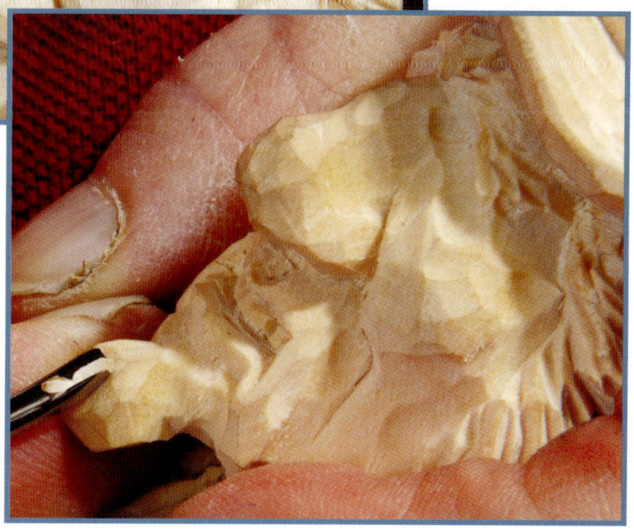

...and the goatee.

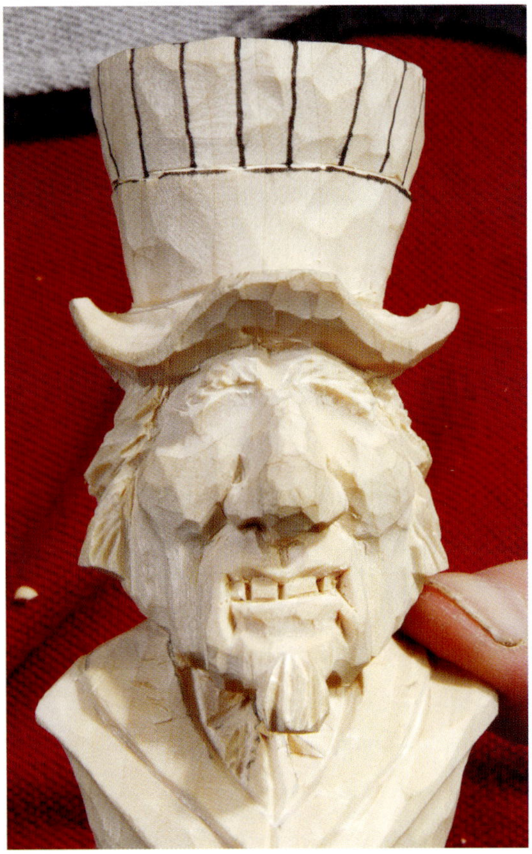

Progress.

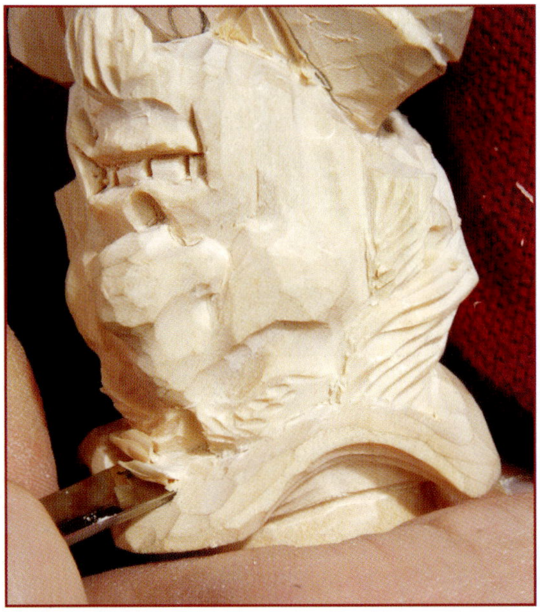

The front brim seems a bit thick, so I am under-cutting it.

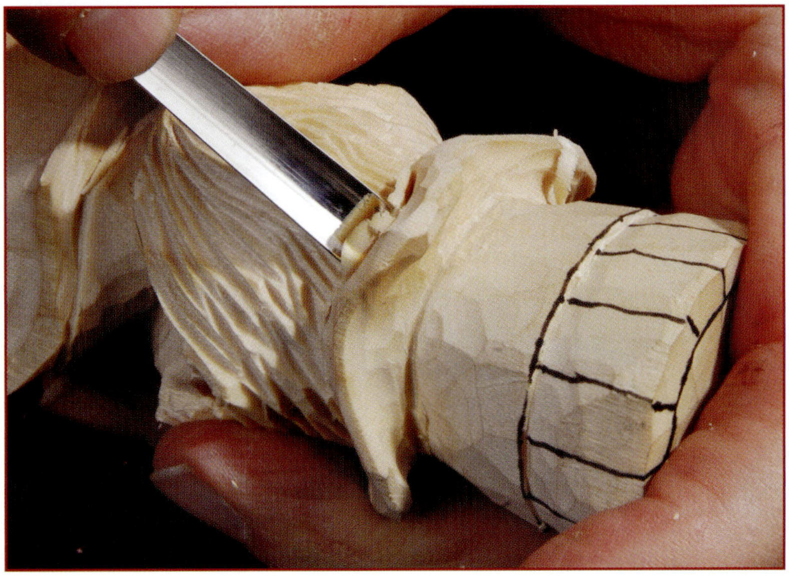

Because of the domino factor, I need to go around the brim doing the same thinning.

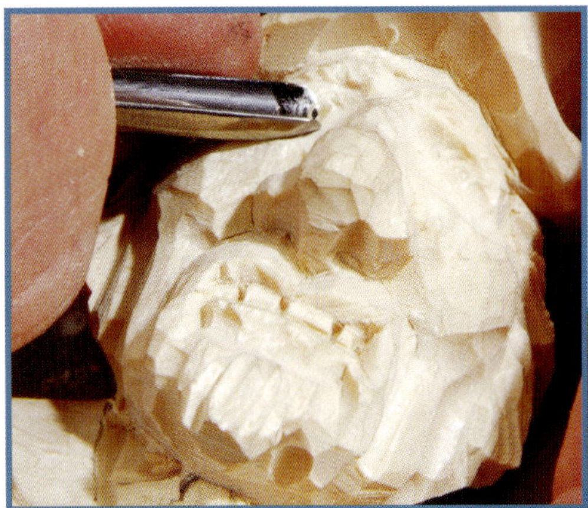

Clean up the eyesockets to get ready for the eyes.

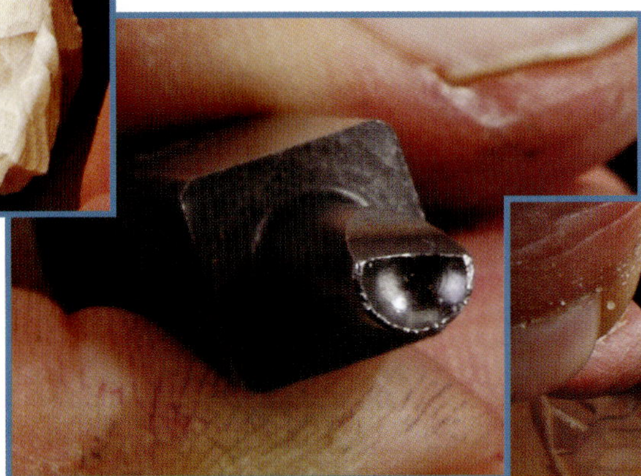

The eyes are formed with this eye punch/

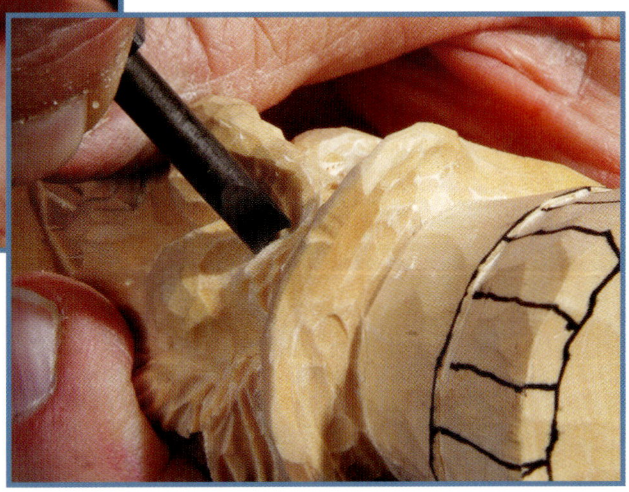

Line the flat edge under the brow and push in, rocking back and forth to form the eyeball.

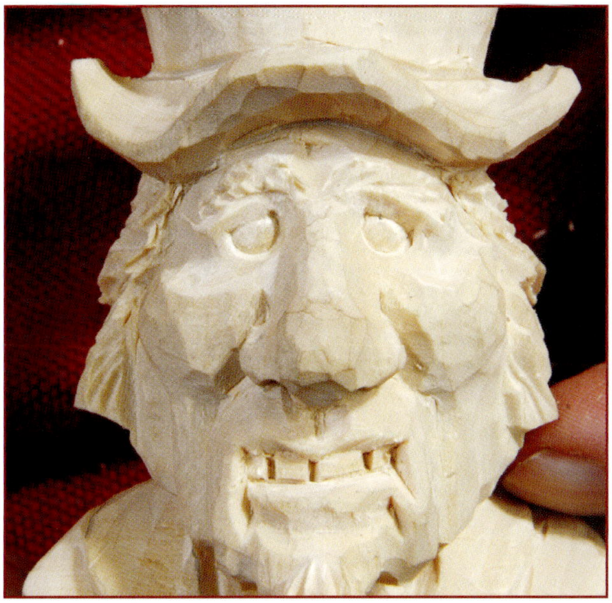

Progress.

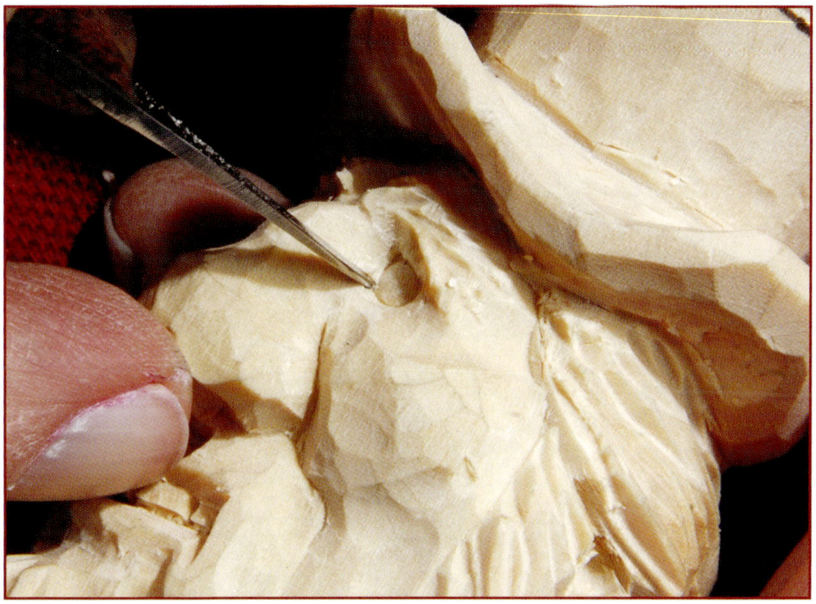

Cut the inside corner with one stop cut along the lower lid...

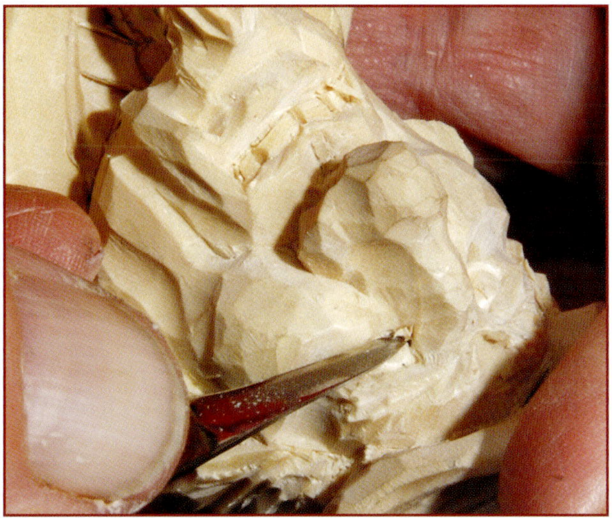

...one along the upper lid...

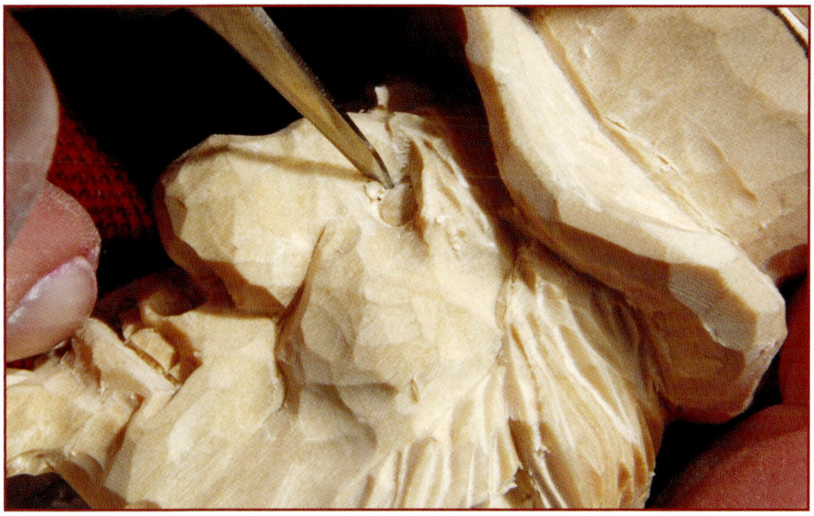

...and a slicing cut back into the corner with the blade against the eyeball. If it doesn't pop out, do all three cuts again. Don't pick at it.

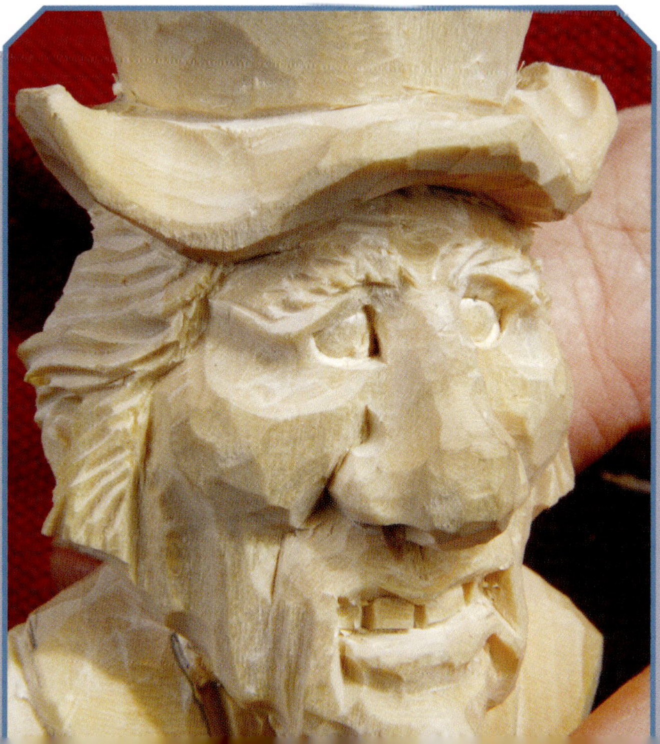

The result

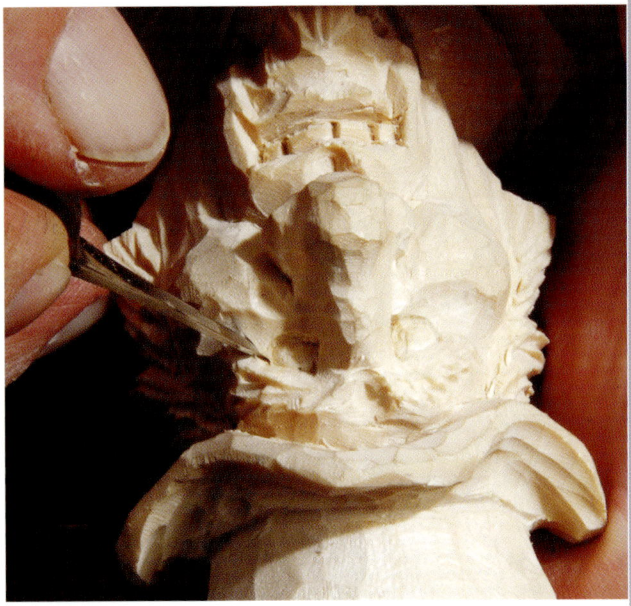

The outside corner is done the same way. A stop along the upper lid...

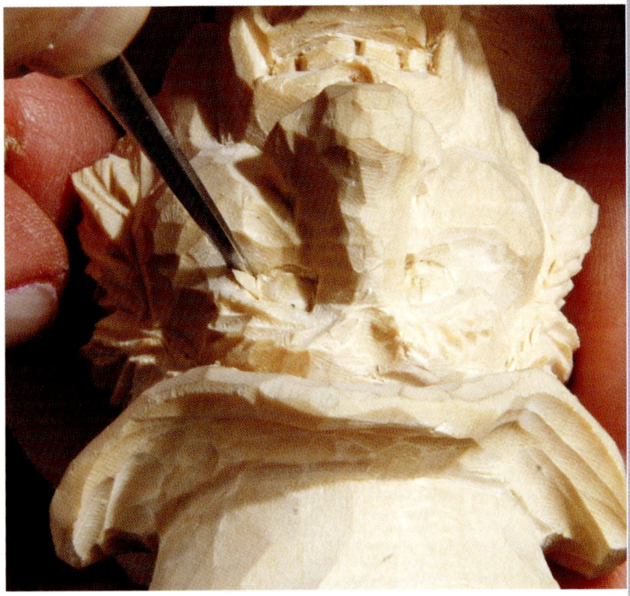

..another along the lower (I want to keep this one flat)

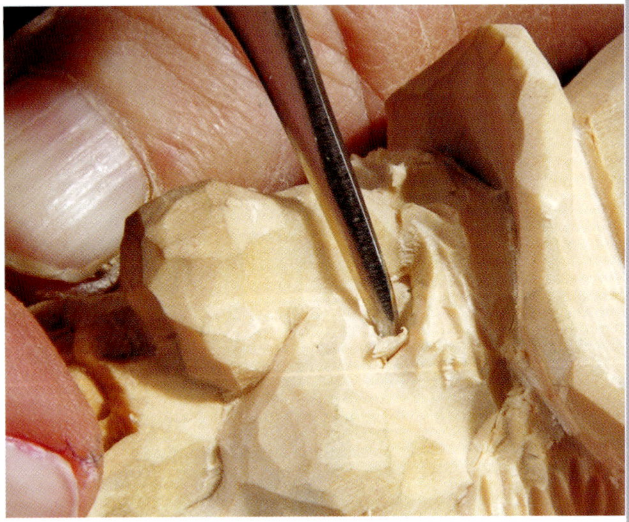

...and slice it out along the eyeball.

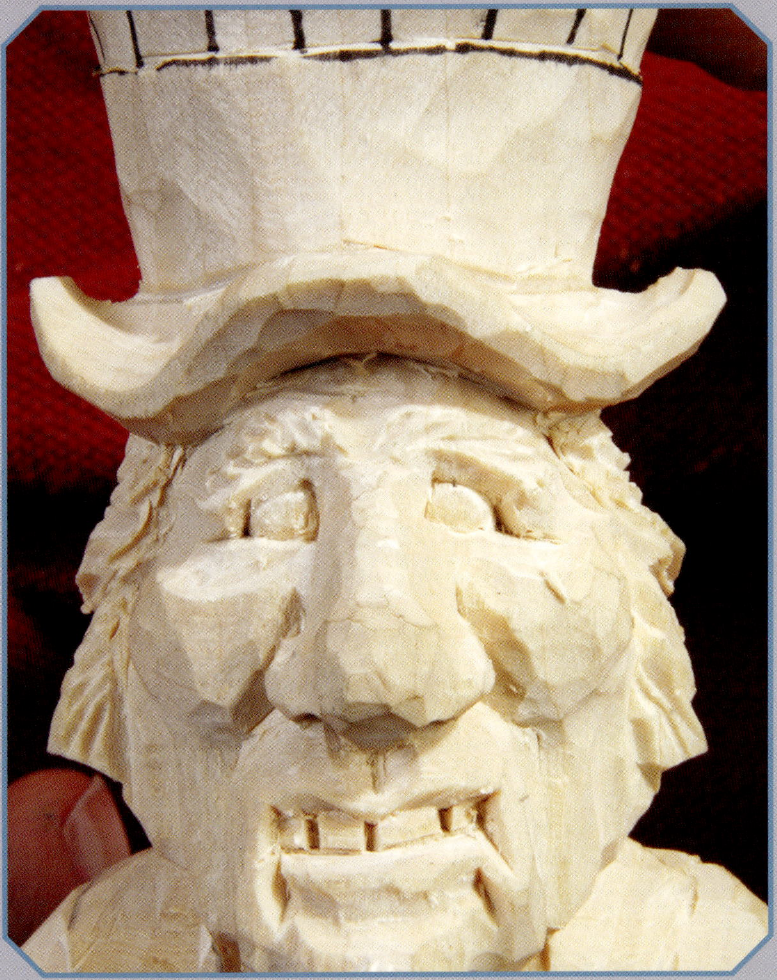

Progress.

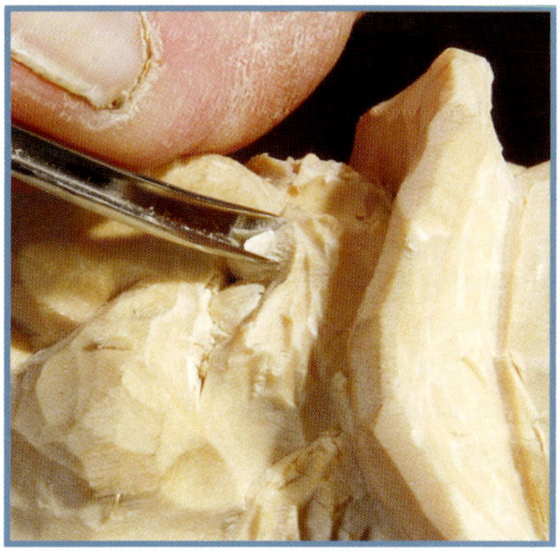

Finally take a V-tool to make a cut beside the nose. Cut up...

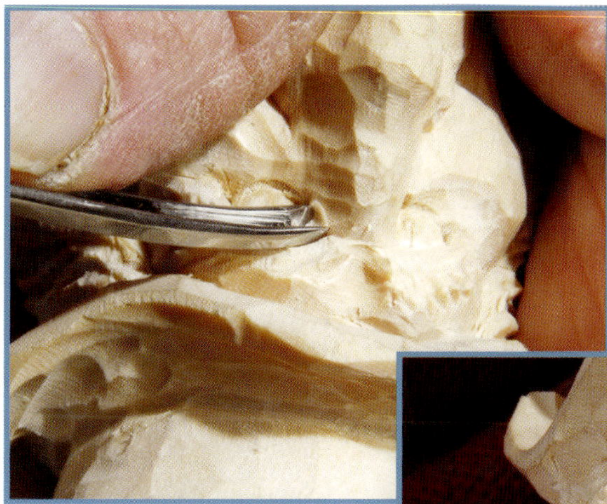

...and nip it off from above.

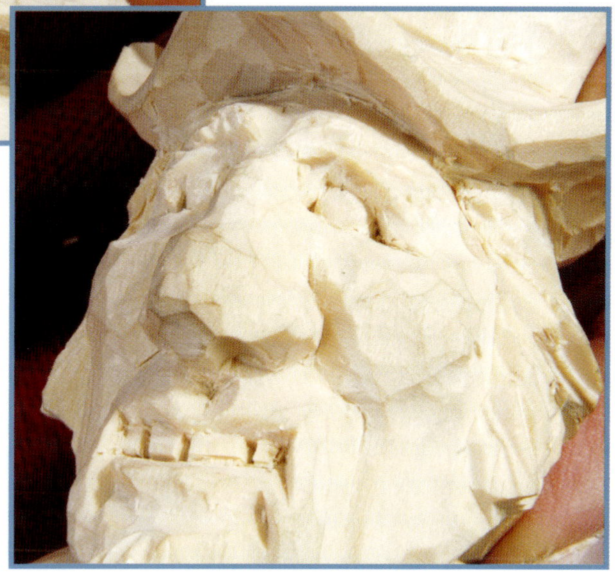

The result.

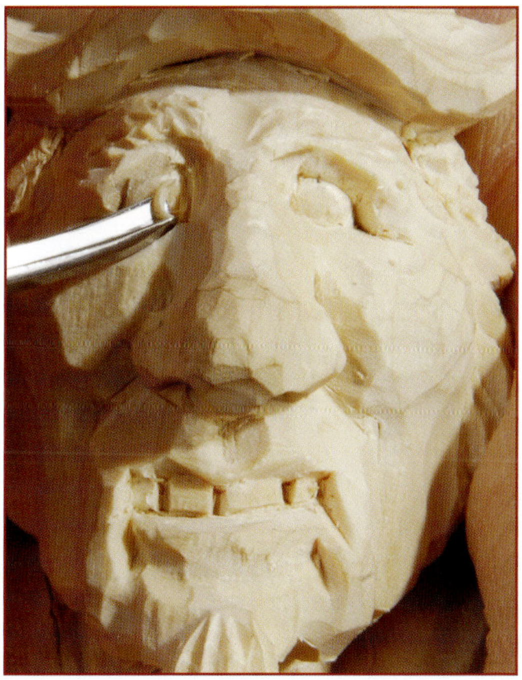

Undercut the bottom eyelid with a small V-tool. It should be started inside the upper lid, so it looks like lower lid comes under the upper lid.

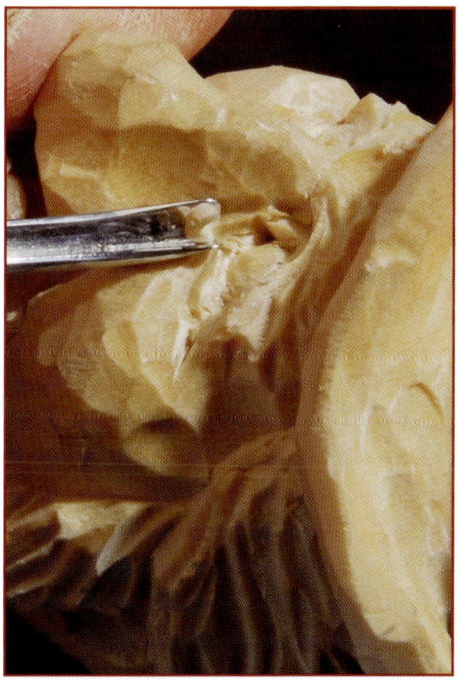

Bags are formed with a V-tool. Work from the middle...

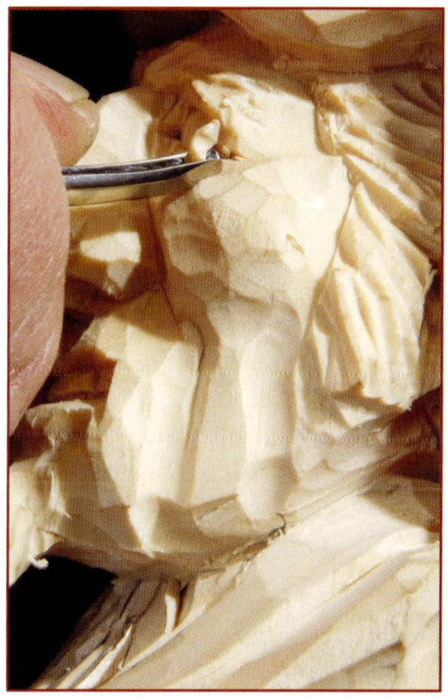

...to the sides. This is a good precaution against busting it out.

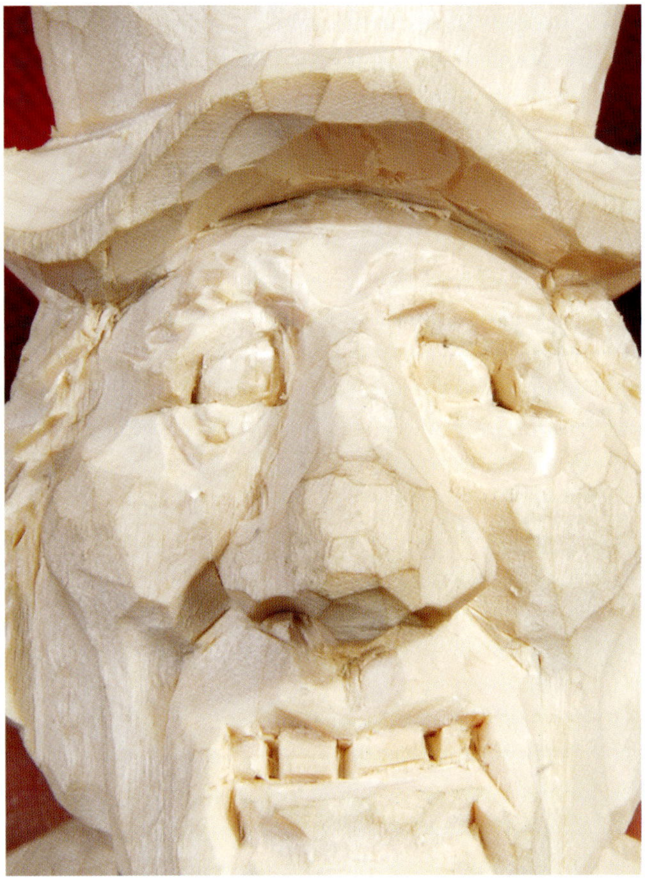

Progress.

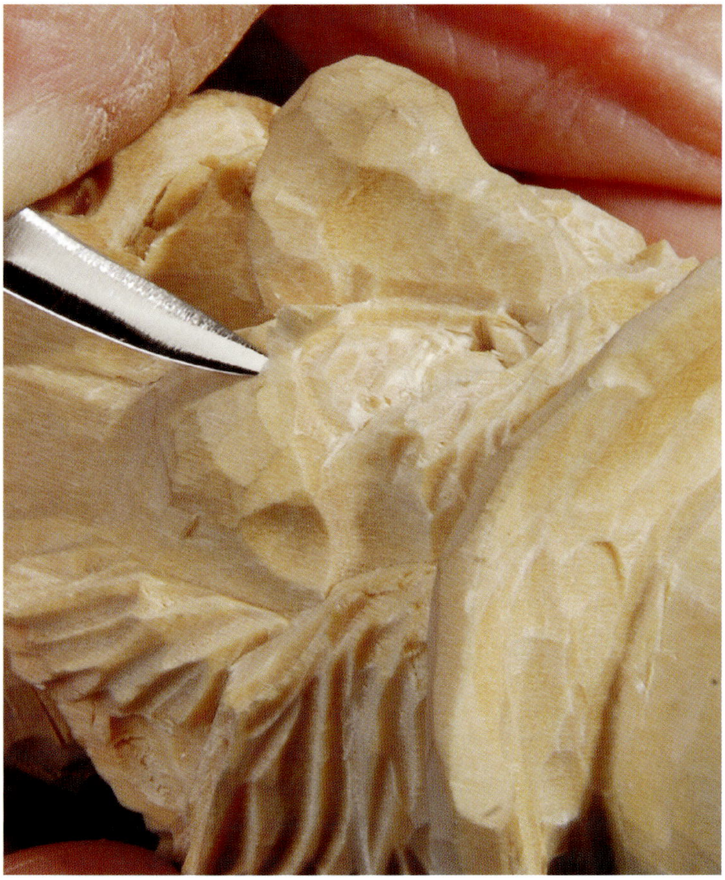

With a knife I want to soften the bags under the eyes.

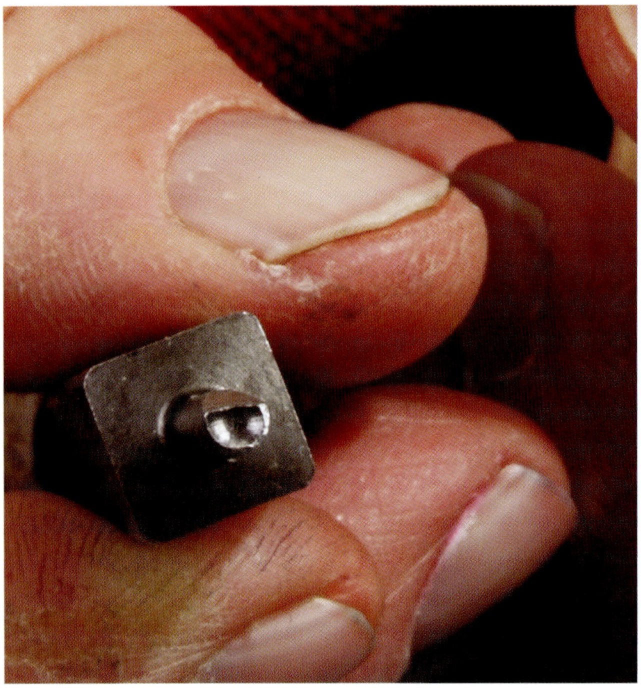

A smaller eyepunch is used for the pupil.

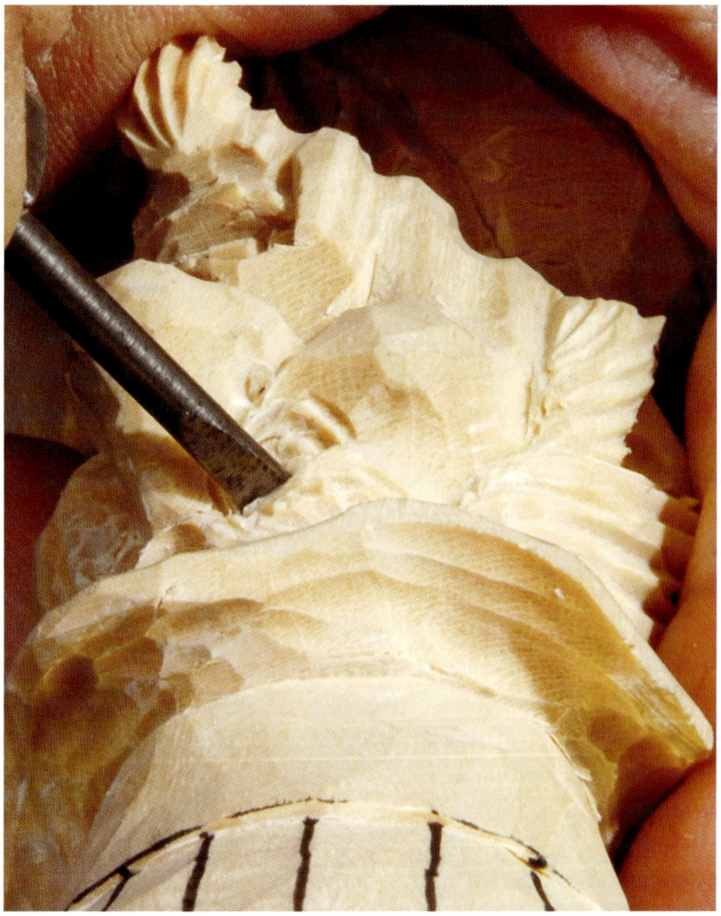

Push it in and rock it.

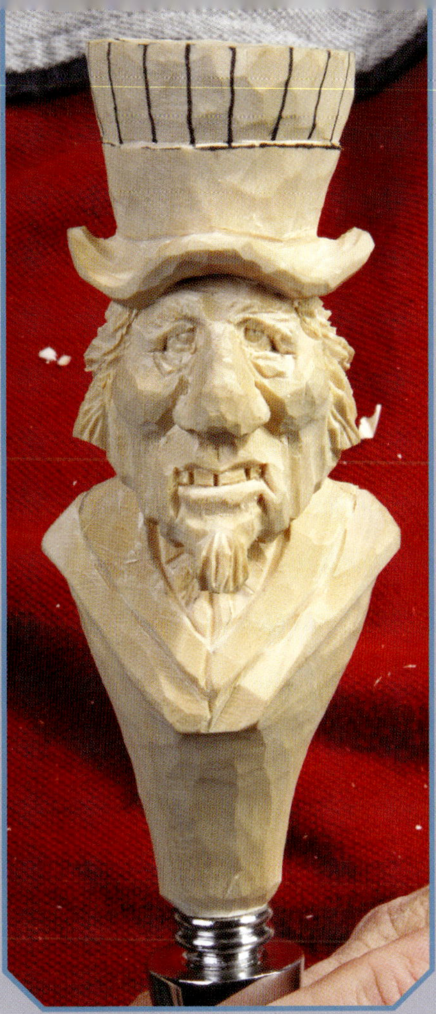

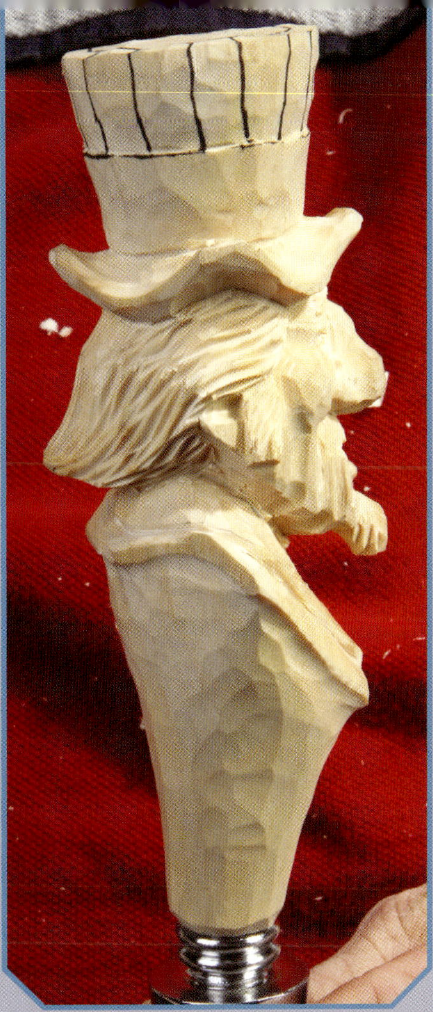

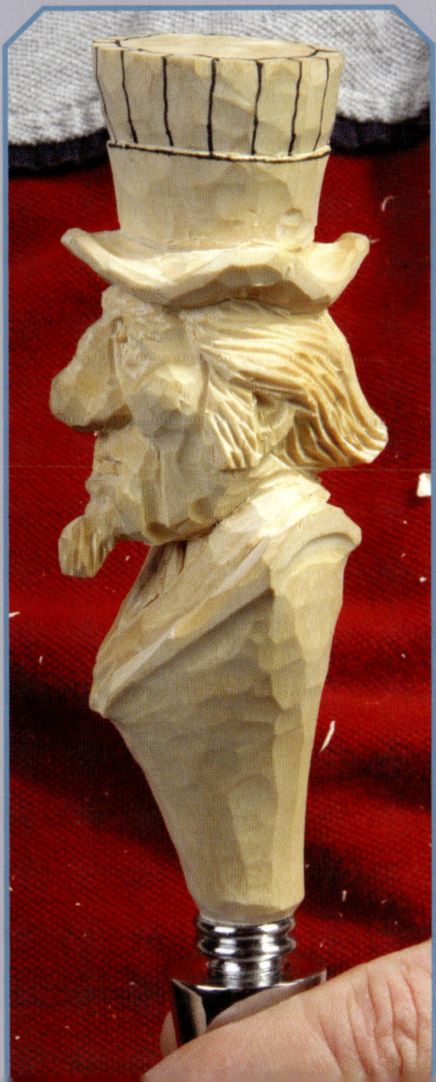

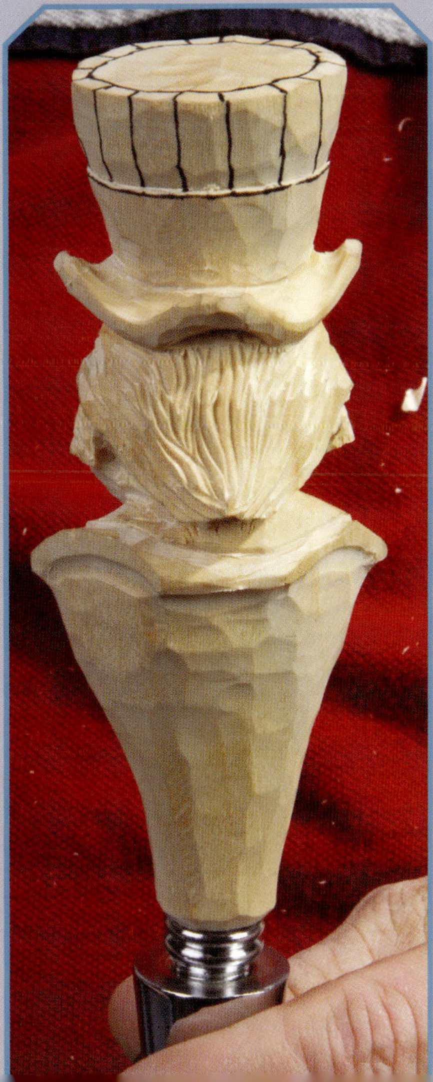

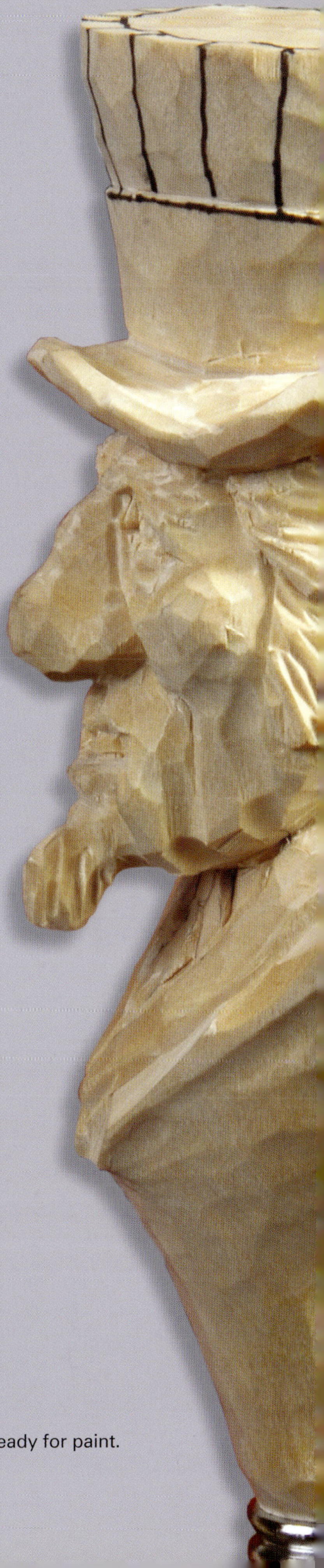

Ready for paint.

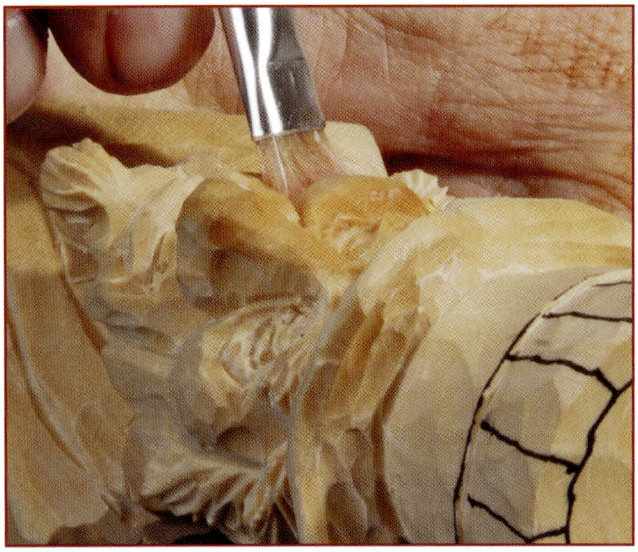

Paint the flesh areas with a good coat of turpentine.

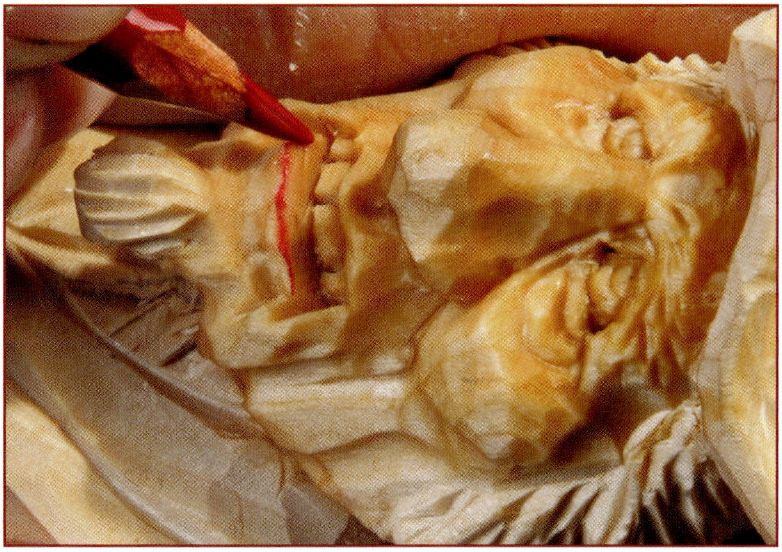

I use paint pencils soaked in turpentine for details. The brand name is Multichrome, by General Pencil Company. I use a lighter red, Carmine, on the flesh first. Apply to the lip.

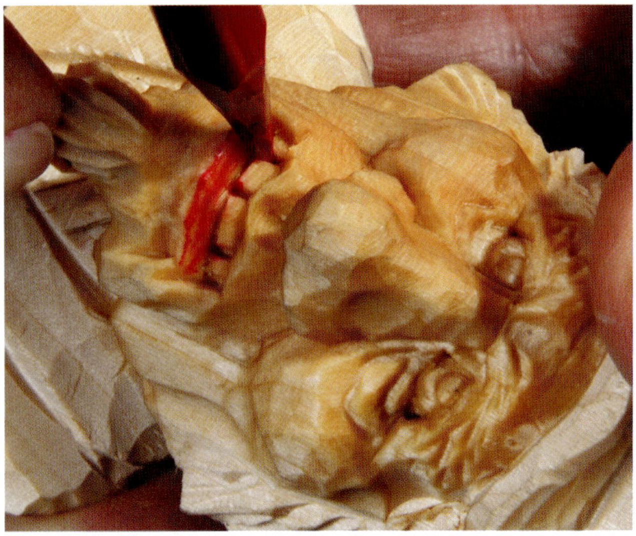

At the corners of the teeth, push the pencil in and rotate it a bit.

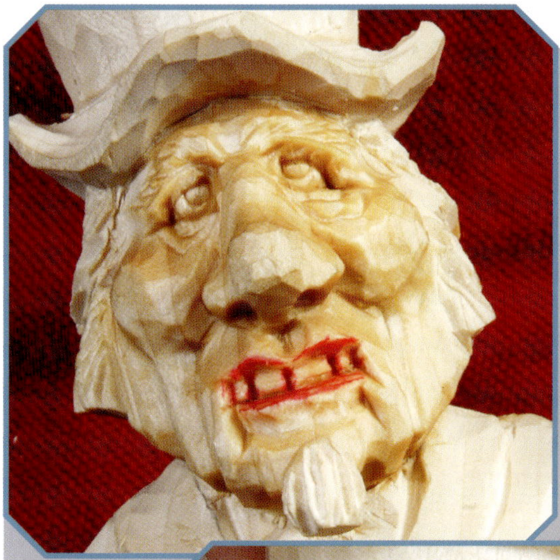

Progress.

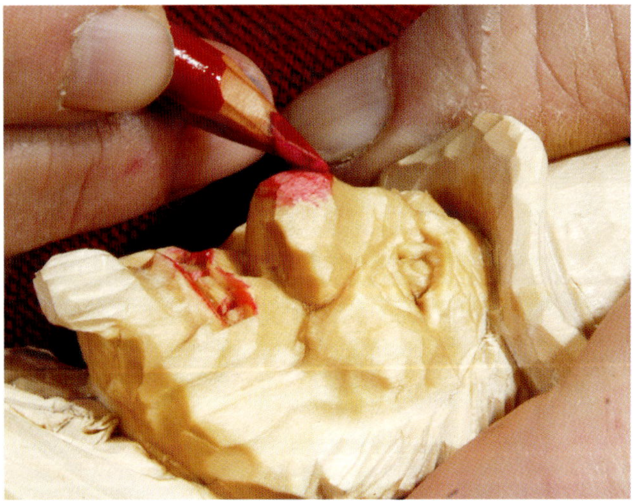

Go over the highlights of the face. I use a crisscross stroke, going one way, then the other.

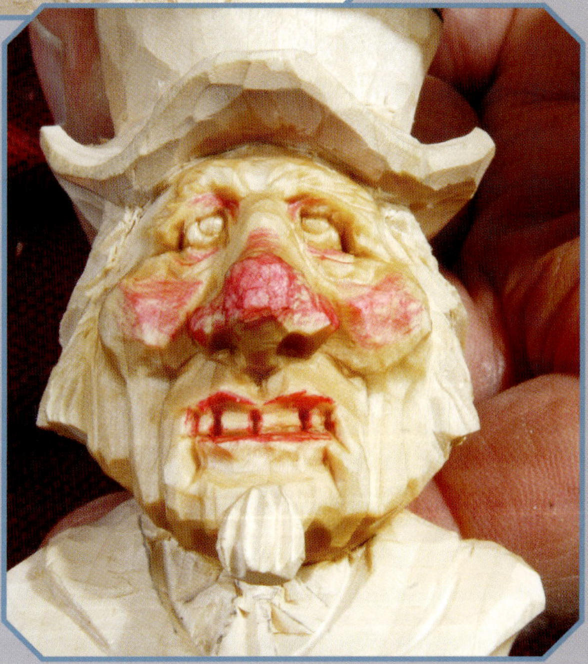

Progress.

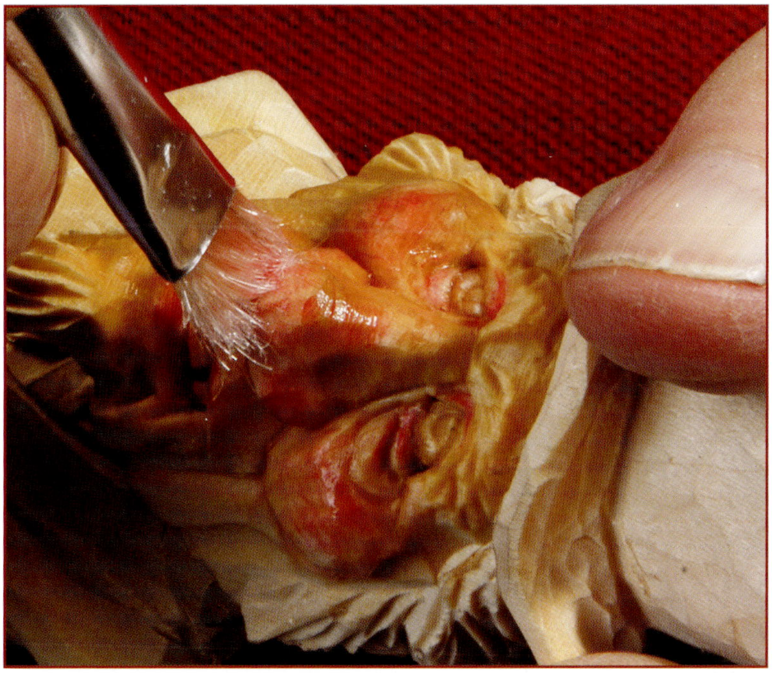

A brush with turpentine is used to smooth it out...

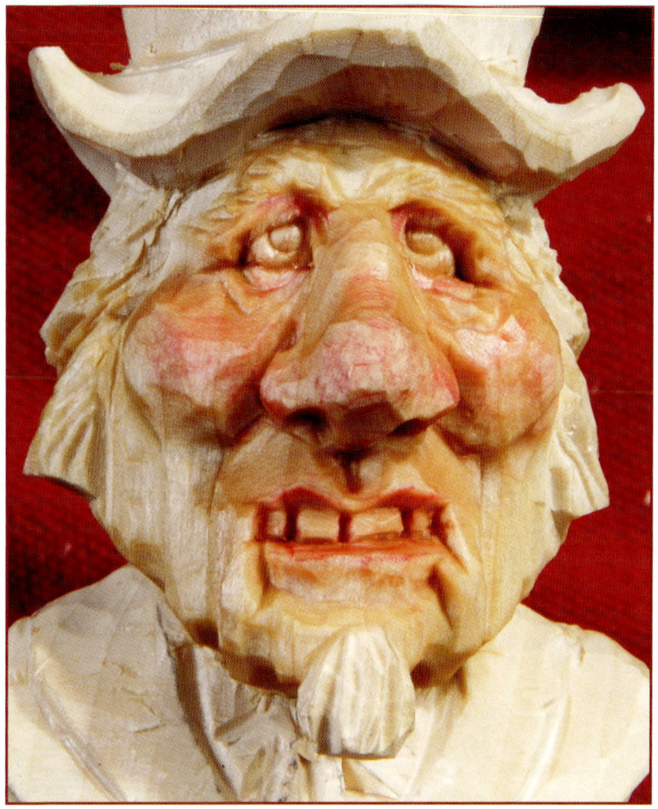

...for this result.

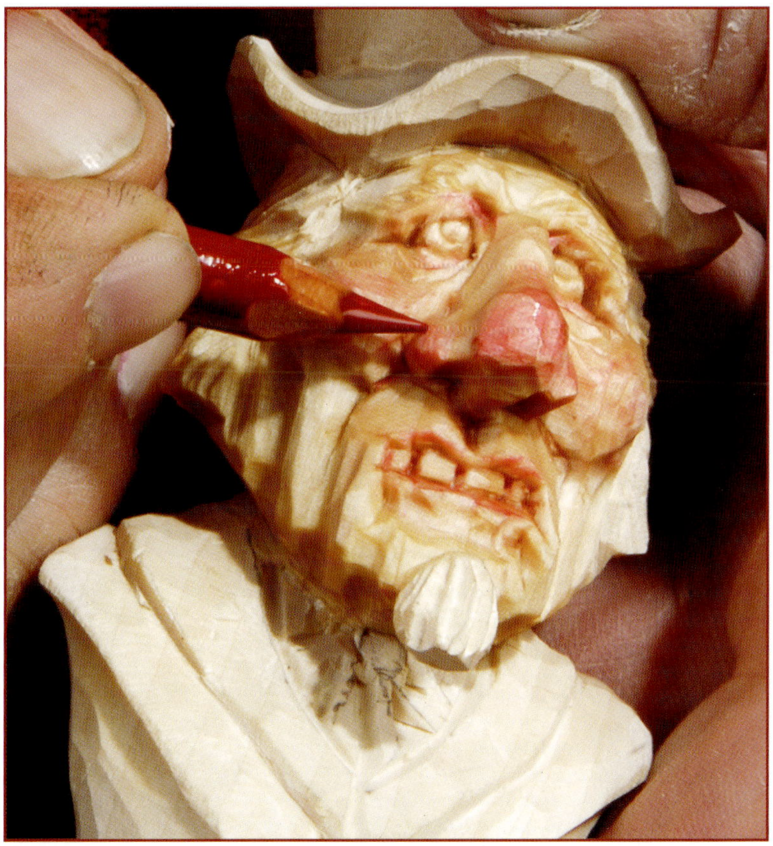

A darker red is applied to the highlights.

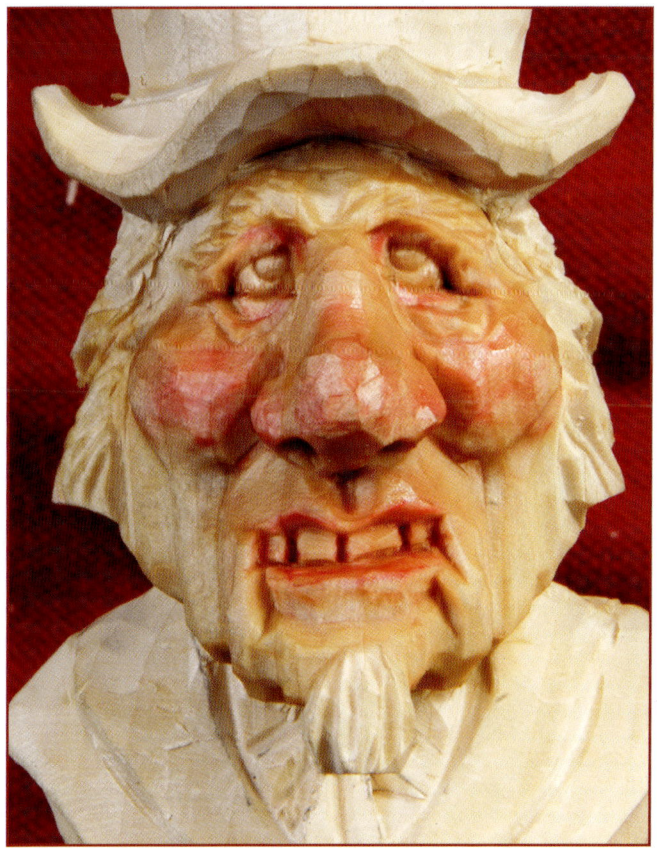

Wash it with turpentine for this effect.

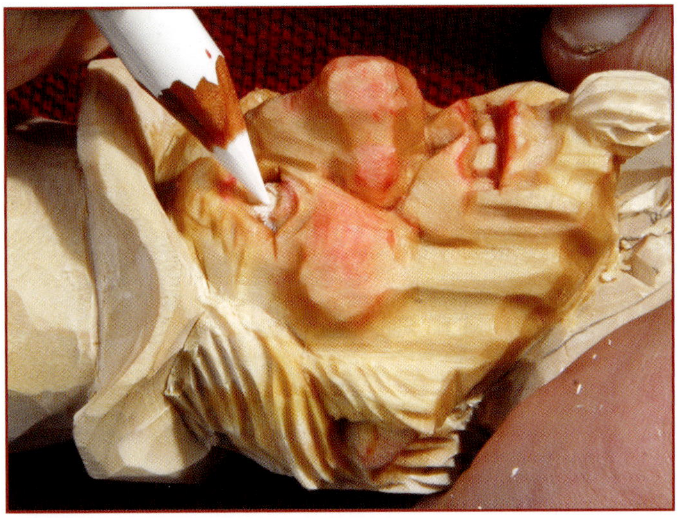

A white pencil is used for the whites of the eyes...

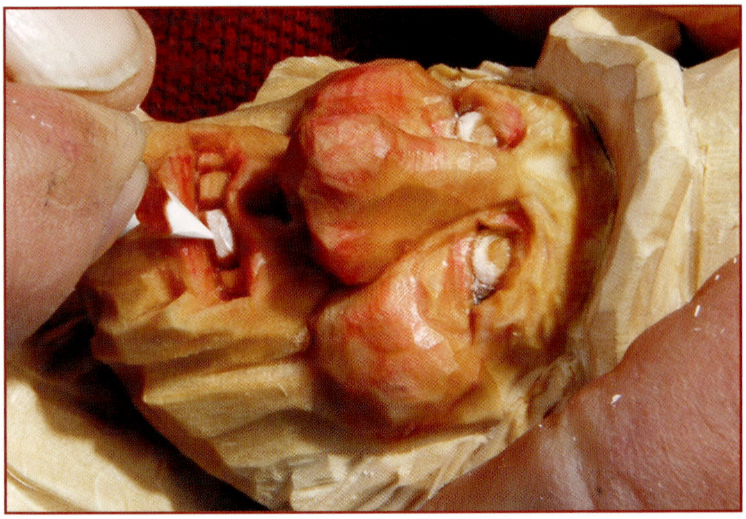

...and the teeth.

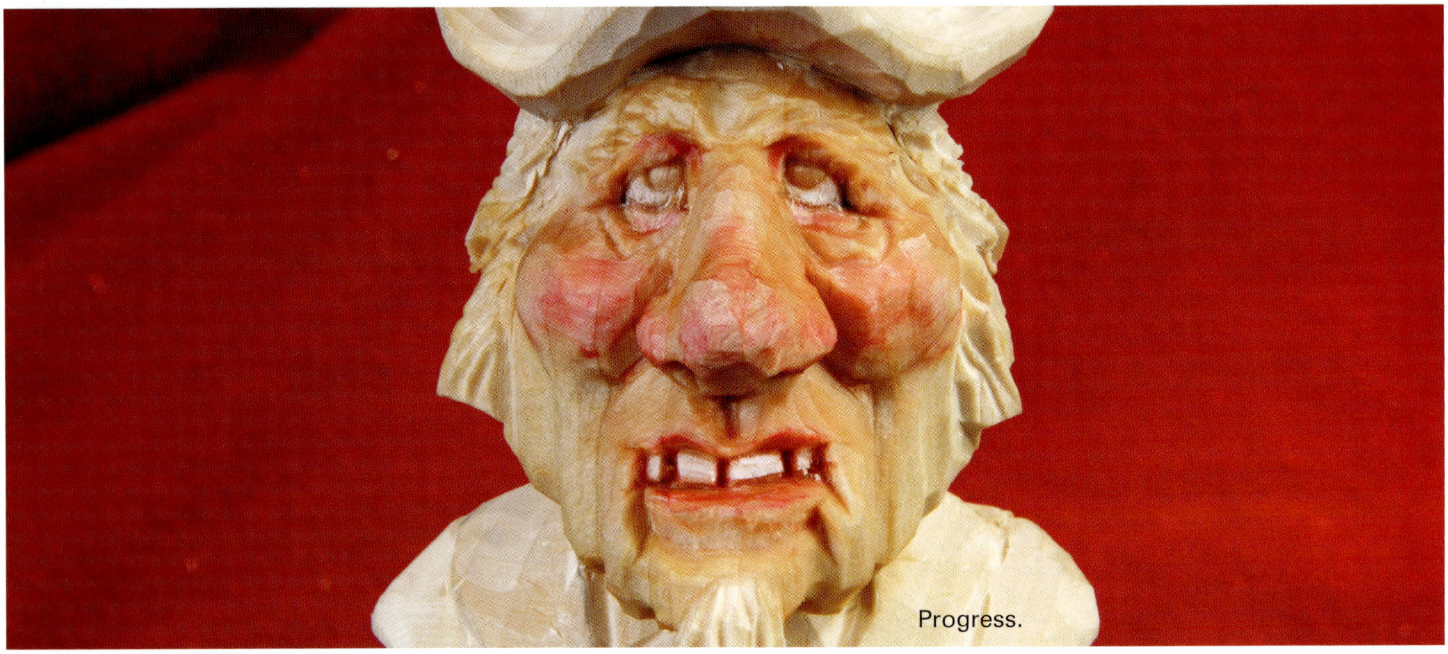

Progress.

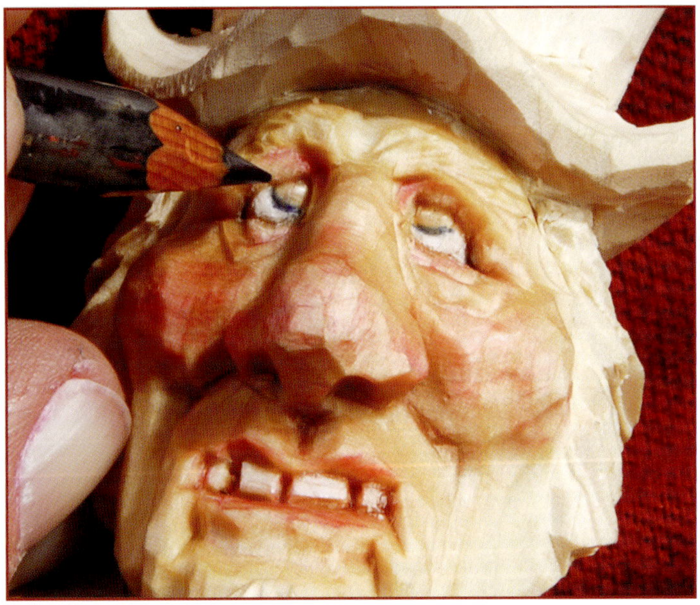

Use a dark blue to outline the bottom of the iris...

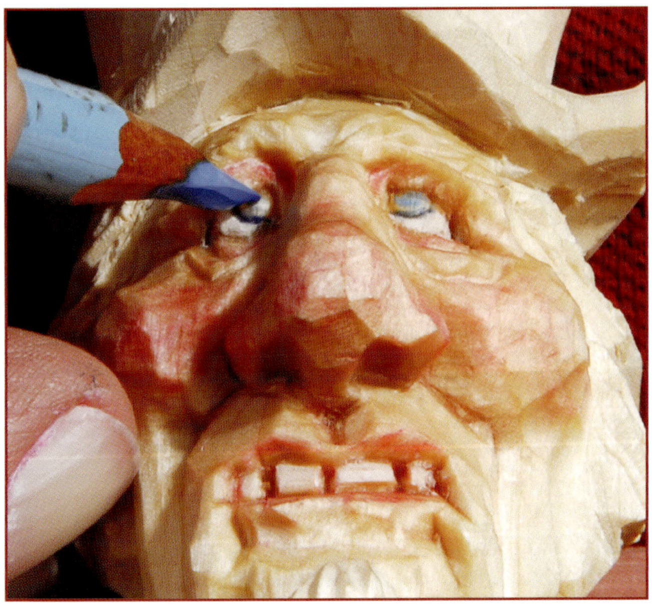

...and a light blue to color it.

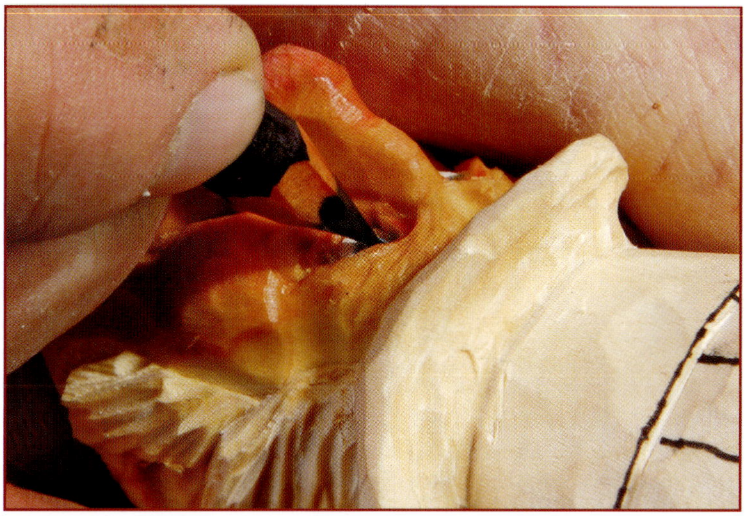

A black pencil makes the pupil.

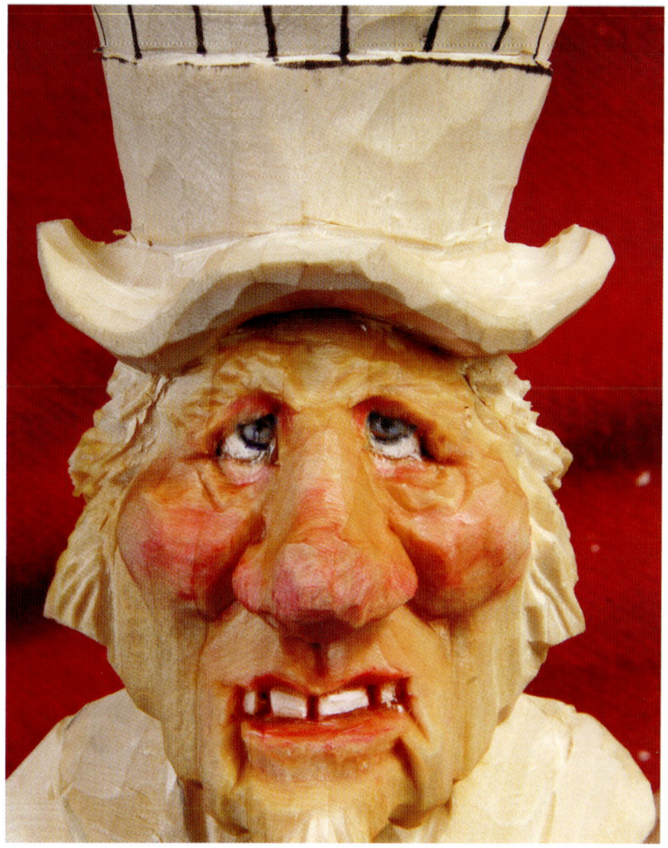

Progress.

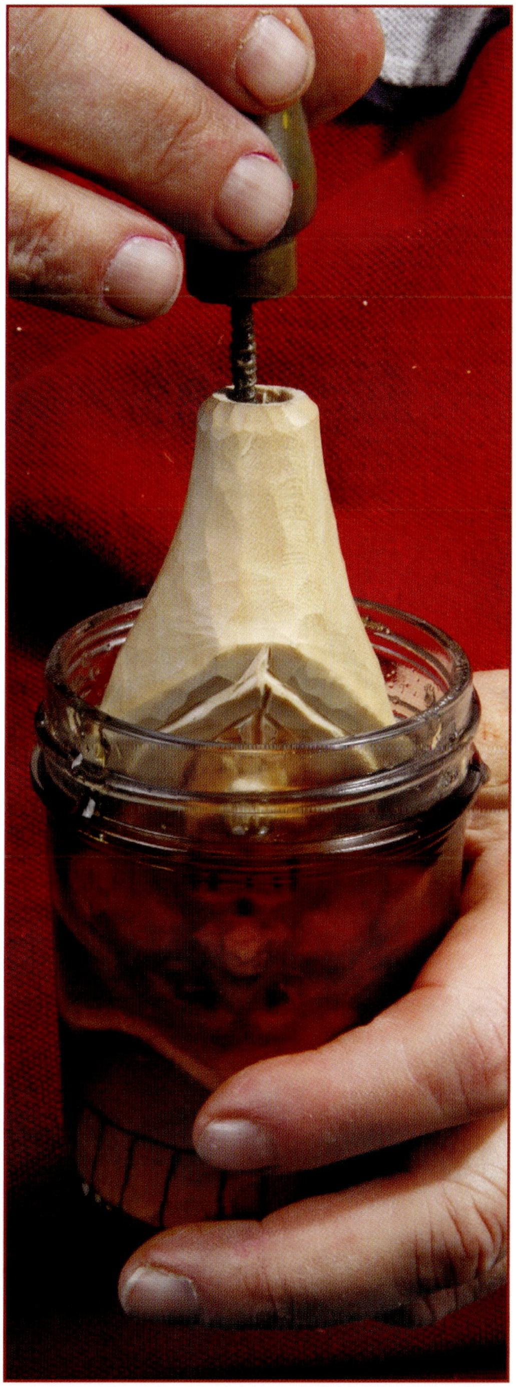

Before I switch to oil paints I dip the figure in boiled linseed oil. This will make the painting easier and better. I'll paint the linseed on the bottom portion so I don't get it into the screw socket.

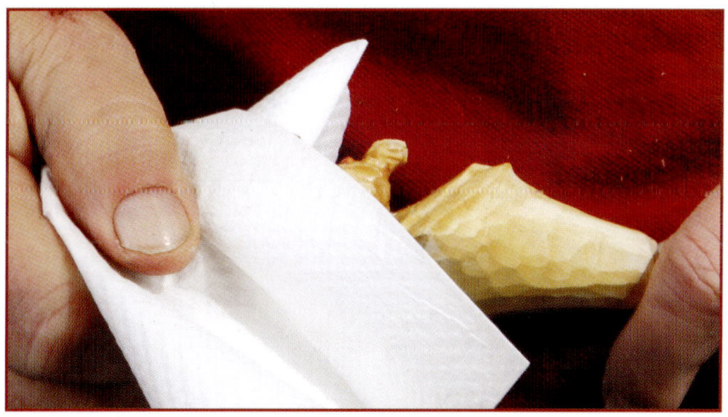

Let it soak in for a bit, then wipe it down with a blotting motion.

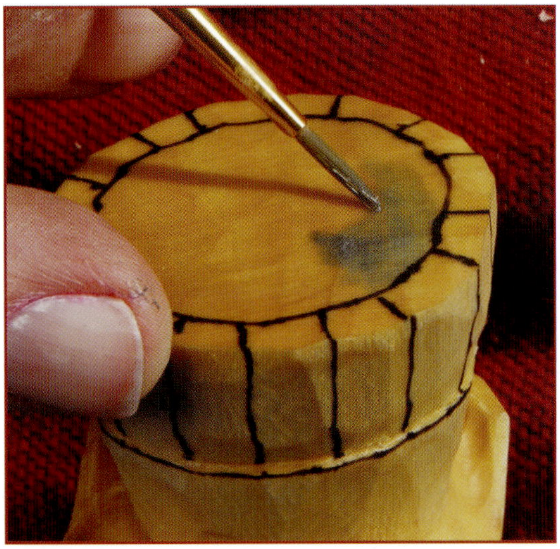

Begin with a good flag blue, painting the top of the hat...

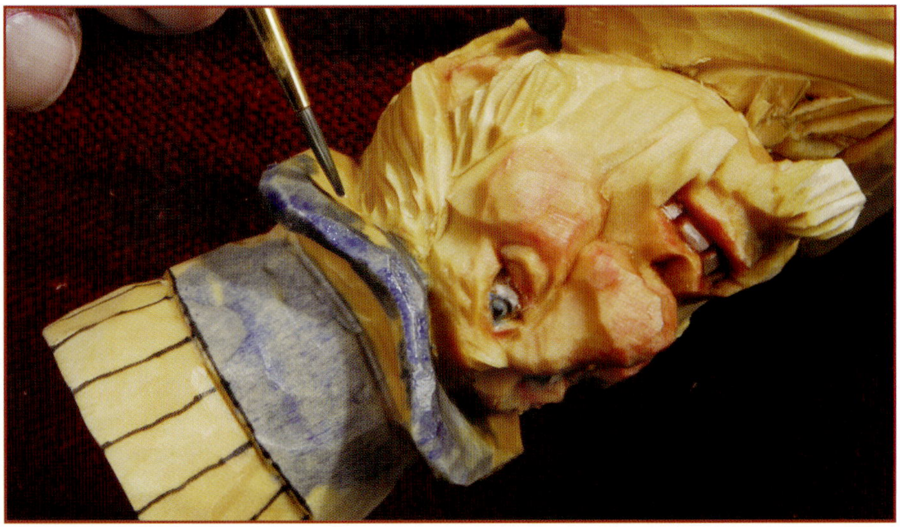

...the lower crown, the brim...

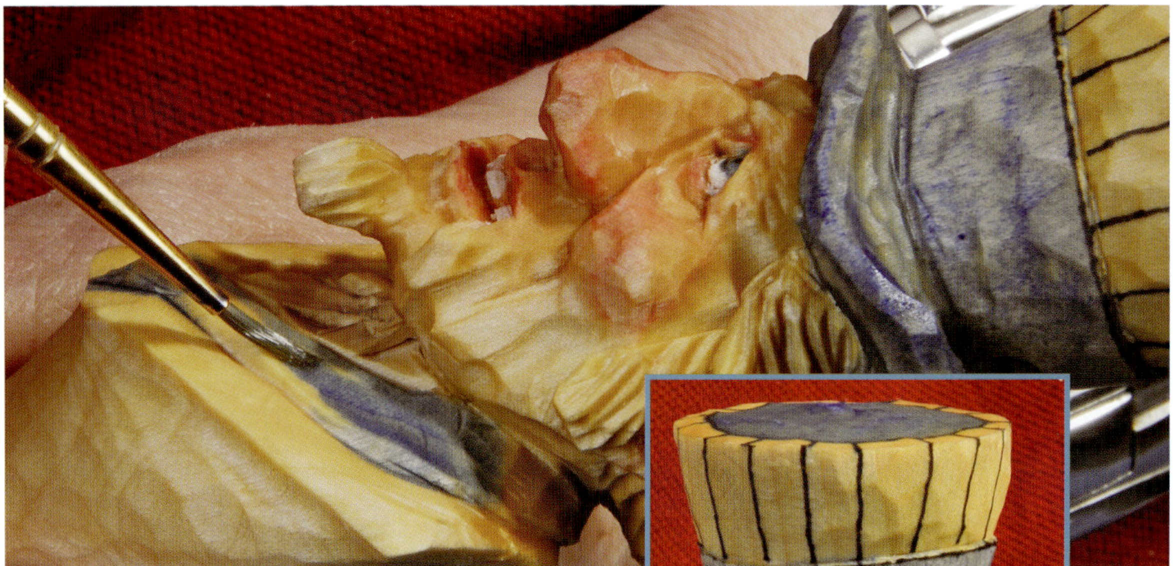

...and the coat

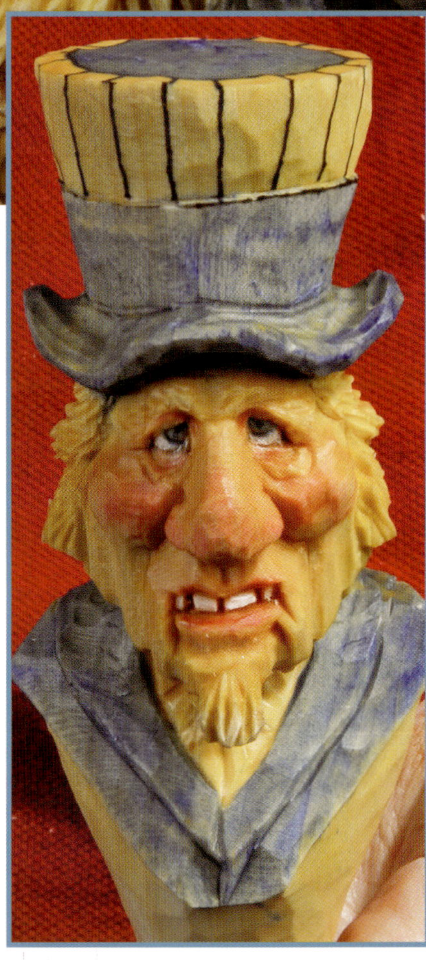

Blue is finished.

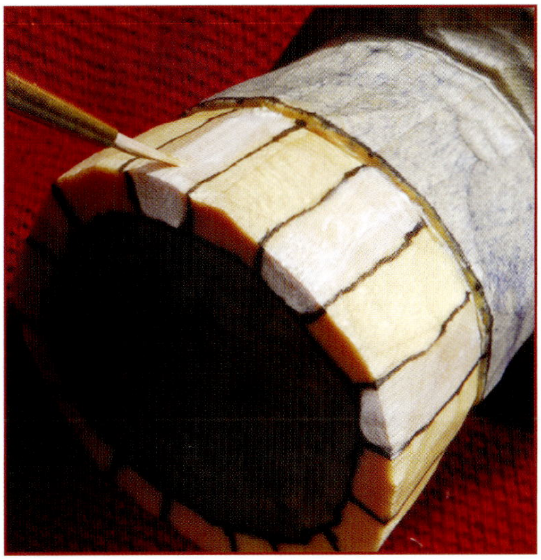

White is next. Start with every other stripe.

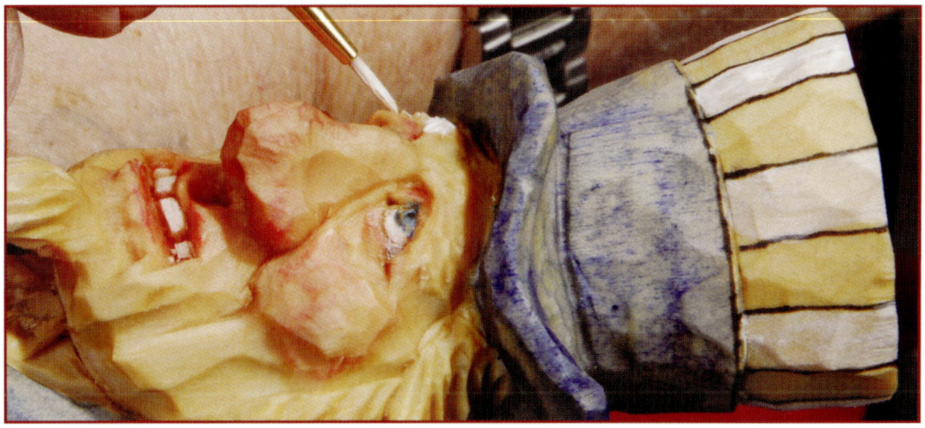

Continue with the eyebrows...

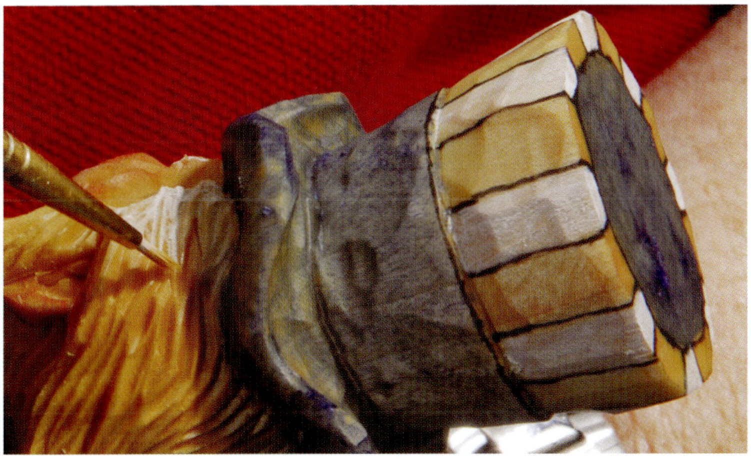

...and the hair.

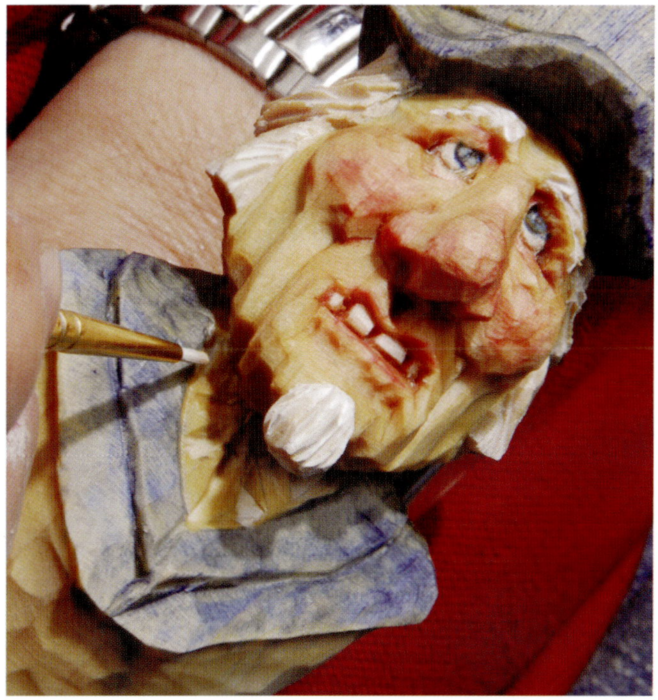

Finally apply white to the little bit of shirt that shows.

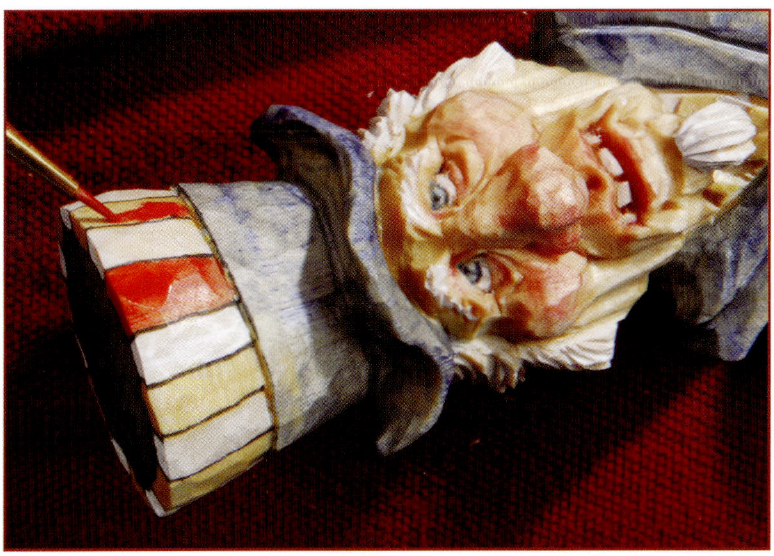

The remaining stripes are painted red.

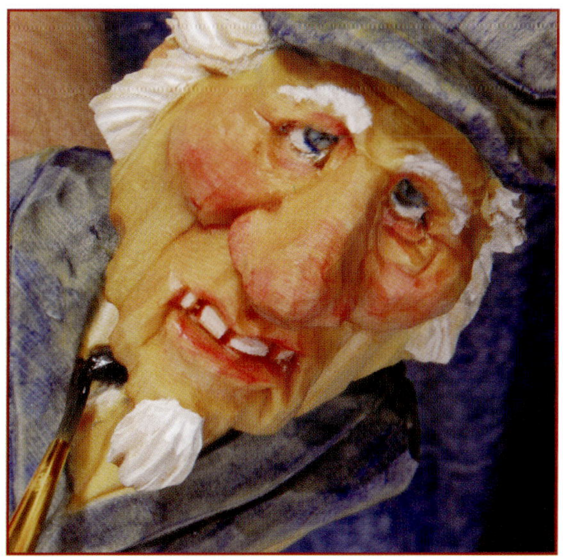

The tie will be black.

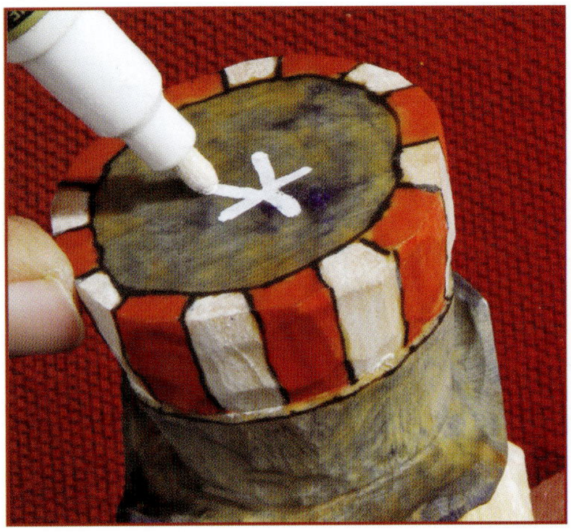

As a finishing touch I'll add some stars to the hat. I find a paint marker to be good for this. Start with the five arms…

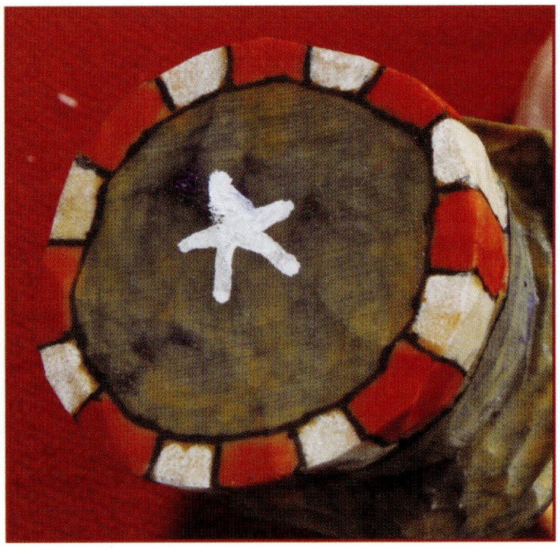

…and thicken the lines for this result.

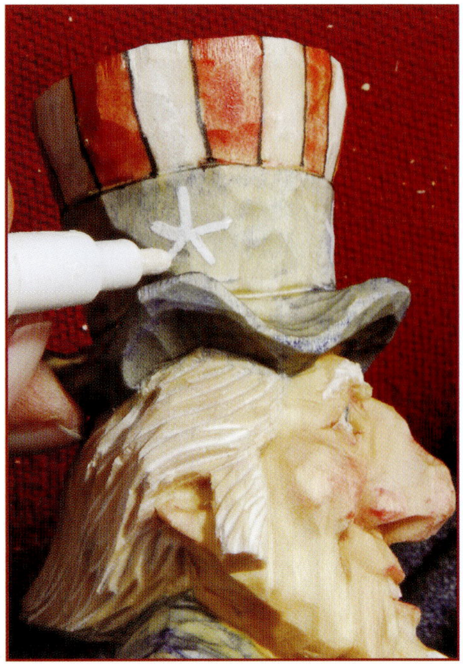

I use four stars on the band, one on each corner.

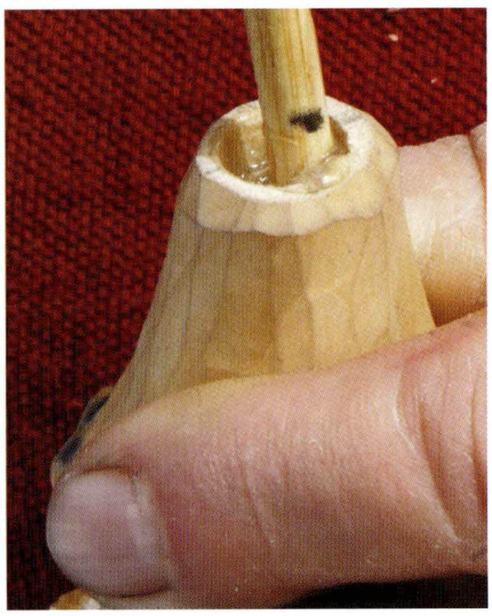

Apply 5-minute epoxy in the base of the carving. Ideally you'll fill the space enough to cover well, but not so much that it will overflow.

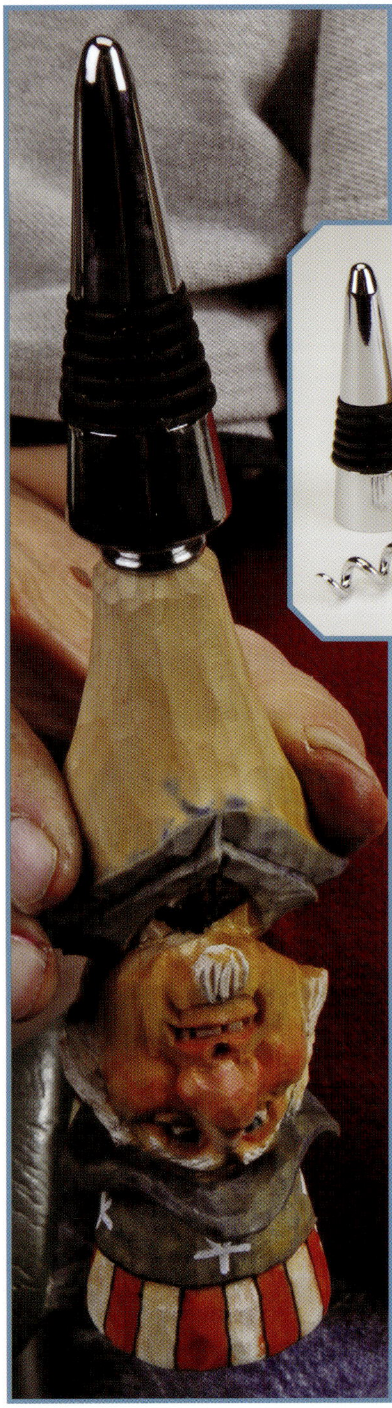

Insert the hardware and clean up any overfill.

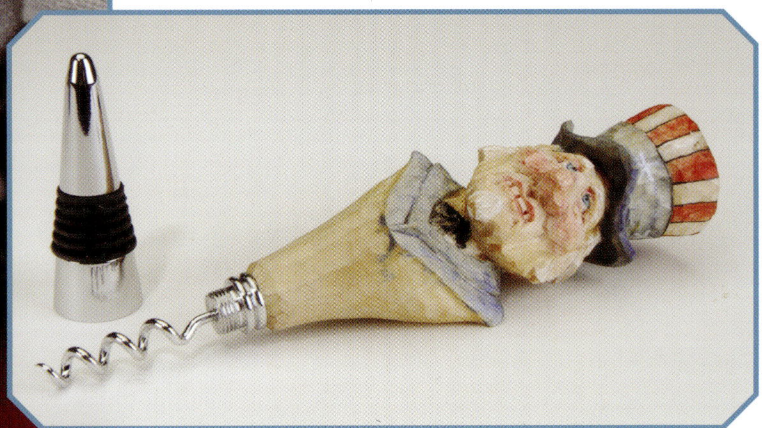

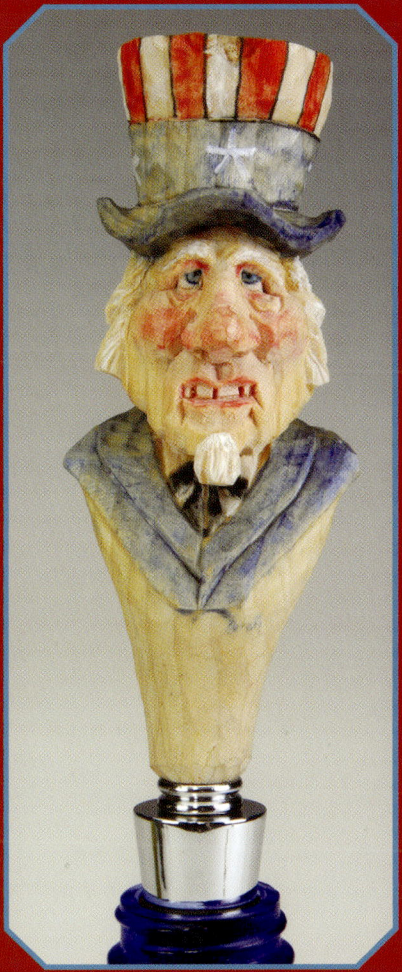
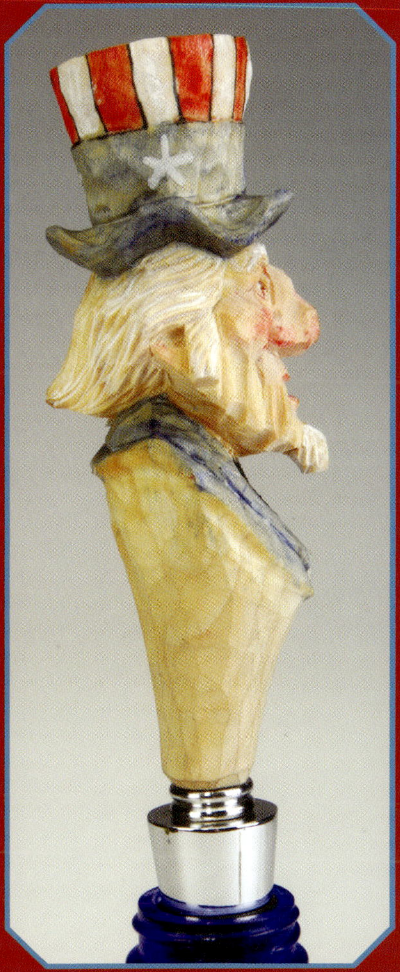
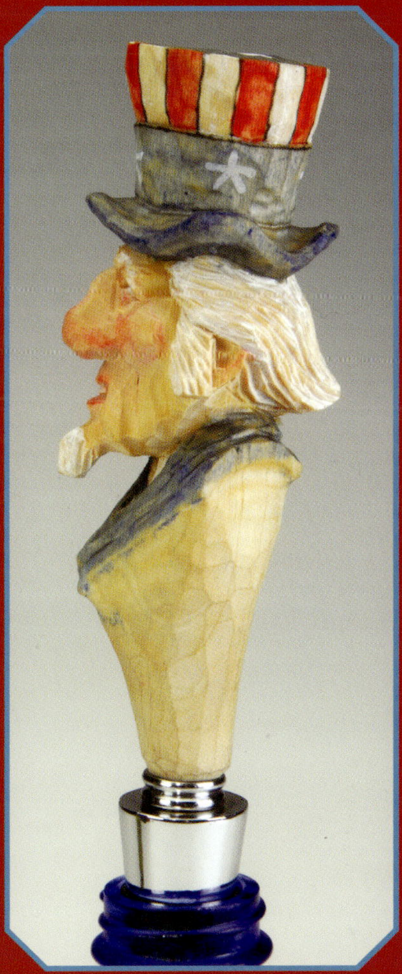
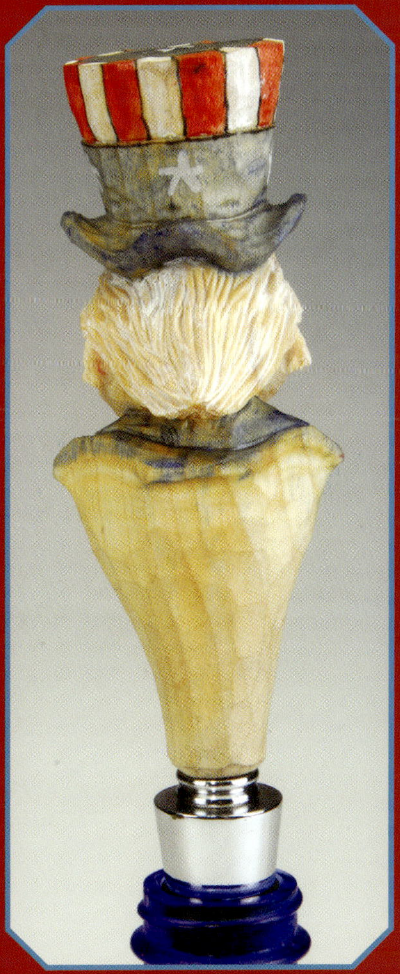

Gallery

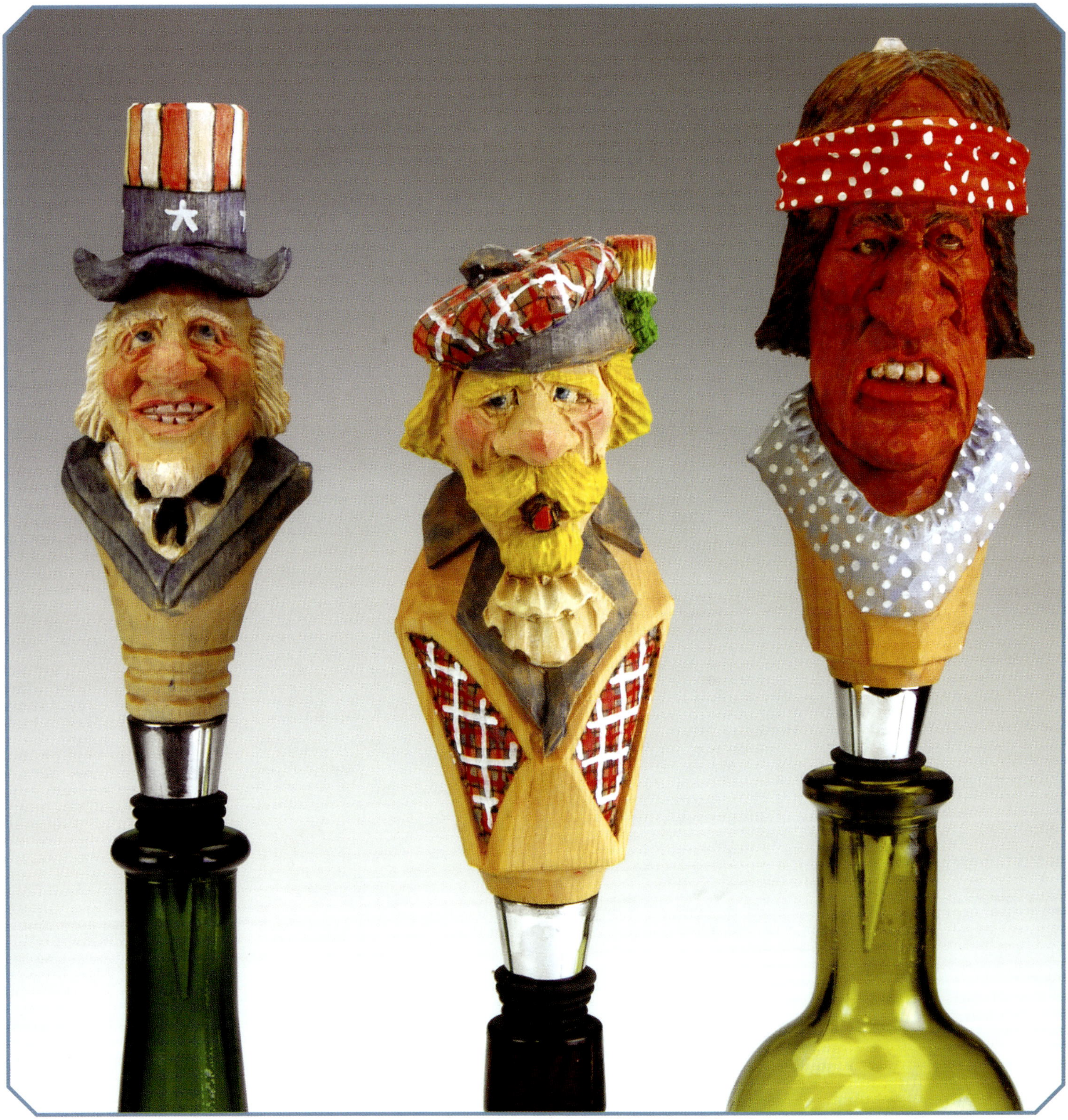

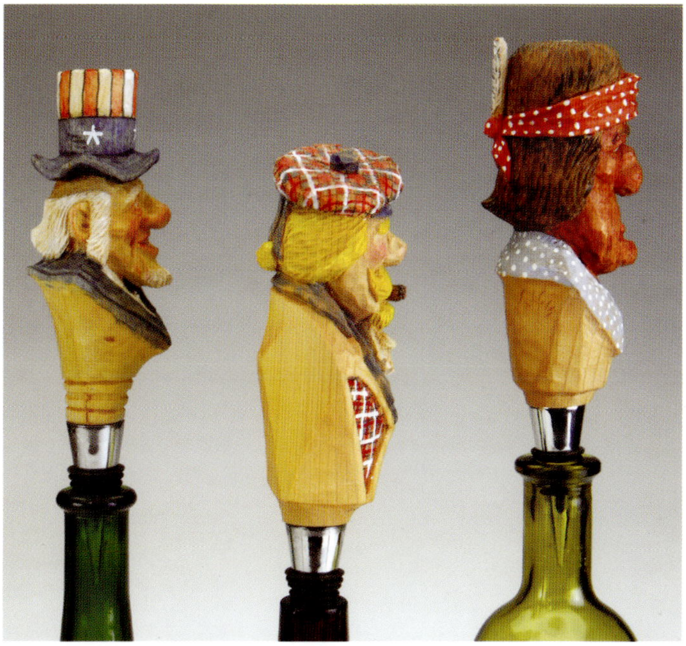

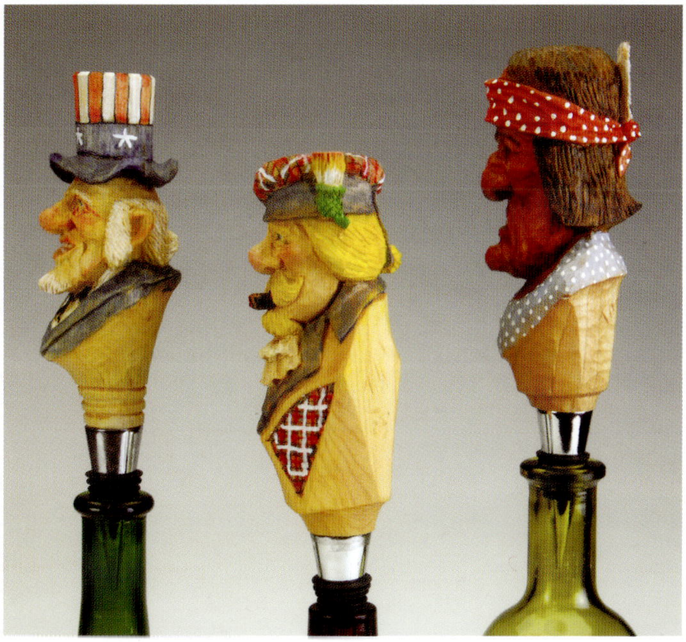

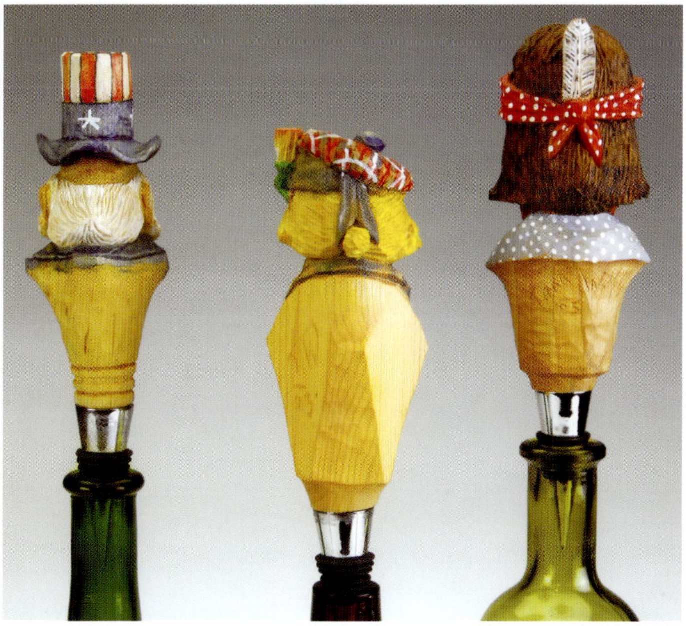

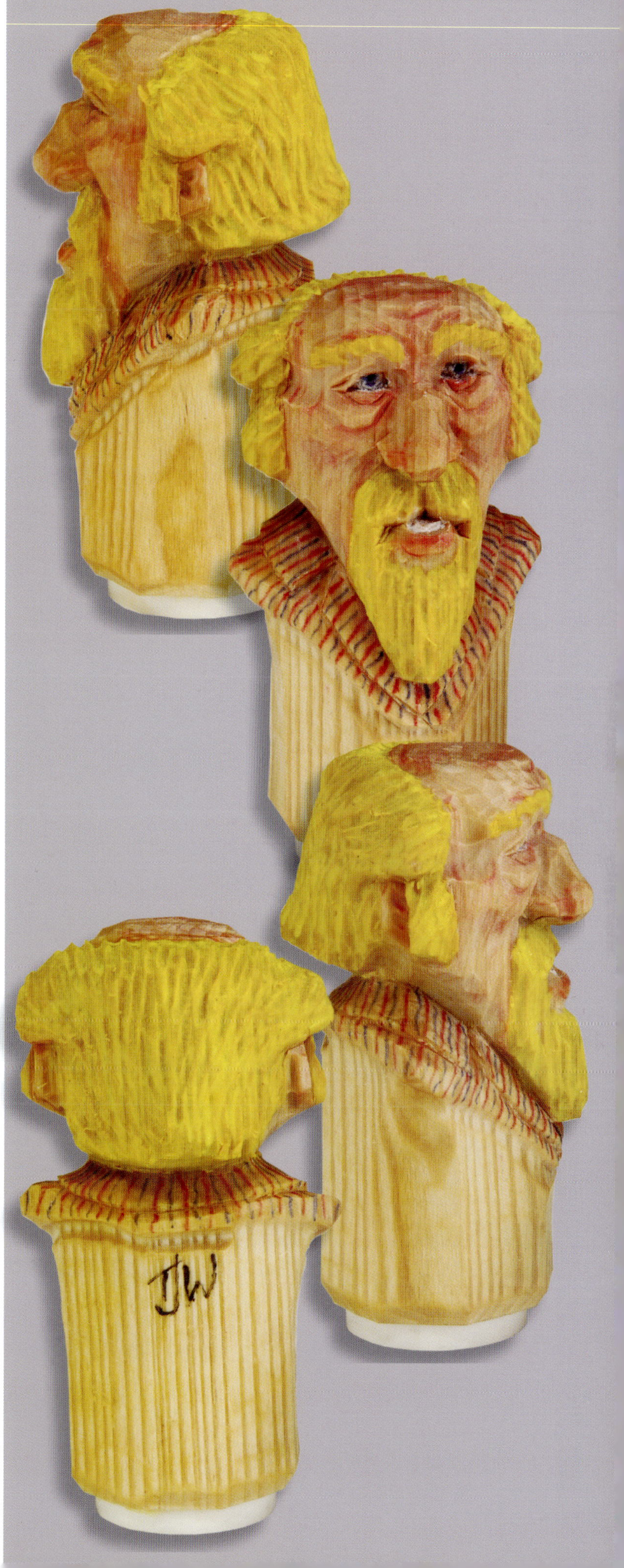
JW

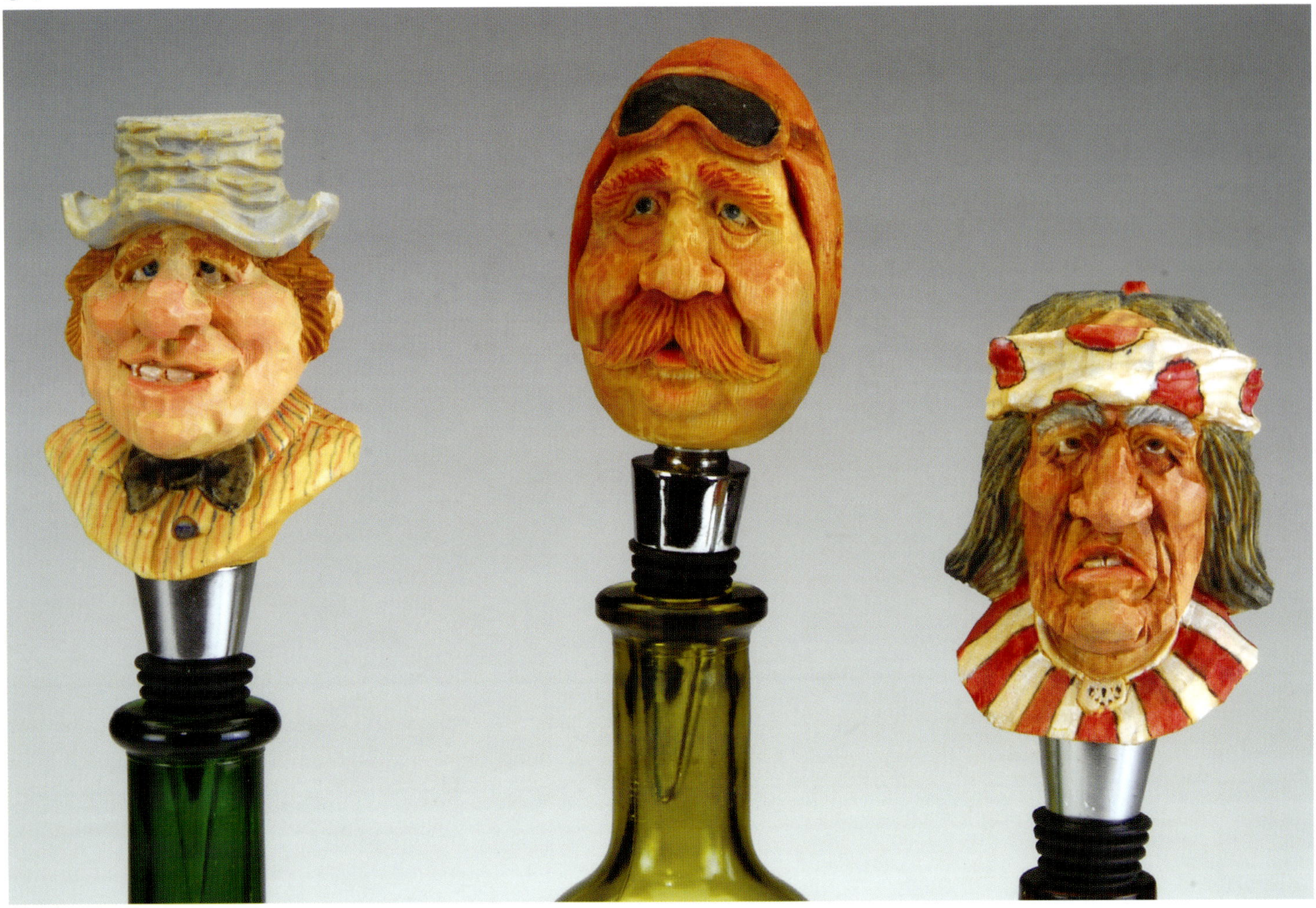

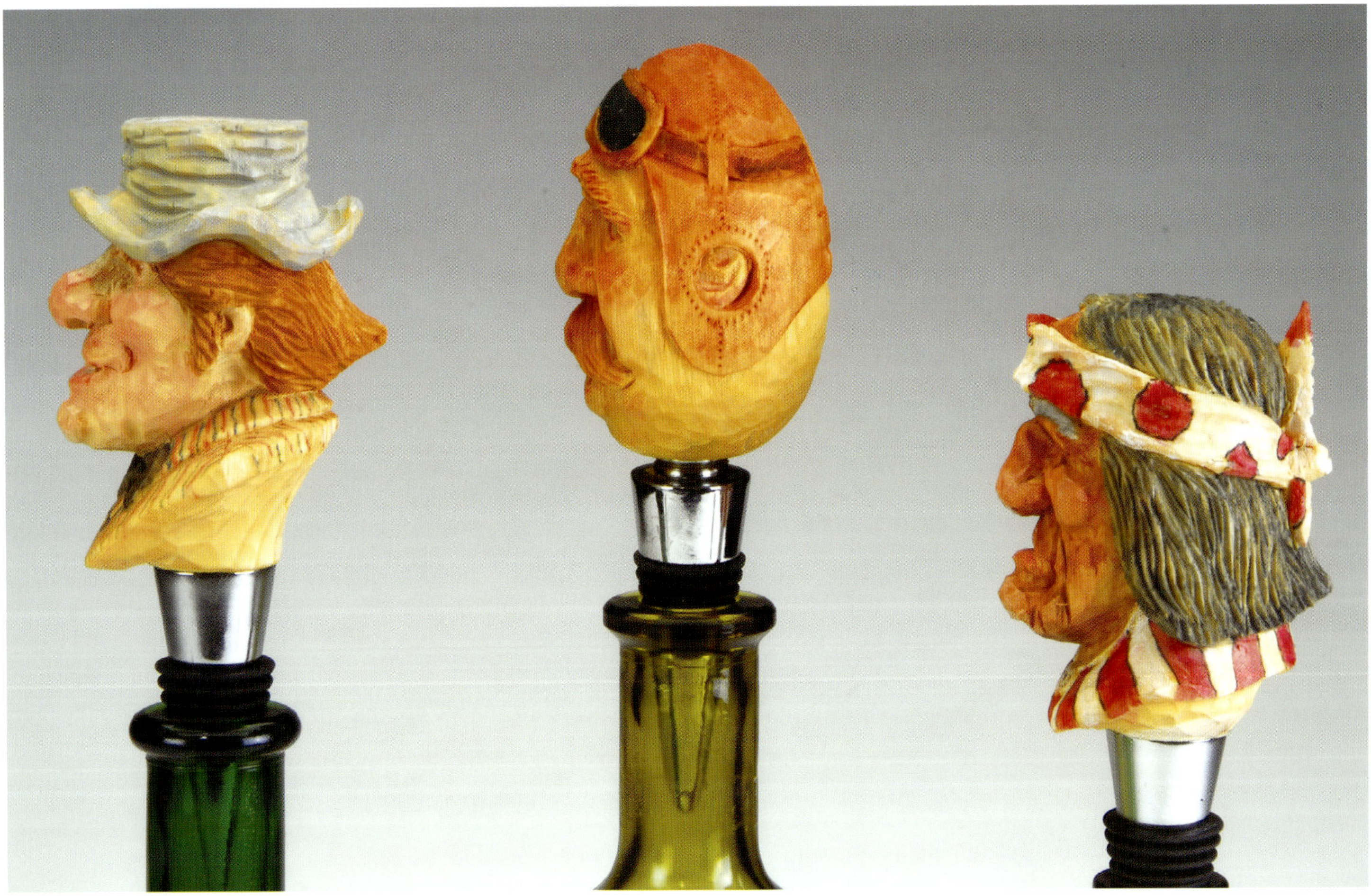

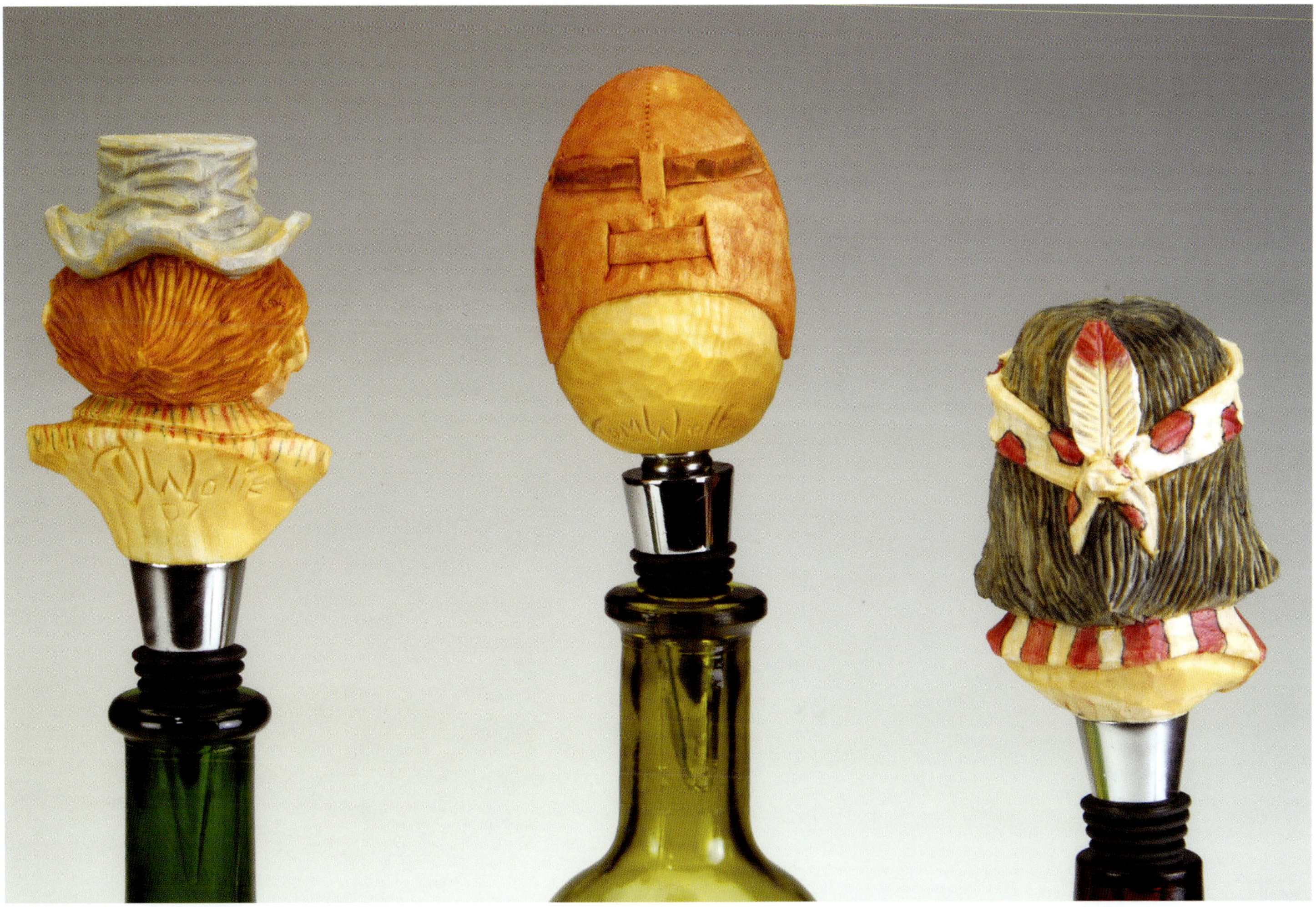

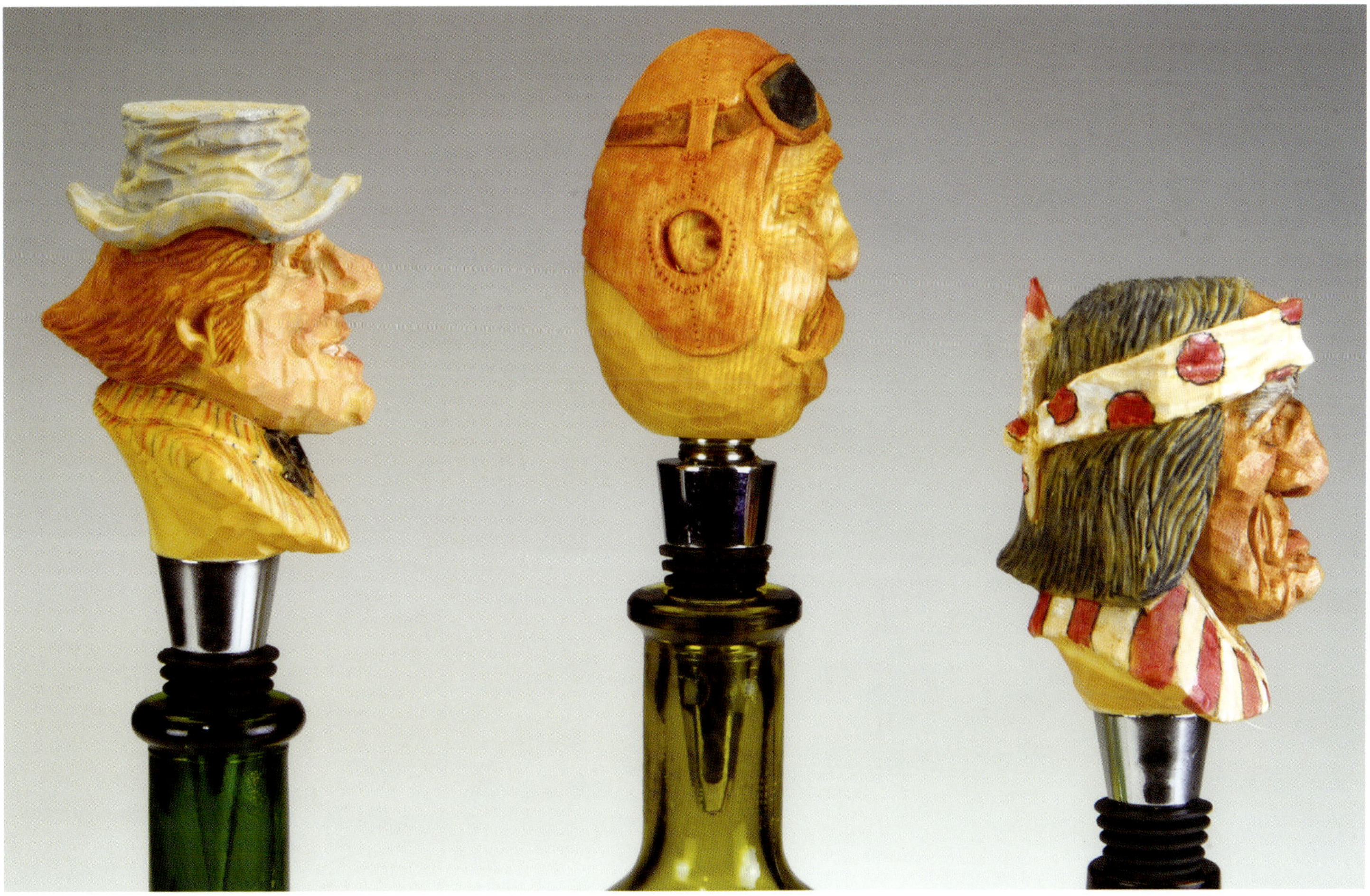

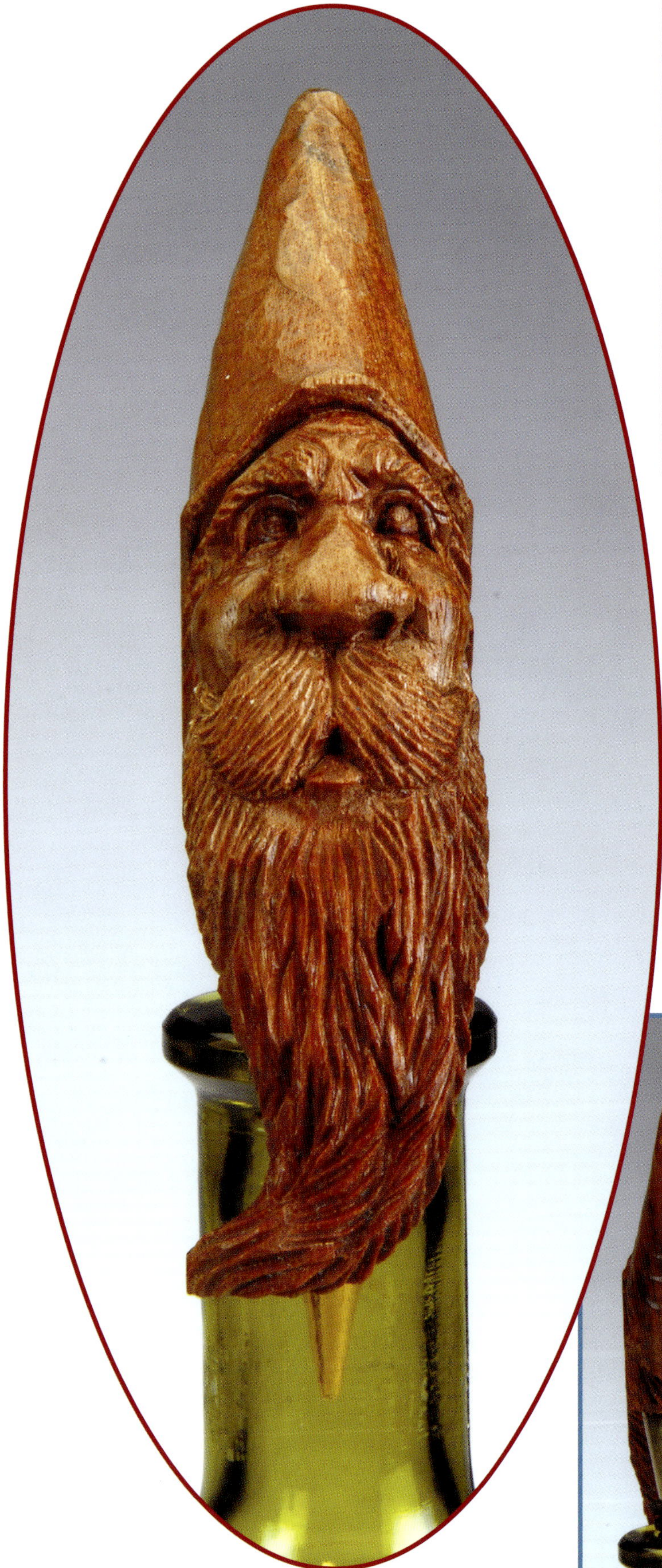

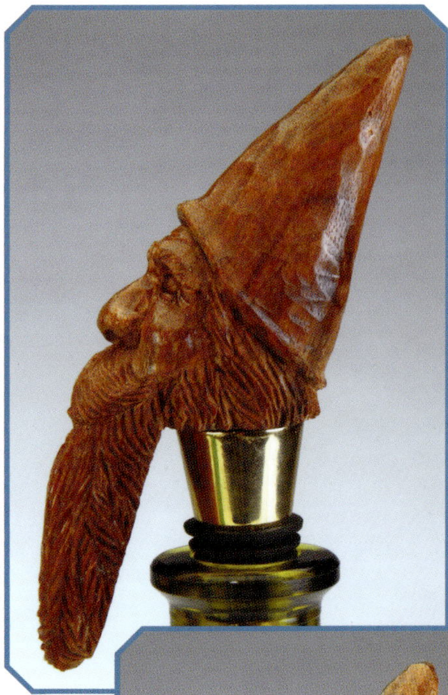

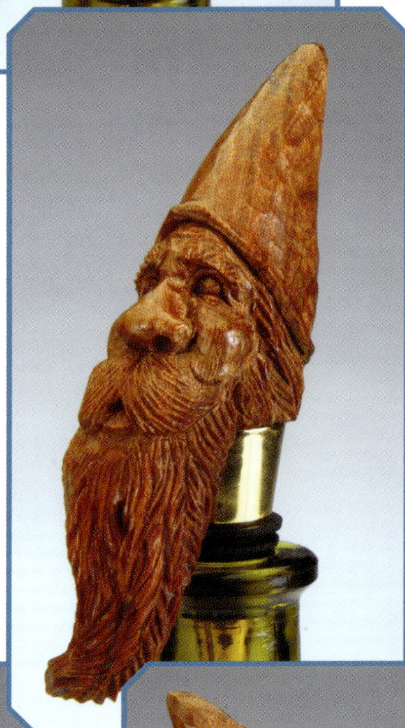

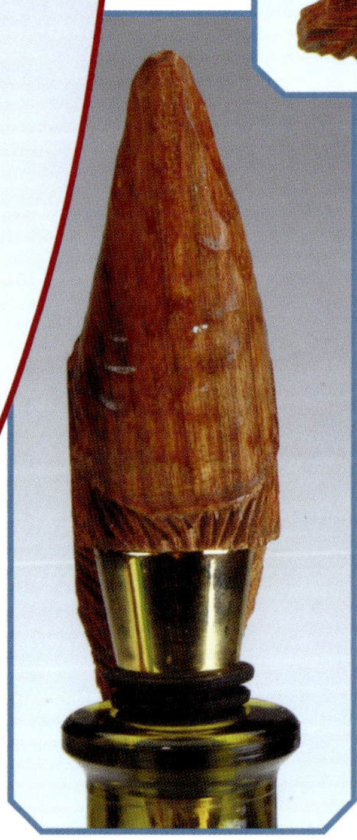

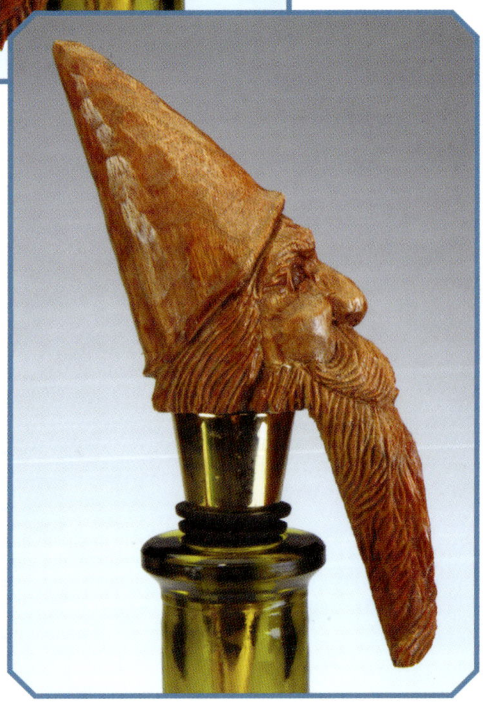

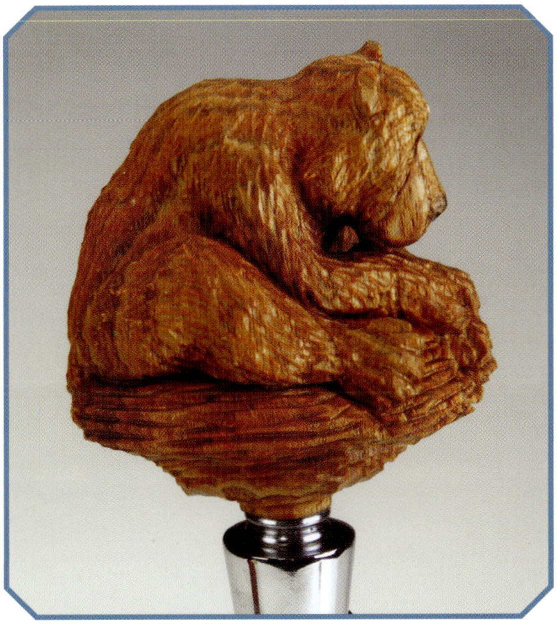

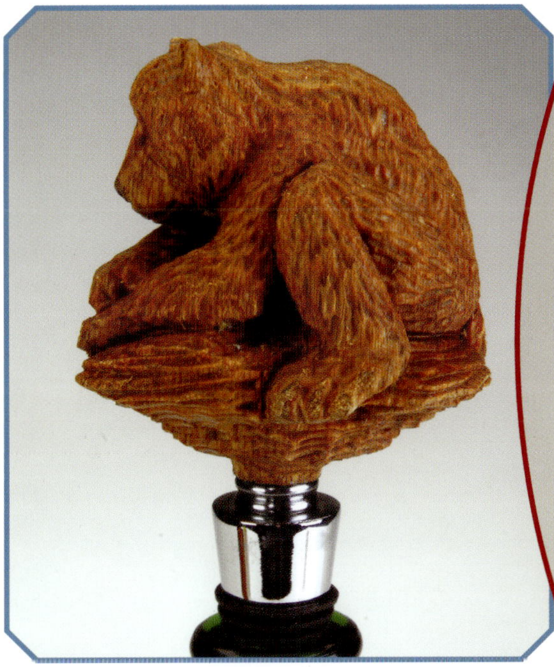

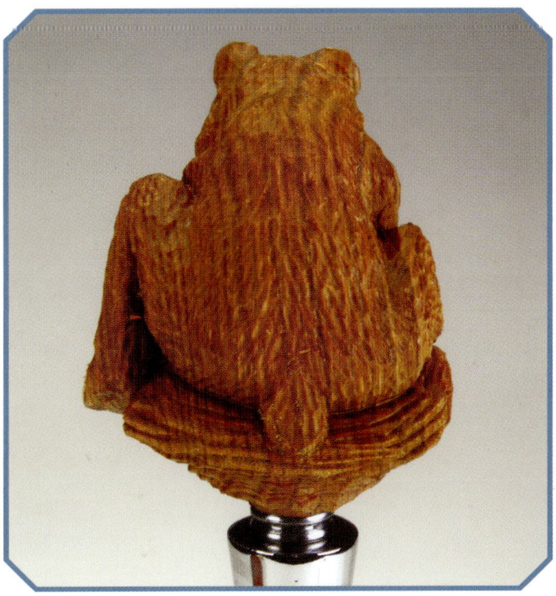

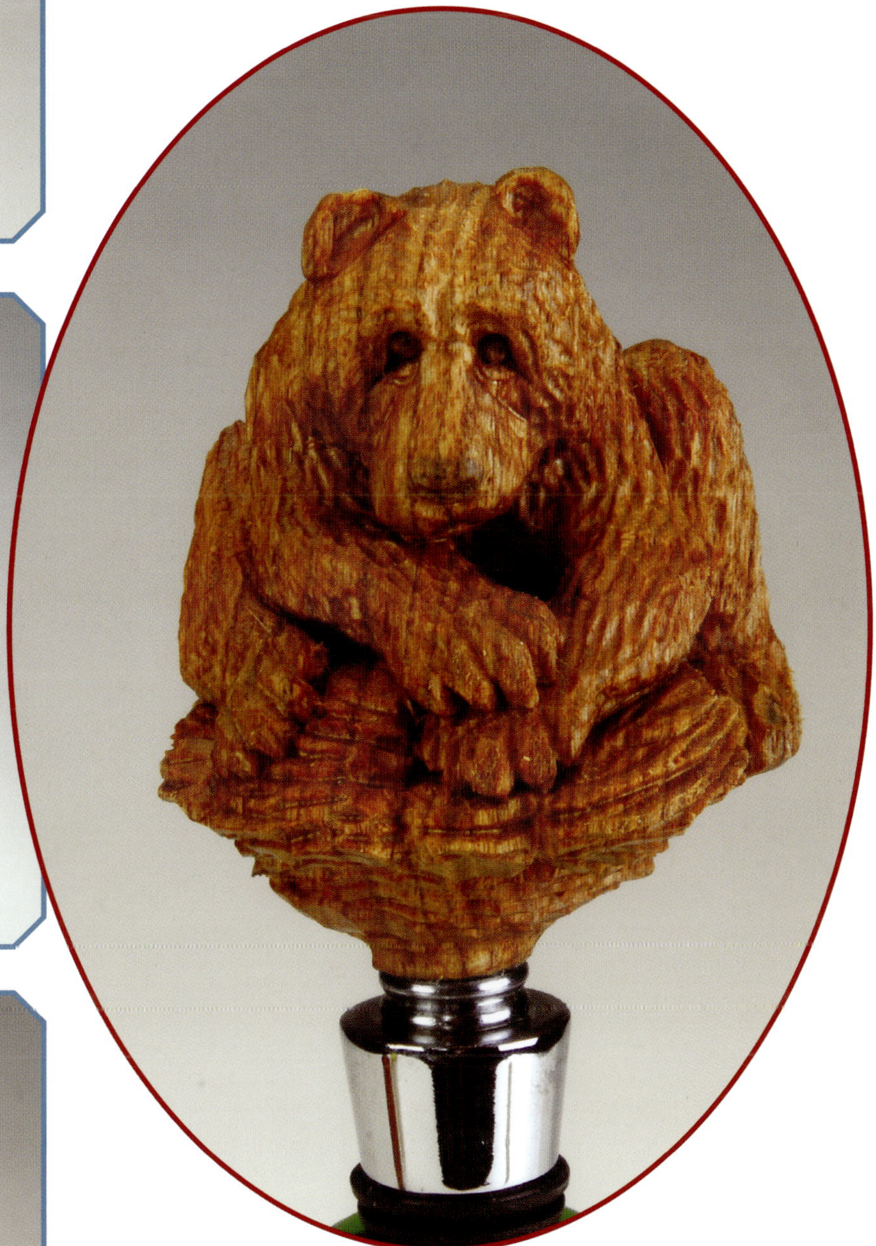

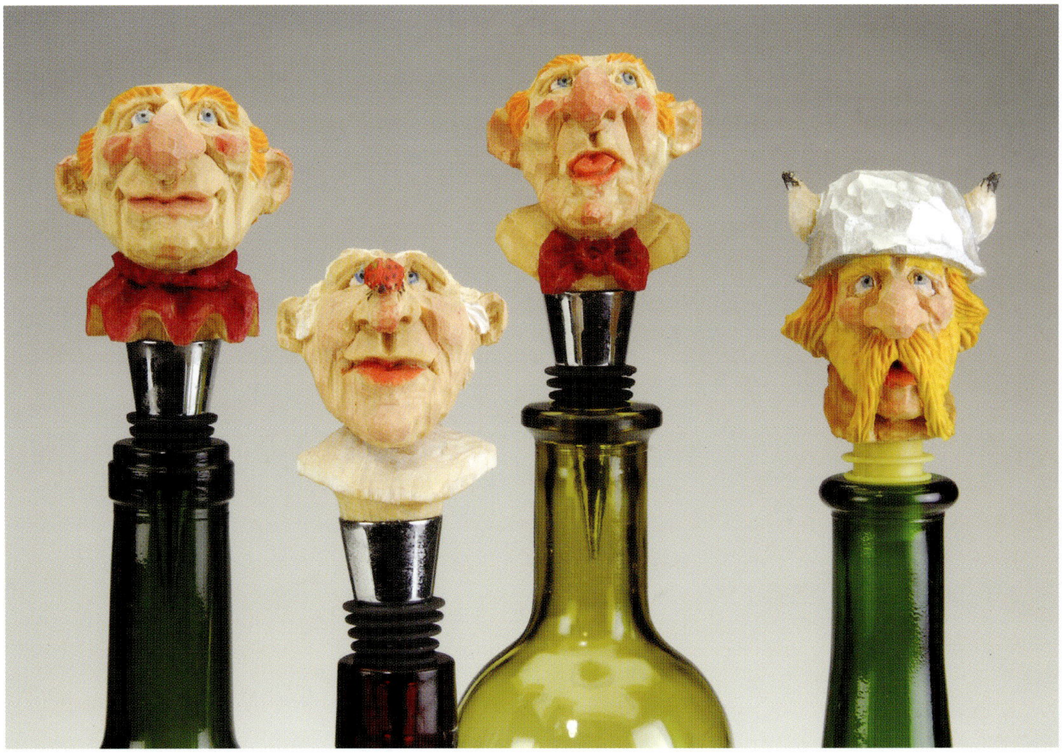

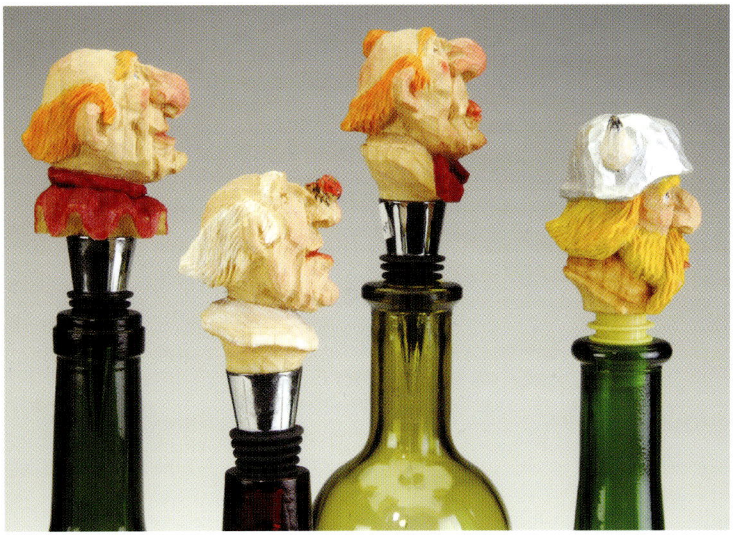

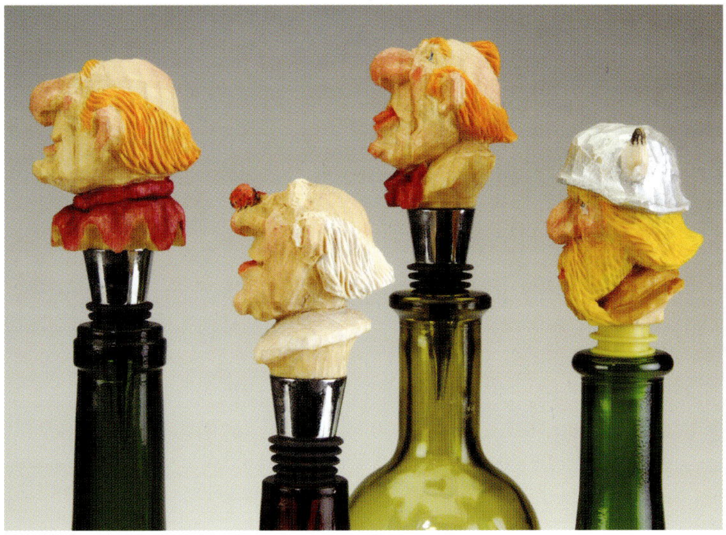

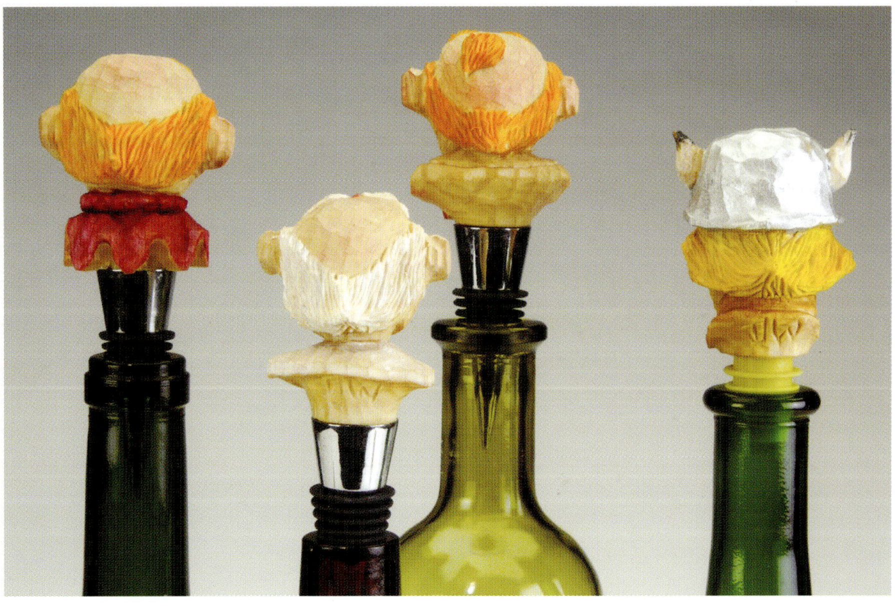

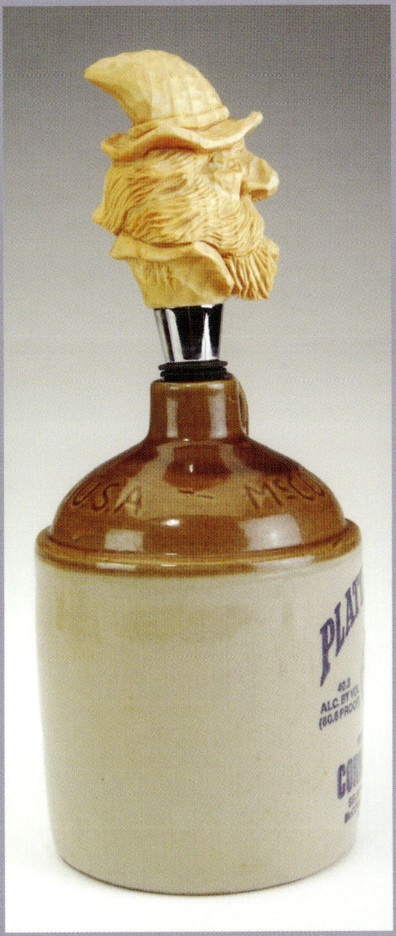

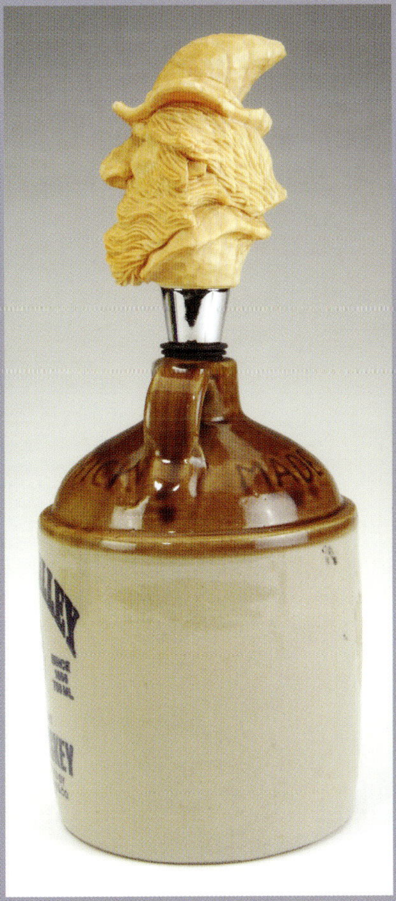

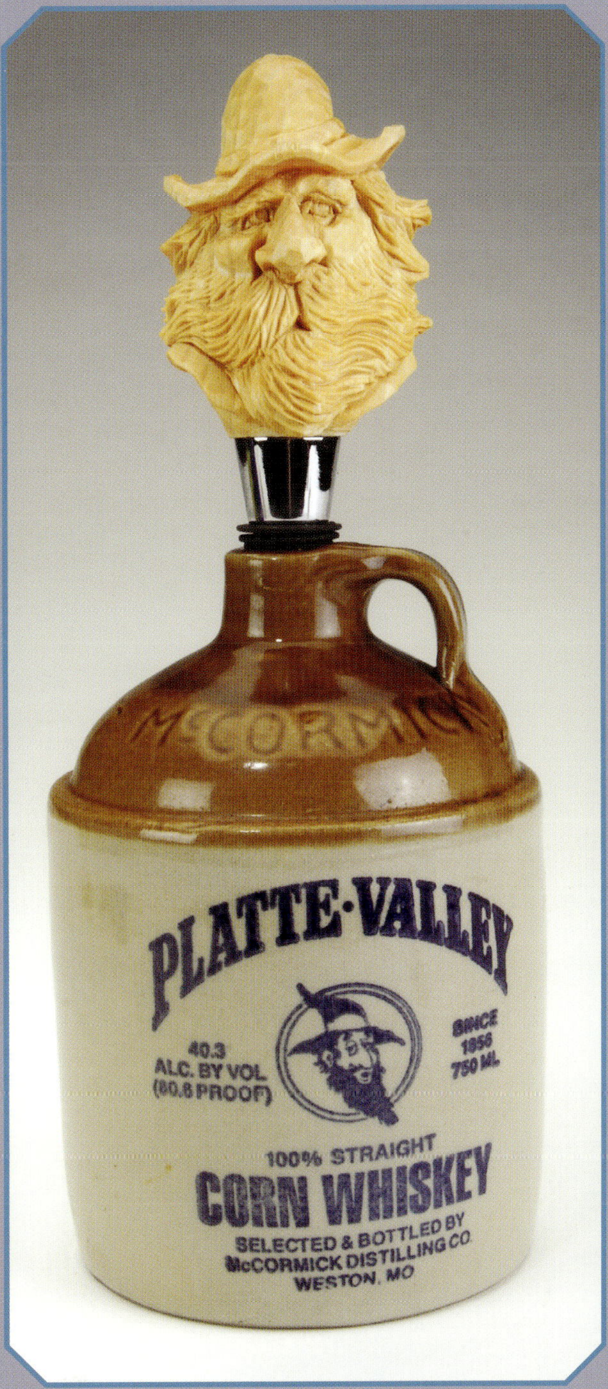
McCORMICK
PLATTE·VALLEY
40.3
ALC. BY VOL.
(80.6 PROOF)
SINCE
1956
750 ML
100% STRAIGHT
CORN WHISKEY
SELECTED & BOTTLED BY
McCORMICK DISTILLING CO.
WESTON, MO

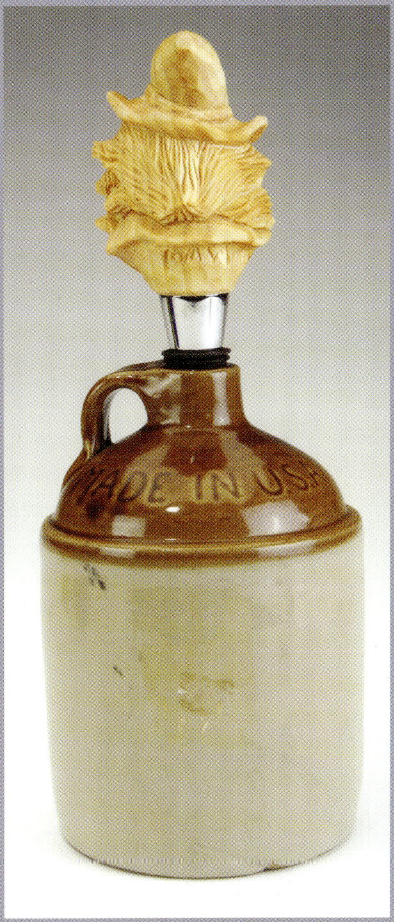
MADE IN USA

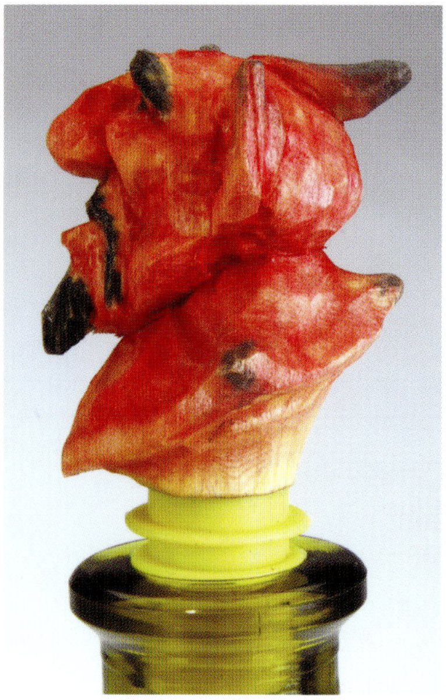

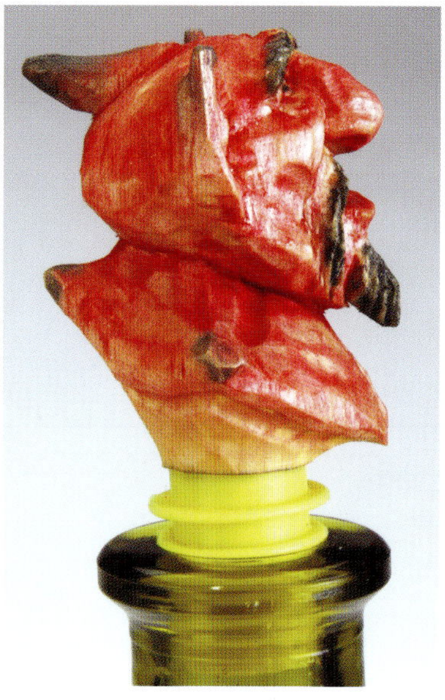

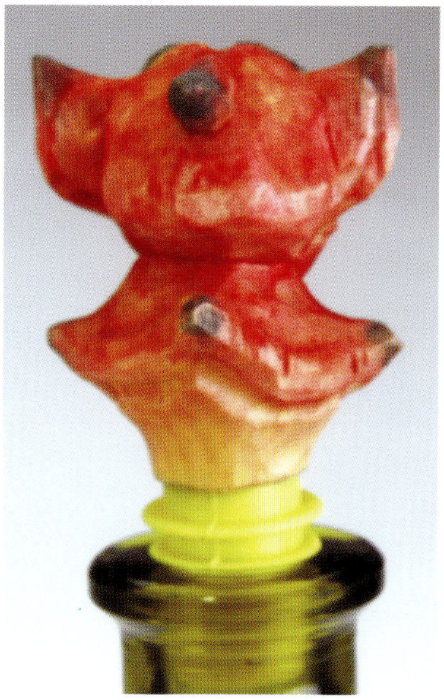

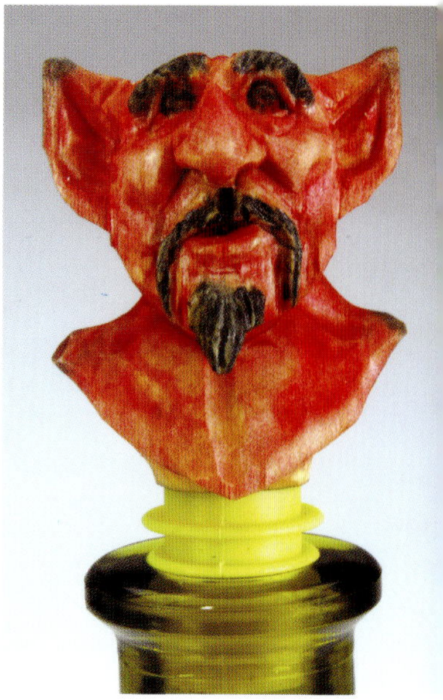

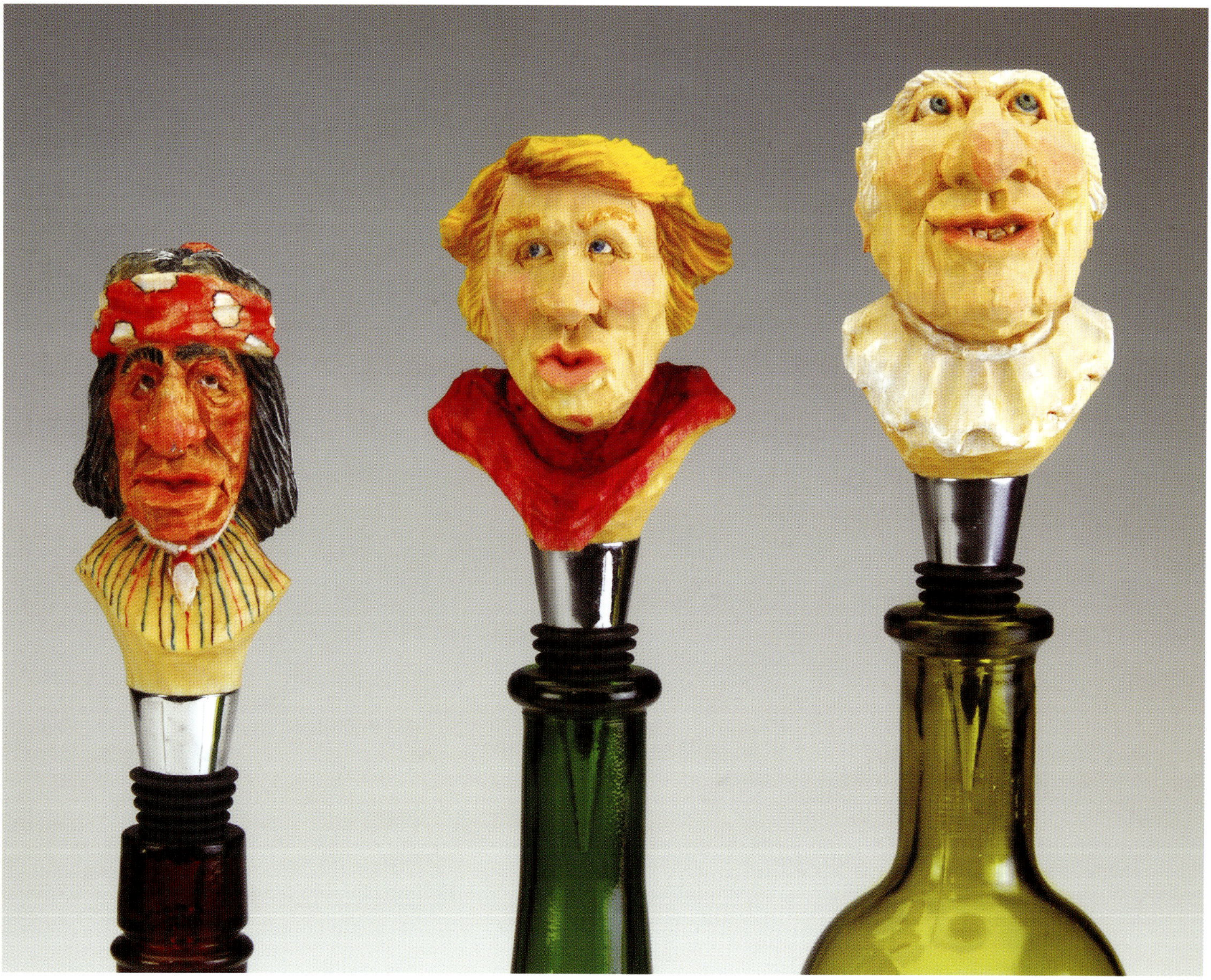

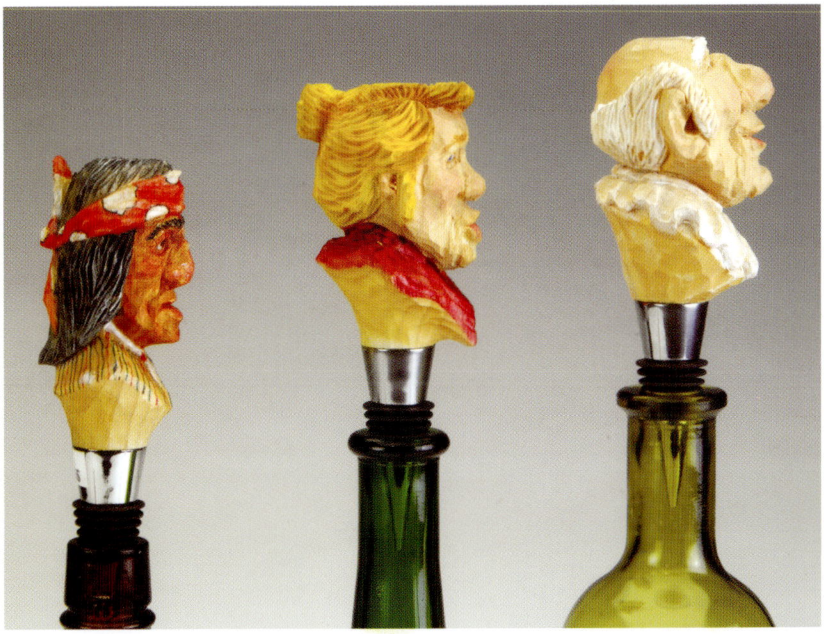
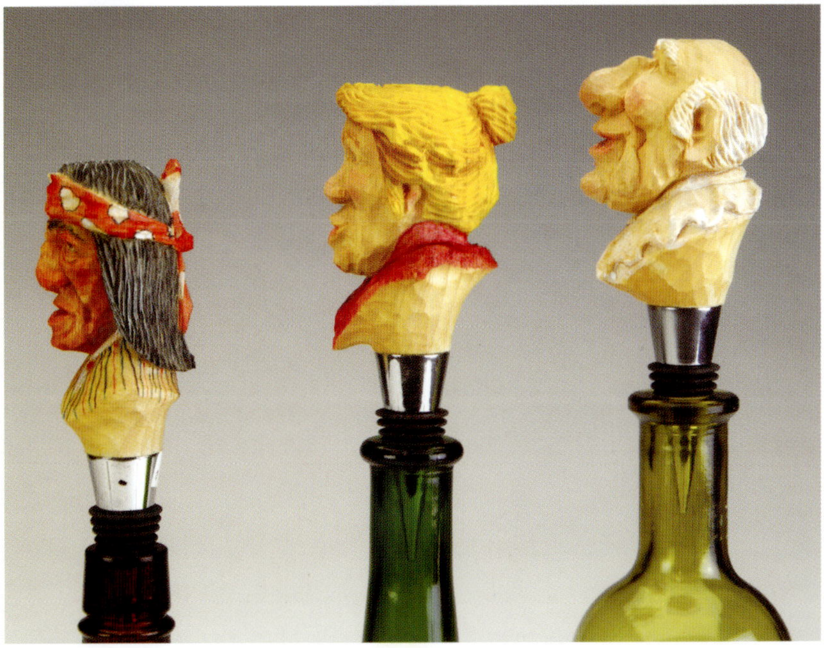
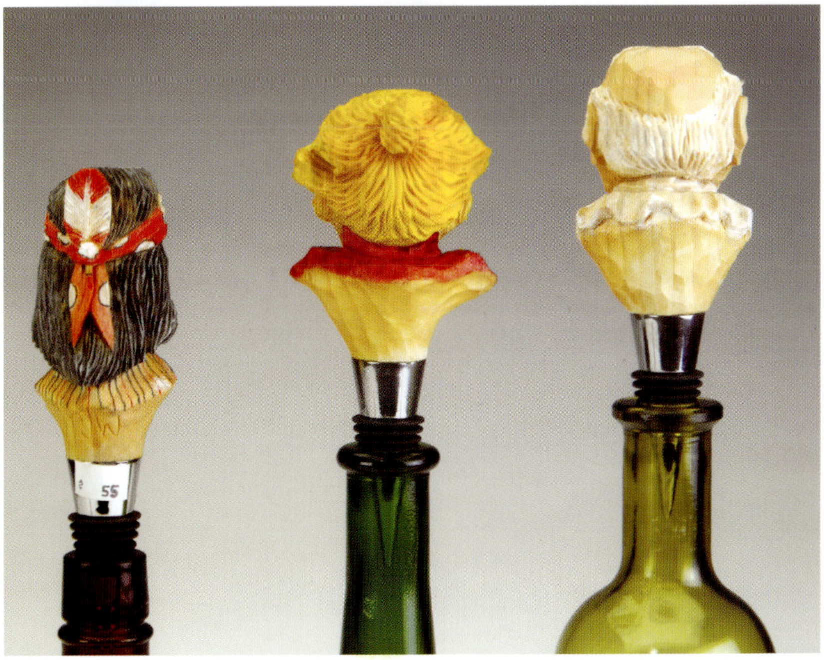
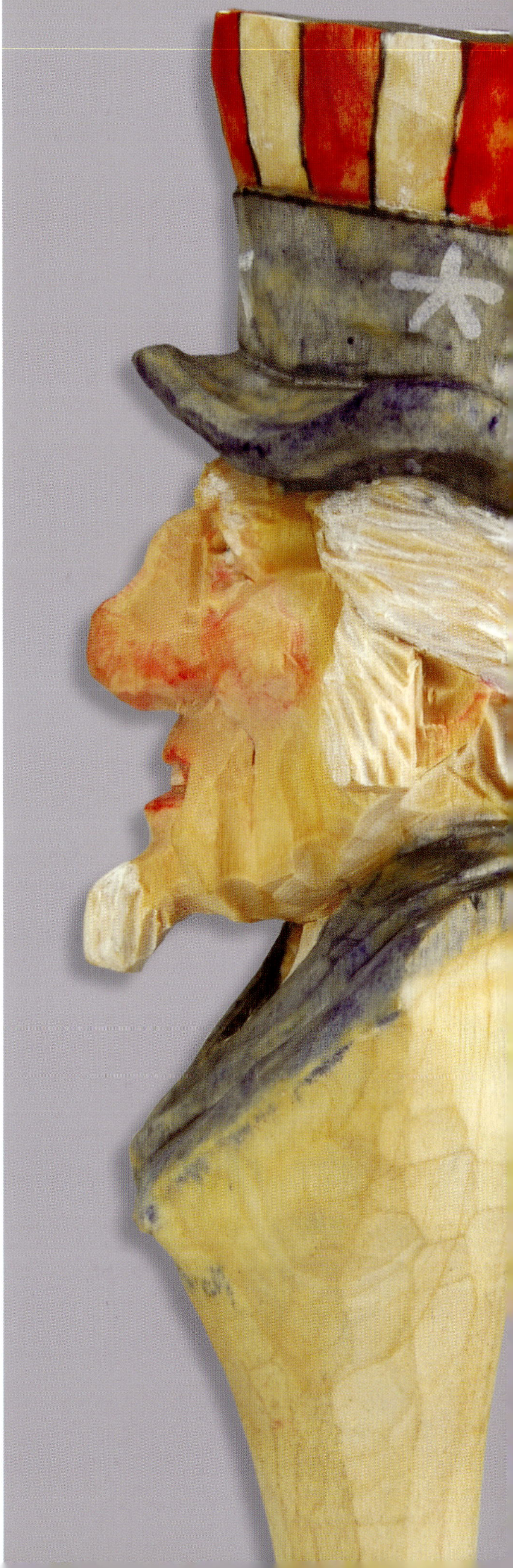

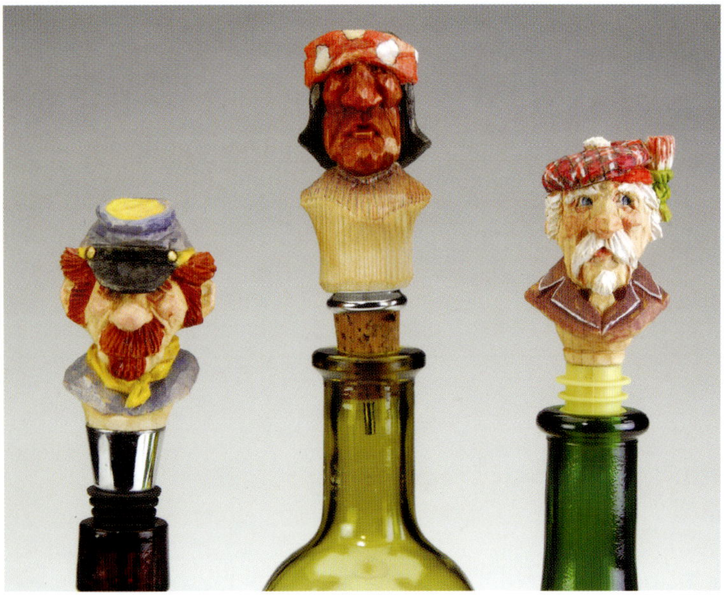

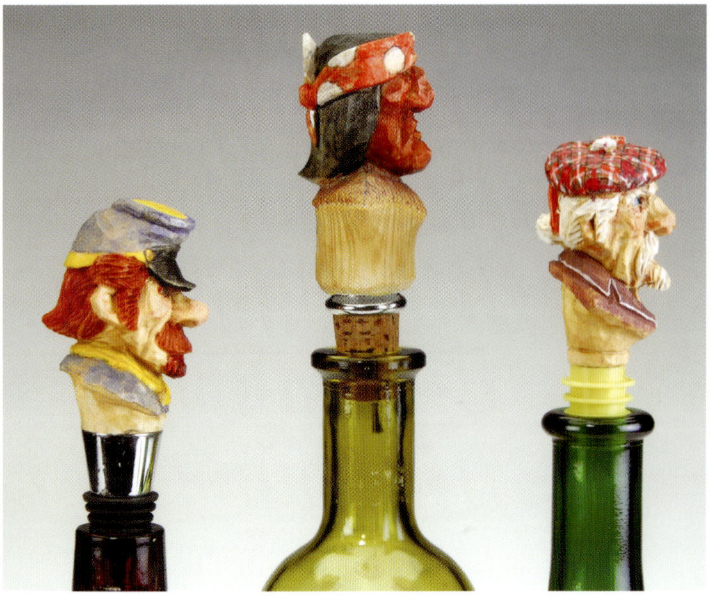

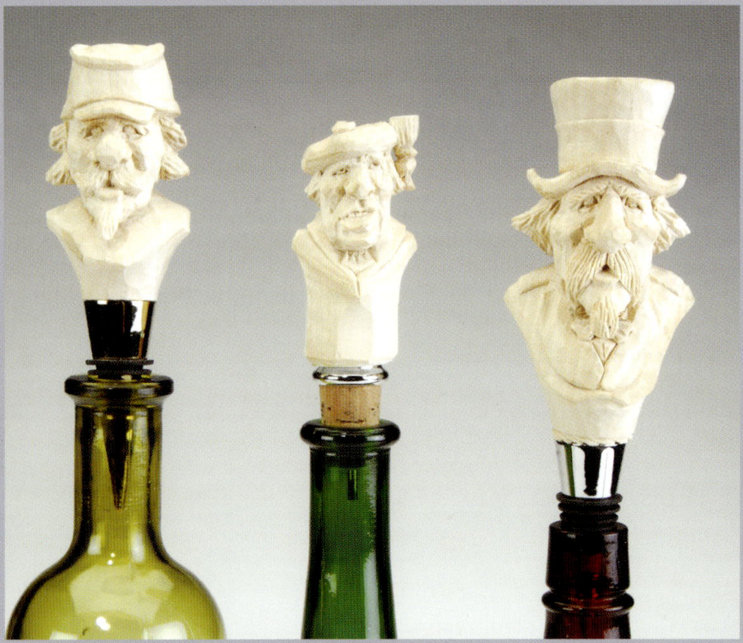

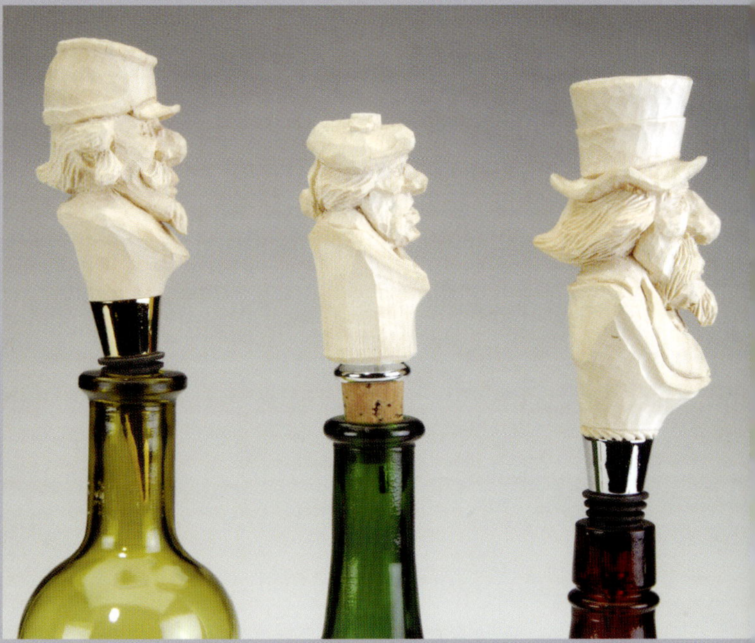

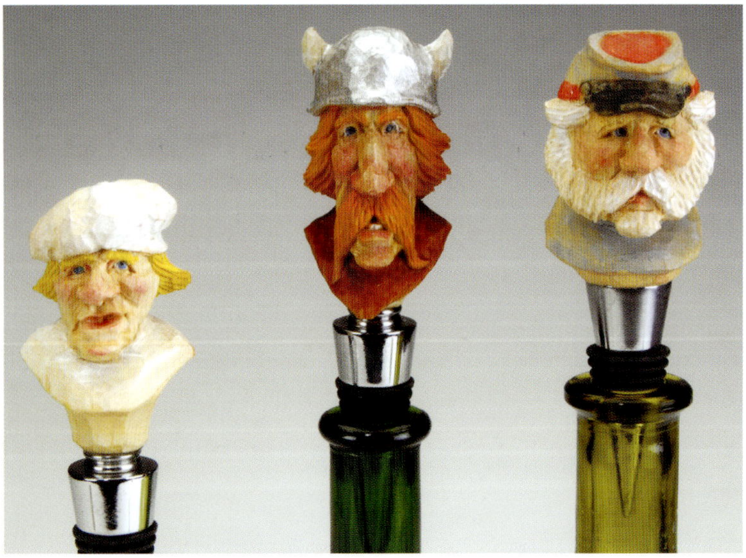

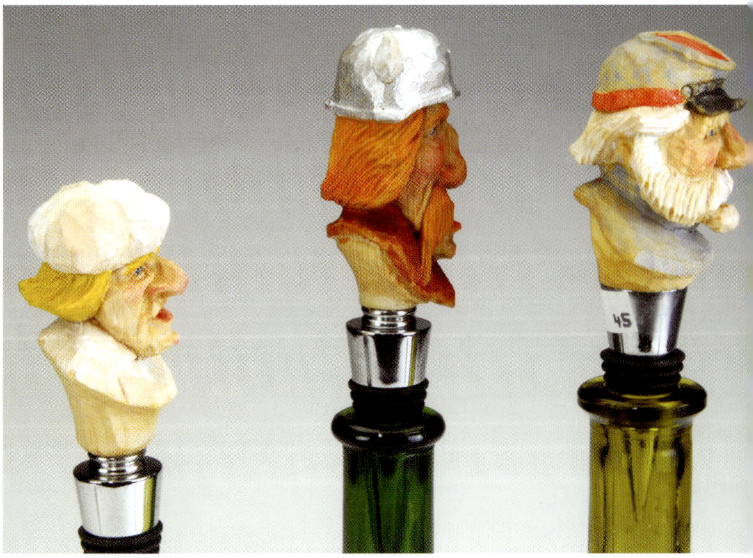

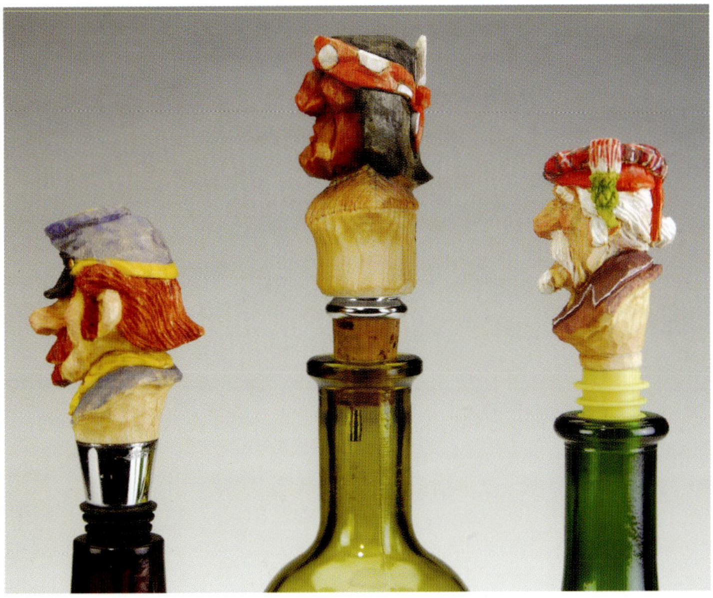

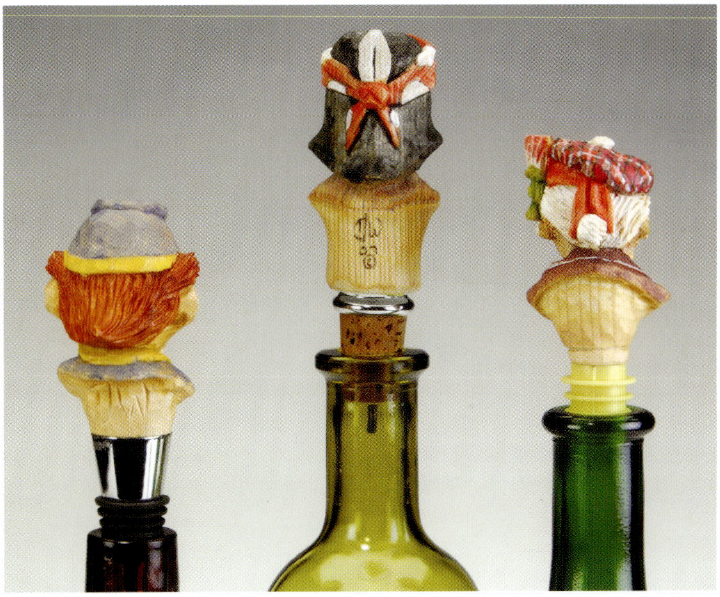

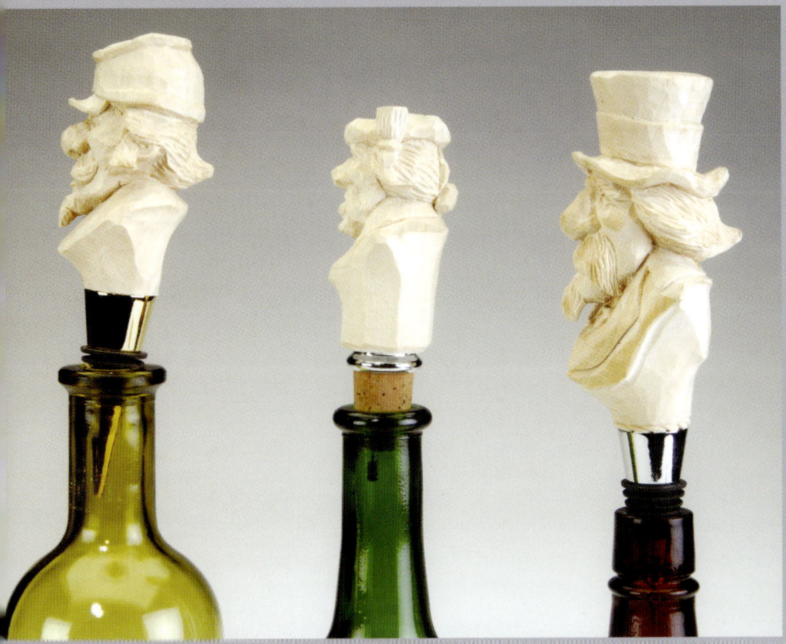

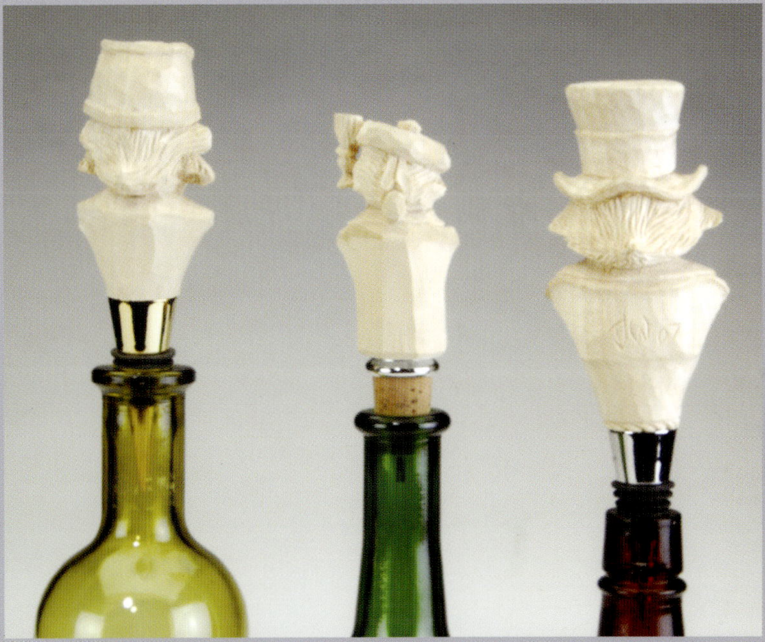

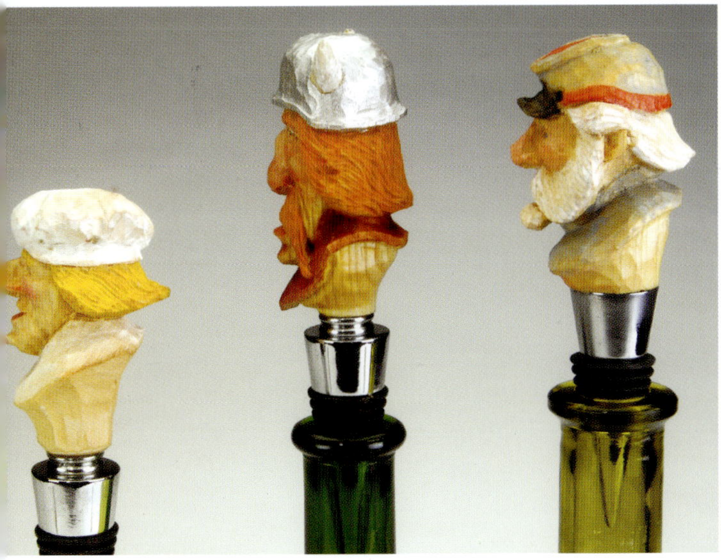

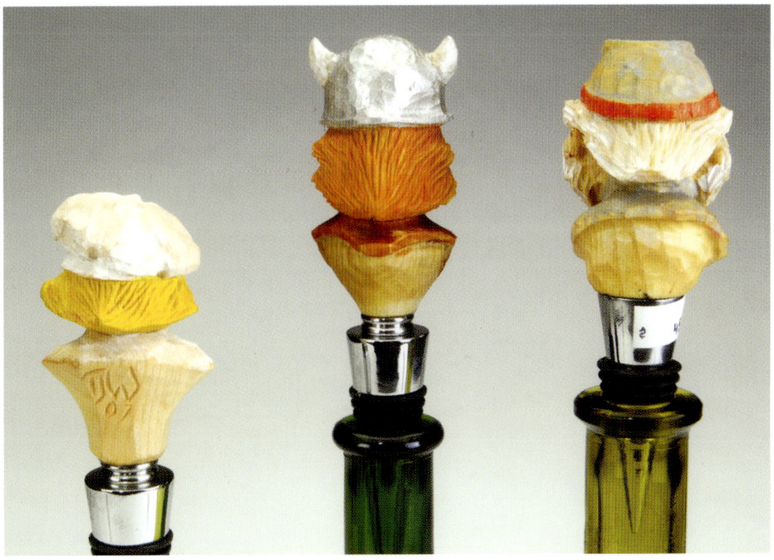

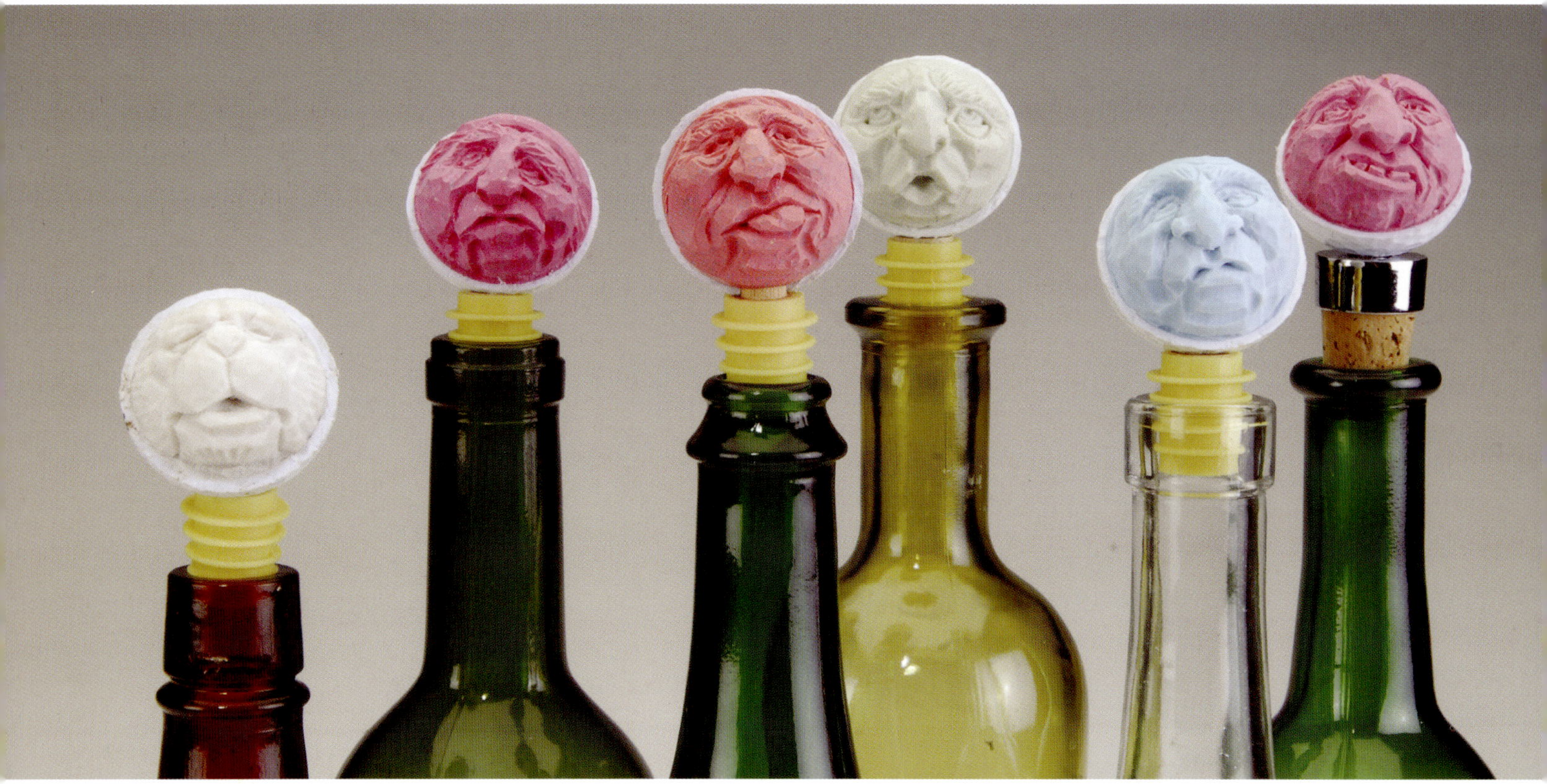

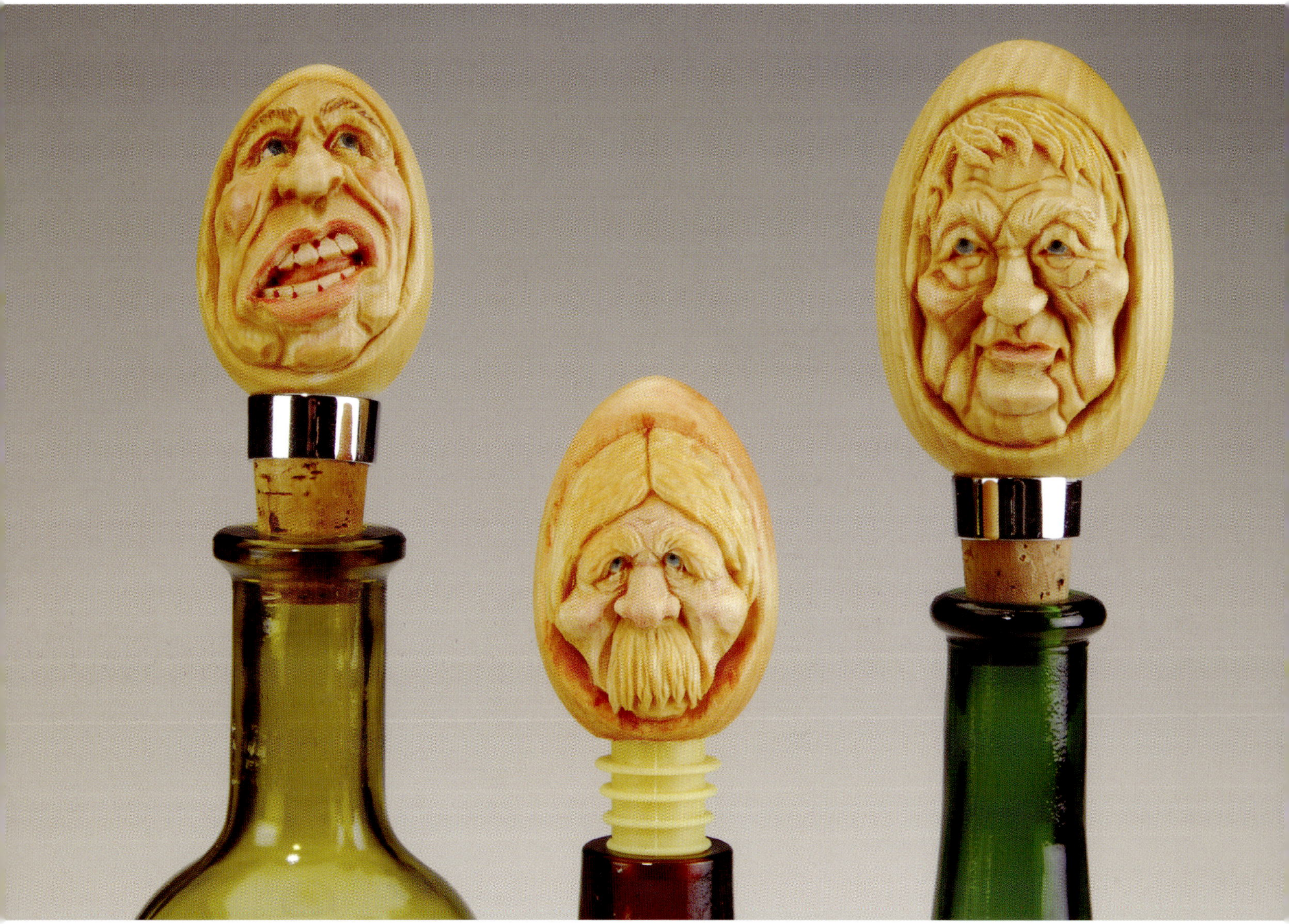